William Nimmo

The history of Stirlingshire

Vol. II

William Nimmo

The history of Stirlingshire
Vol. II

ISBN/EAN: 9783337141783

Printed in Europe, USA, Canada, Australia, Japan

Cover: Foto ©ninafisch / pixelio.de

More available books at **www.hansebooks.com**

THE HISTORY

OF

STIRLINGSHIRE.

By WILLIAM NIMMO.

THIRD EDITION,
Revised, Enlarged, and brought down to the Present Time.

IN TWO VOLUMES.

VOLUME II.

LONDON: HAMILTON, ADAMS & CO.
GLASGOW: THOMAS D. MORISON.
1880.

CONTENTS

OF

VOLUME II.

CHAPTER XXIII.

PARISHES, - - - - - - - PAGE 1

CHAPTER XXIV.

MISCELLANEOUS, - - - - - - 20

CHAPTER XXV.

EMINENT MEN, - - - - - - 45

CHAPTER XXVI.

OLD COUNTY FAMILIES, - - - 85

CHAPTER XXVII.

TITLED AND UNTITLED ARISTOCRACY, - - 107

CHAPTER XXVIII.

ROBERT ROY MACGREGOR, - - - 136

CHAPTER XXIX.

BLACK MAIL, - - - - - - 152

CHAPTER XXX.

SMUGGLING, - - - - - - 165

CHAPTER XXXI.

GEOLOGICAL LANDMARKS, - - - 171

CHAPTER XXXII.

RIVERS AND LOCHS, - - - - 185

CHAPTER XXXIII.

HILLS, - - - - - - - 211

CONTENTS.

CHAPTER XXXIV.
BOTANY, - - - - - - - 219

CHAPTER XXXV.
ZOOLOGY, - - - - - - - 232

CHAPTER XXXVI.
AGRICULTURE, - - - - - 241

CHAPTER XXXVII.
LANDOWNERS, - - - - - - 259

CHAPTER XXXVIII.
IRON INDUSTRIES, - - - - 293

CHAPTER XXXIX.
MINING, - - - - - - - 311

CHAPTER XL.
GENERAL INDUSTRIES, - - - - 322

CHAPTER XLI.

SPORTS AND GAMES, - - - - - - 357

CHAPTER XLII.

SOCIAL FEATURES, - - - - - - 374

INDEX

TO THE TWO VOLUMES. - - - - 390

THE HISTORY
OF
STIRLINGSHIRE.

CHAPTER XXIII.

PARISHES.

THE county is divided into twenty-four parishes. The figure of Airth resembles that of a parallelogram, and is consequently somewhat irregular. Its length, from north to south, is about 7 miles, and its breadth, from east to west, about $3\frac{1}{2}$ miles—the whole comprehending a surface of 30 square miles. It is bounded on the north by the Firth of Forth, on the east by the same firth and the parish of Bothkennar, on the south by Bothkennar and Larbert, and on the west by the parish of St. Ninians. The church was first opened for public worship on 20th February, 1820, and is built for the accommodation of 800 persons. The population of the parish in 1841 was 1,498; in 1851, 1,319; in 1861, 1,194; and in 1871, 1,395.

Alva belonged in ancient times to Clackmannanshire, with which it has been politically incorporated since the passing of the Reform Bill. Since the beginning of the seventeenth century, however, it has been attached for judicial purposes to Stirlingshire, although upwards of four miles distant from its nearest point. The barony is surrounded on all sides by the shire of Clackmannan, except on the north, where it is bounded by a part of the county of Perth. From the chartulary of Cambuskenneth, we learn that Alva was a parish nearly 600 years ago, although it does not appear certain when the building of the village was first started. In the year 1795, the latter only contained 130 families, including a few single persons, each of whom occupied part of a house. The population of the parish in 1791 was 611; in 1801, 787; in 1811, 921; in 1821, 1,197; in 1831, 1,300; in 1836, 1,470; in 1841, 2,136; in 1851, 3,204; in 1861, 3,618; and in 1871, 4,296. For a considerable period prior to the Reformation, Alva was in the diocese of Dunkeld, and under the ecclesiastical jurisdiction of the bishop of that see. By an extract taken from the chartulary of Cambuskenneth, it appears that it was a mensel church *(de mensa Episcopi)*, belonging to that abbacy; and that the monks, who were of the order of St. Augustine, performed duty there, from want of a sufficient fund to maintain a resident and regular clergyman in the parish. In 1260, Richard, bishop of Dunkeld, made a donation to the monks of the church of St. Mary, at Cambuskenneth, of "the church of Alva with all its legal pertinents," and dispensed with their employing a vicar to officiate statedly. From 1581, till 1632, this parish was united to the neighbouring one of Tillicoultry—the minister of Alva officiating in both. The fabric of the present church was erected in 1632, by Alexander Bruce, proprietor of Alva, who afterwards, making a small addition to the stipend, procured its disjunction from Tillicoultry. In the year 1815, at the expense of Mr. James Raymond Johnstone, it was wholly rebuilt, and fitted up so as to accommodate 600 sitters.

Baldernock, in shape, is a very irregular, three-sided figure. It is bounded, on the west side, by New Kilpatrick and Strathblane; on the south, by the rivers Allander and Kelvin; and on north and east by Campsie. The first records of session bear date 1690; but the present church was not built till 1795. It is still in good repair, and is seated for 406. The population of the parish in 1794 was 620; in 1801, 796; in 1811, 806; in 1821, 892; in 1831, 805; in 1841, 809; in 1851, 801; in 1861, 729; and in 1871, 616.

Balfron parish, which runs very nearly east and west, is about 11 miles in length, and 3 in breadth. It is bounded on the east and south-east, by Gargunnock and Fintry; on the south and north-west, by Killearn and Drymen; and on the north and north-east, by Drymen and Kippen. The church was rebuilt in 1833, and seats 700. The population in 1841, was 2,057; in 1851, 1,900; in 1861, 1,836; and in 1871, 1,502.

Bothkennar is bounded on the north, by the parish of Airth; on the east, by the Firth of Forth; on the south by the river Carron; and on the west, by the parish of Larbert. Its population in 1811, was 821; in 1821, 895; in 1831, 905; in 1841, 849; in 1851, 1,179; in 1861, 1,565; and in 1871, 2,377. Since the last census was taken, Grangemouth has been formed into a police burgh partly from the parishes of Bothkennar, Falkirk, and Polmont. In that year (1871) the population of the Bothkennar part of Grangemouth was 651; and what is now the landward part, 1,726. It is worthy of notice that, while in every other parish in Scotland there was a great aversion to episcopacy, this parish was so much attached to it that they kept their minister, Mr. Skinner, a most worthy man, from 1688 till 1721; and had he not resigned his situation it is probable he would have died among them in the full exercise of his ministerial functions. There have been only six presbyterian ministers in this parish, of whom Mr. Nimmo was one, since episcopacy was abolished.

Buchanan has not yet been measured. It is supposed, however, to be about 24 miles in length, and 5 in breadth; while its area, including the islands and mainland, may be stated at 120 square miles. It is bounded by Lochlomond on the west; by the parish of Arrochar on the north; by Loch Katrine, and the parishes of Aberfoyle and Drymen on the east; and by the river Endrick on the south. Its population in 1755 was 1,699; in 1793, 1,611; in 1801, 748; in 1831, 600; in 1841, 619; in 1851, 632; in 1861, 622; and in 1871, 591.

Campsie (Lennoxtown) was reduced to its present dimensions, in 1649, by the annexation of its eastern extremity to Kilsyth, and of its southern extremity to Baldernock. Its length is about 7 miles, and its breadth about 6. It is bounded by the parish of Fintry on the north; by Baldernock and Strathblane on the west; by Cadder and Kirkintilloch on the south; and on the east by Kilsyth. The "clachan" has been treated ecclesiastically in a previous chapter. The population of the parish in 1789 was 1,627; in 1793, 2,517; in 1831, 5,109; in 1836, 5,653; in 1841, 6,396; in 1851, 6,918; in 1861, 6,483; and in 1871, 6,739. The great increase of inhabitants, during the first decade noted, arose from the establishment of the Lennox mill and the Kincaid printfields.

Denny is 6 miles in length, and, on an average, 4 in breadth. On the west, it is bounded by Darroch hill; on the east by Dunipace; on the north by the river Carron; on the south by the Bonny; and on the south-west by Kilsyth. As already mentioned, this parish was originally part of the parish of Falkirk. The parochial registers commence about 1679. The minister of Polmont draws from the heritors, in Temple Denny, the equivalent for his grass glebe—a satisfactory evidence that both parishes were at one time portions of Falkirk. The population in 1755 was 1,392; in 1790, 1,416; in 1801, 1,967; in 1821, 3,364; in 1831, 3,843; in 1837, 4,300; in 1841, 4,428; in 1851, 4,754; in 1861, 4,821; and in 1871, 4,993.

Drymen is bounded on the north by Aberfoyle and Port; on the east, by Kippen, Balfron, and Killearn; on the south, by Killearn, Kilmaronock, and Dumbarton; and on the west, by Buchanan and Kilmaronock. Its extreme length is 15 miles, and breadth 10. It contains about 50 square miles. The church was erected in 1771. It is a plain substantial building, and affords accommodation for about 400. The population in 1755 was 2,780; in 1791, 1,607; in 1811, 1,500; in 1821, 1,652; in 1831, 1,690; in 1841, 1,523; in 1851, 1,481; in 1861, 1,469; and in 1871, 1,405.

Dunipace, in form, approaches to that of a triangle. It is bounded on the west and north by the parish of St. Ninians; on the east by Larbert; and on the south by the parishes of

Falkirk and Denny—the Carron separating it from the latter for nearly 5 miles. It is a curious fact that forty years ago there was neither a medical man nor a clergyman, a smith nor a wright, nor even a resident beggar in this parish; and it was only in 1838 that there was either a baker or a tailor. In the latter part of the thirteenth century an uncle of Sir William Wallace was parson of Dunipace, which was originally a chapel of the parish of Ecclis, now St. Ninians. At the time of the Reformation Dunipace and Larbert were erected into two separate parishes—the former then being both the more populous, and by far the more wealthy of the two—so much so, that the latter could not maintain a minister. A union, therefore, with Dunipace was desired, and accomplished under the authority of two Acts of the Scottish Parliament in 1617 and 1624. The present church stands on the top of one of those little knolls with which the whole district abounds. It is built in the Gothic style, with a tower, in which there is a fine bell. It is seated for 604 persons, and was first opened for worship on the 29th June, 1834. The old church stood a mile and a half to the eastward. The population of the parish in 1831 was 1,278; in 1841, 1,578; in 1851, 1,472; in 1861, 1,601; and in 1871, 1,733.

Falkirk is situated in the eastern division of

the county, and is separated from the Firth of Forth by a small part of the parish of Polmont. It extends about 9 miles in length, and from 2 to 5 in breadth. It is bounded on the east by the parishes of Polmont and Muiravonside; on the south by Muiravonside and Slamannan; on the west by Cumbernauld and Denny; and on the north by the river Carron, which divides it from Dunipace, Larbert, and Bothkennar. The parish is of an oblong shape, stretching from the north-east to the north-west. Ancient documents show that at one time Denny, Slamannan, Muiravonside, and Polmont formed parts of the then existing parsonage of Falkirk. Of the period when the first three of these parishes were disjoined no record has been found; but Polmont was created a distinct parish in 1724. Here the parochial records are voluminous, and have been regularly kept until the present time. The date of the earliest entry is 4th January, 1594. The old church, which was founded by Malcolm, in 1057, and rebuilt in 1810, with sittings for 1,500 hearers, has already been mentioned. Falkirk is the only market town in the parish, and in 1841 contained nearly 5,000 inhabitants; but the population of the parliamentary burgh, in 1835, was ascertained to be 7,445. At the last census, in 1871, it was 9,547; and, on the lowest calculation, it must now be over 12,000. The population of the parish in 1755 was 3,932; in

1792, 8,020; in 1801, 8,838; in 1811, 10,395; in 1821, 11,536; in 1831, 12,748; in 1835, 13,037; in 1841, 14,108; in 1851, 16,438; in 1861, 17,026; and in 1871, 18,051.

Fintry, irregular in figure, extends from east to west about 6 miles, and its breadth, from north to south, is 5. It contains nearly 20 square miles. The parish is bounded on the north by Balfron and Gargunnock; on the east by St. Ninians and Kilsyth; on the south by Campsie; and on the west by Killearn and Strathblane. The parochial registers belonging to the session have been kept from a remote date. The oldest is dated 1632. The Established Church, which is a plain but neat building, with a tower on the west end, was erected in 1823, and contains 500 sittings. The population in 1755 was 891; in 1791, 348; in 1801, 958; in 1811, 1,003; in 1821, 1,002; in 1831, 1,051; in 1851, 823; in 1861, 685; and in 1871, 499. After 1755 the farms of the parish were enlarged by the union of several small farms; and the consequence was, that many of the tenants were ejected, and had to seek a subsistence for themselves and families elsewhere. . Accordingly, in 1791, there is a decrease of population to the extent of 543. About this time, however, a change of an opposite nature caused a great increase. Mr. Speirs built a large cotton factory; and, to accommodate the many hands employed, a village was erected, which, in 1841, contained about 650 inhabitants.

Gargunnock contains about 20 square miles. Its length is 6 miles, and breadth 4. It is bounded on the east and south by St. Ninians; on the west by Fintry, Balfron, and Kippen; and on the north by Kincardine and Kilmaronock. The earliest entry in the parish registers is dated 1615. Although built in 1774, the church is still in a state of good repair. It accommodates 500 sitters. The population in 1755 was 956; in 1793, 830; in 1833, 908; in 1841, 826; in 1851, 754; in 1861, 729; and in 1871, 675.

Killearn contains 27 square miles. Its length is 12 miles; and its breadth, where greatest, 4; but at an average $2\frac{1}{2}$. It is situated in Strathendrick, now the western district of Stirlingshire. It was originally, however, a part of Lennox or Dumbartonshire. The population in 1755 was 959; in 1769, 948; in 1794, 973; in 1831, 1,206; in 1841, 1,187; in 1851, 1,176; in 1861, 1,145; and in 1871, 1,111. A temporary diminution was also occasioned here by the union of small farms.

Kilsyth, in form, approaches to an irregular oblong. It runs for 7 miles along the north high road from Edinburgh to Glasgow, and its mean breadth is fully half of its length. It contains nearly 24 square miles. The natural boundaries are the Carron, on the north; the Kelvin and the Bonnyburn, on the south; Inchwood burn on the west; and the Bush burn on the east. The population in 1801 was 1,762; in 1811, 3,206; in 1821, 4,260; in 1831, 4,297; in 1841, 4,683; in 1851, 5,346; in 1861, 5,828; and in 1871, 6,313.

Kippen lies chiefly in Stirlingshire, but in different places is intersected by portions of Perthshire which run across it from north to south, for nearly a third part of the parish. Its greatest length is about 8 miles, and its breadth from 2 to nearly 4 miles. It is bounded on the north by the river Forth, which separates it from the parishes of Port and Norriestown; on the east by Gargunnock; on the south by Balfron; and on the west by the parish of Drymen. The church was built in 1825, and seats 800. The population in 1793 was 1,777; in 1801, 1,722; in 1811, 1,893; in 1821, 2,029; in 1831, 2,085; in 1851, 1,892; in 1861, 1,736; and in 1871, 1,568.

Larbert parish proper is nearly elliptical in form—the measures of the transverse and conjugate axis being about 3 and $2\frac{1}{2}$ miles; while the superficial extent is close upon $4\frac{1}{2}$ square miles. The river Carron is the boundary on the S. & S. S. E., for $2\frac{1}{4}$ miles; Dunipace on the west and north-west for $2\frac{1}{2}$ miles; the little rivulet the Pow, of Airth, on the north; and for $1\frac{1}{4}$ mile, on the north-east and south-east, the parishes of Airth and Bothkennar form the marches. On account of its early poverty, Larbert, as we have already said, was united *quoad sacra* to Dunipace; but the establishment of the iron works at Carron changed matters entirely. Its population in 1831 was 4,262; in 1841, 4,411; in 1851, 4,606; in 1861, 4,999; and in 1871, 5,280.

Logie is bounded on the north by the parish of Dunblane; on the south by the river Forth, which divides it from Stirling and St. Ninians; on the west by Lecropt and Dunblane; and on the east by Alva and Alloa. Its extreme length, from north to south, is between 6 and 7 miles; and its extreme breadth, from east to west, about 6. The present church, which was built in 1805, is a plain unpretending structure, but neat and commodious. It is seated for 644 people. Its situation is peculiarly romantic and beautiful; and that of the old kirk (now an interesting ruin) still more so. The population in 1831 was 1,943; in 1841, 2,198; in 1851, 2,551; in 1861, 3,468; and in 1871, 4,553.

Muiravonside, or Moranside, is about 7 miles in length, and its irregular breadth may average 2. The river Avon descending towards the north-east, till it turns to the north and west not far from Linlithgow Bridge, bounds its extreme length on the south-east, and forms the border of its breadth on the north-east, separating it from the parishes of Slamannan, Torphichen, Linlithgow, and Bo'ness. It is said to have been, in ancient times, annexed to the parish of Falkirk; but we find it named a separate parish in 1606, the date of the oldest presbytery record. In several returns, too, of the earldom of Linlithgow, which were made in the seventeenth century, Muiravonside is reckoned amongst its patronages. The population in 1801 was 1,070; in 1811, 1,330; in 1821, 1,678; in 1831, 1,540; in 1851, 2,644; in 1861, 2,662; and in 1871, 2,653.

Polmont is about $6\frac{1}{2}$ miles in length, and its utmost breadth is nearly 3. It is bounded on the north by the firth of Forth; on the east, partly by the river Avon, which separates the county of Stirling from the county of Linlithgow, and partly by the parish of Muiravonside; on the south by Muiravonside and Slamannan; and on the west by the parish of Falkirk, from which it was disjoined in 1724. Its name, however, must be at least of long standing, for among the titles of the Duke of Hamilton, he is called Lord Polmont. The population in 1755 was 1,094; in 1791, 1,400; in 1801, 2,194; in 1811, 1,827; in 1821, 2,171; in 1831, 3,200; in 1835, 3,107; in 1841, 3,412; in 1851, 3,764; in 1861, 3,892; and in 1871, 3,910. In 1801, the colliery at Shieldhill was in active operation, and hence the large increase at that period compared with the census in 1791. In 1811, work there was almost discontinued: consequently the decrease. Again, from 1821 to 1831, the Redding Colliery was conducted on an extensive scale; and in 1835, the diminution was occasioned by fewer men being employed.

St. Ninians once comprehended the whole district between the Forth and Carron. With the exception of the small space occupied by the parish of Stirling, the Forth is still its northern boundary for many miles, by which it is separated from Kincardine, Lecropt, Logie and Alloa. On the east, it is bounded by Airth; on the west by Gargunnock and Fintry. The Carron on the south, for nearly 6 miles, separates it from Kilsyth and Denny; while Dunipace and Larbert form the remainder of its southern boundary. A parallelogram of 10 miles by 6 is more than the parish would fill up. 11 miles by 5 is nearer the mark. It contains about 55 square miles. From the church to Randieford, on the west, is a distance of fully 11 miles; and to Powbridge, on the east, about 7, though in a direct line the distance between these extreme points may not be over 15 or 16 miles; but owing to the windings of the Forth and other causes it is very irregular, and at both extremities is not more than 3 miles. The church was built in 1750, and contains upwards of 1,500 sittings. The population in 1645 was 4,760; in

1745, 5,916; in 1755, 6,491; in 1792, 7,079; in 1801, 6,849; in 1811, 7,636; in 1821, 8,274; in 1831, 9,552; in 1841, 10,080; in 1851, 9,851; in 1861, 8,946; and in 1871, 10,146.

Slamannan is bounded on the north-west by the parish of Cumbernauld; on the west and south-west by New Monkland; on the east and south-east by Torphichen; and on the north and north-east by Muiravonside, Polmont, and Falkirk. At the north-western extremity, there is a point where three counties meet, viz., Stirling, Dumbarton, and Lanark; and on the south there is another point where the counties of Stirling and Lanark meet with the county of Linlithgow. The parish lies on the south of the water of Avon, and is from 5 to 6 miles in length, and about 3 in breadth. In 1724, when Polmont was disjoined from Falkirk, a considerable portion of the former, which lies on the north of the Avon, was annexed *quoad sacra* to Slamannan, making the whole parish upwards of 6 miles in length and nearly 5 in breadth. The church, which was rebuilt in 1810, accommodates upwards of 700 persons. The population in 1801 was 923; in 1811, 993; in 1821, 981; in 1831, 1,093; in 1851, 1,655; in 1861, 2,916; and in 1871, 4,164.

Strathblane lies in the south-west corner of the shire, and is bounded on the east by the parish of Campsie; on the south by Baldernock and New

Kilpatrick; and on the west and north by Kilwarn. Its average length is rather more than 5 miles, and breadth about 4. The surface comprises nearly 20 square miles. The church, which was built in 1803, is a handsome edifice of modern Gothic, and is seated for 450. The population in 1755 was 797; in 1795, 620; in 1811, 795; in 1821, 748; in 1831, 1,030; in 1841, 1,045; in 1851, 1,010; in 1861, 1,122; and in 1871, 1,235.

Stirling parish is 2 miles in length from west to east, and $1\frac{1}{2}$ mile in breadth from north to south. Its figure is very irregular, depending in some places on the waving line of the Forth, in others on the deep indentations made in it by the parish of St. Ninians. By the latter it is bounded on the west, south, and east, by Logie on the north-east, and north, and by Lecropt on the north. The population in 1755, was 3,951; in 1792, 4,698; in 1801, 5,256; in 1811, 5,993; in 1821, 7,333; in 1831, 8,499; in 1841, 8,860; in 1851, 12,837; in 1861, 13,846; and in 1871, 14,279. With the Reformation, came the abolition of the Popish ritual, and the establishment of the Protestant worship. From this period, until 1607, the parish was under the spiritual charge of one minister. A second minister was then appointed, but it was not till 1643 that a fixed endowment was given by the magistrates and others. In 1731, upon an application from the inhabitants, the third charge was created, when consent was granted to a multure, which had been levied for some years, being perpetuated for its support. From this time, the ministers of the first and second charges were colleagues together in the east church, the minister of the third charge preaching in the west, until, upon the deposition of Ebenezer Erskine, in 1740, for whom this charge had been instituted, that church was disused as an ordinary place of worship, and only opened on sacramental occasions for the accommodation of those who could not find access to the east church. This state of things, notwithstanding petitions from the inhabitants, continued till 1817, when the third charge was revived, and the west church re-opened with Archibald Bruce ordained and admitted as minister. The arrangement, in other respects, continued the same down till 1825, when the then minister of the third charge being appointed to the second, remained in the west church, instead of being transferred to the east, and on being appointed in 1829, to the first charge still remained in the west. After that date, the minister of the first charge was fixed in the west church, the minister of the second charge in the east, while he of the third charge preached in each church alternately as colleague to both the others. The first person who appears to have occupied any ministerial office in the parish was Thomas Duncanson, *Reader*, who was, for uncleanness, suspended by the General Assembly, December 31st, 1563. The earliest appointment of a second minister was, as we have already said, in 1607, when Robert Mure was admitted coadjutor to Patrick Simpson. The dissenters from the national religious establishment were, seventy years ago, perhaps more numerous, proportionally, in Stirling than in most parts of Scotland. It was here, indeed, that, in 1738, that secession began which afterwards spread over the country under the name of "The Associated Synod," and, ten years after, branched into burghers and antiburghers. The prime mover, however, in a party which has been considered as unfavourable to loyalty, where the reigning prince has not signed "the Solemn League and Covenant," Mr. Ebenezer Erskine, eight years after his expulsion from the bosom of the national church, demonstrated his attachment to the civil government, by assuming the military character in the defence of Stirling against the insurgent army in 1746, when he gallantly headed two companies of his affectionate flock.

A census table, dry as the look of it may seem, tells an interesting tale of its own. The social history of a district may, in part, be read from it. An increase of population means industrial prosperity. A decrease, industrial depression. In the previous pages of this chapter, we have given the number of inhabitants in each of the parochial divisions of the shire. We close with the populations of the county itself, at intervals from 1765 till 1871.

1765,	-	- 39,761	1831,	-	- 72,621
1768,	-	- 47,373	1841,	-	- 82,057
.1801,	-	- 50,825	1851,	-	- 86,237
1811,	-	- 58,174	1861,	-	- 91,926
1821,	-	- 65,376	1871,	-	- 98,179

CHAPTER XXIV.

MISCELLANEOUS.

SHIRE, or scire, comes, according to Bailey, from the Saxon verb *scyran*, "to divide." The word is said to have been anciently applied to parishes. "Hadintunschire," says Mr. Chalmers, "is mentioned in the charters of David I., but meant merely the parish, then, probably, of very large extent. It did so also under Malcolm IV. and William the Lion."

The area of Stirlingshire comprehends about 480 square miles, or 312,960 acres (exclusive of the parish of Alva), of which about 200,000 are cultivated, 50,000 uncultivated, and 62,960 unproductive. Its greatest length is 45 miles, and its extreme breadth 18 miles. It is bounded on the north by Perthshire, and part of Clackmannanshire; on the west by Argyleshire; on the south by Dumbartonshire and Lanarkshire; and on the east by the county of Linlithgow. In general, the Forth divides it from Perthshire. The latter crosses the Forth from the water of Duchray above Aberfoyle, to the south end of the barony of Gartmore in the parish of Port; and extends about a mile and a half on the average. It again encroaches beyond the confines of proper Caledonia opposite to Cardross; and runs towards the hill of Fintry, in a breadth of two miles, and length of four. An insulated portion, about two miles long and half a mile broad, embraces the village of Kippen. The minister's manse stands on the eastern march, so that his dinner is cooked in Perthshire and eaten in Stirlingshire. A small detachment of the latter, about a furlong from the main body, which here crosses the Forth, occurs in Sheriff-moor. The whole of Alva parish is in Stirlingshire, though about 3 miles from the nearest point of the parent county. Ochtertyre seems to have belonged to it anciently. In Robert Duke of Albany's Register, we find a charter of confirmation by that regent " of a grant by John Drummond of Cargill, knight, to John Forster of Corstorfyne, of the lands of Uchtertyre in the barony of Kyncardyne, in Stirlingshire."

ROYAL BURGH.—The nature of the subjects with which the Convention of the Royal Burghs of Scotland had to deal, was wide, large, and important. The following formed part of its recognised business —" The imposition and application of rates for local purposes; the maintenance of burghal rights and privileges against assault from whatever quarter; the protection of the rights and privileges of Scottish traders both at home and abroad, and the negotiation of treaties with foreign governments.

Extract from Minute of the General Convention of Burghs at Stirling, on 2nd, 3rd, 4th, and 5th July, 1611.

"CITATIOUN.—The samin day, the commissioner for the burgh of Striviling verefeit the citatioun of the burrows to the present convention, exceptant for the burgh of Nairne.

"MODERATOUR.—The samin day, the saidis commissioners makis and constitutis Johne Scherer, first in the commissioun for the burgh of Striviling, thair moderator for this present conventioun, quha exceptit the samin and gaif his aith *de fidelj administratione*.

"CONVENTIOUN.—The saimin day, the saidis commissioners appointis thair houris of meiting to be and begin at aucht houris in the morning quhill sex at nicht, and the personis absent at the calling of the rollis to pay ane vulaw of sex schillings, and they that depairtis furth of the house quhill the conventioune dissolve to be unlayit as said is, and sik as sall depairt fra this present conventioune before the desolving thairof without licence to be unlayit as absentis, and that nane speik onrequirit or without licence askit and given, nor mixt thair ressoning with their voting for avoyding of confusion, under the payne of (blank) onforgivin."

The following is a literal copy of a burgess ticket granted by Lord Livingstone, who possessed the barony of Callendar; and which also bears the sign and subscription manual of the clerk of the court of regality :—

BURGESS TICKET FOR ANDREW HUTTON, WRIGHT, 1679.

"*At Ffalkirk, the second day of September, the year of God, jajvj and thriescore nynteine years.*

" The quhilk day, ane noble and potent Earle, Alexander Earle of Callender, Lord Livingstone of Almond and Ffalkirk, freilie receives and admits Andrew Hutton, wright in Ffalkirk, to libertie and freadome of ane neightbour and burges within the burgh of Ffalkirk, with power to him to bruik joyse use and exerce the haill liberties, priveleges, and immunities pertaining yrto; siclyke and als frielie in all respects as any oyr nightbour and burges may exerce and use within the said burghe of barronie and regalitie in tyme comeing; in suae far as concerneth the said noble and potent Earle his lops; present liberties yrof allenerlie venting and running of wyne, being alwayes excepted and reserved furth heirof; and with this speciall and express provisione, that the said Andrew Huttone shall use noe other tread nor calling, but onlie his owne tread of wright, and noe other; and yt he shall concur and assist the sd noble Earle and his lops, baillies and officers in all things necessar and requisite to be done be ane nightbour and burges in assisting of them. And the said Andrew Huttone has made faith hereupon as use is subscrived be the said noble and potent Earle, and extracted furth of the court books of the said regalitie of Ffalkirk.—By me John Brown, noy, poblict and clerk yreof, witnessing heirto my signe and subt-ne manuell, &c., &c., &c.

"CALANDER.

"Jo. Brown."

POLICE.—Sheriffs are mentioned under Alexander I. and David I., though they did not extend over North Britain. But many places—Scone, Edinburgh castle, and other fortresses, and some towns—had sheriffs, without forming sheriffdoms. Galloway, Argyll, Ross, and the Western Isles, had remained, till later times, without sheriffs; while sheriffships, in other quarters, had become hereditary. At first, the king appointed sheriffs, as servants and deputies; afterwards they came to be formally installed by the parliament. Bernard Frazer of Touch, a frequent witness to charters by Alexander II., was appointed sheriff of Stirling in 1234, in which year he swore to the performance of the Treaty of York. He was alive in November, 1247, and then witnessed a royal charter. Bernard seems to have been succeeded by his relative Gilbert Frazer, sheriff of Traquair, who had three sons—Symon, sheriff of Peebles from 1262 till 1268; Andrew *de Touch*, sheriff of Stirling in 1291-3; and William, bishop of St. Andrews and chancellor of Scotland. Andrew *Dominus de Touch* swore fealty to Edward I. at Dunfermline on the 17th of June, 1296. The sheriffship of Stirling remained among those Frazers till 1630, when David II. conferred it upon Sir Robert de Erskine, who was also constable and keeper of Edinburgh and Dumbarton castles, "*Justiciar* benorth the Forth, and great chamberlain of Scotland." It remained, with some interruptions, arising partly from civil commotion, in his family, till 1638; when John, eighth Earl of Marr of his surname, was induced to sell, to Charles I., the sheriffdom of Stirlingshire and baillary of the Forth, for £8,000 sterling. Sir James Livingston, first Earl of Callendar, was now made sheriff of the county. Under Cromwell, Sir William Bruce, baronet of Stenhouse, exercised the function. After the Restoration, it fell to George, third Earl of Linlithgow; and, upon the forfeiture of Alexander, fifth earl, in 1715, it was conferred upon his cousin-german, James, first Duke of Montrose.

Justices of the peace were instituted over Scotland, by Act of Parliament, in 1587. Their powers were further extended by another six years subsequent to the union of the crowns. The Act 1617 confirmed those of 1587 and 1609; and, expressing more particularly the powers and duties of justices and their constables, is, properly, the first general code of instructions for their regulation and guidance. The statute 1617 was ratified and confirmed by the parliament of Charles I., 1633; and empowered the lords of the privy council to enlarge the authority of the justices, and enforce obedience by penalty. Oliver Cromwell followed out the system; and was the first who, by the vigour of his measures, gave efficacy to it. One of his generals, afterwards celebrated as the restorer of the house of Stuart, Monck, on the 17th of May, 1654, from the garrison of Cardross, in the neighbourhood of Stirlingshire, desired the Earl of Airth "to order the cutting down of the woods of Milton and Gleshart in Aberfoyle, which (the general remarked) were great shelter to the rebels and mossers, and did thereby bring great inconveniences to the country thereabouts." Cromwell seems, also, to have availed himself of an institution of an earlier date, and sometimes abused under the semblance of order. A curious voucher to this effect was preserved by Archibald Edmonstone, Esq. of Spittal, a cadet of the family, and hereditary baron-bailie on the estate of Duntreath. "The Justices of his Highness' Peace" met, in quarter sessions at Stirling on the 3rd of February, 1658-9, enforced a contract, between Captain Hew MacGregor and the heritors and inhabitants of more than six parishes in the sheriffdom of Stirling, of which protection to their property on his part, and a certain remuneration on theirs, were the mutual stipulations. We subjoin a copy, the only accurate one, we believe, that has hitherto appeared in print. The difficulty of decyphering the word "Hew" had led to an unfortunate error in the statistical account, and its epitome, the "Beauties of Scotland." Captain MacGregor's petition, however it may, according to Dr. Jamieson, " show the weakness of the executive government " (a point not quite clear), illustrates the respect paid to the judicial, even during the Usurpation.

"At Stirling, in ane quarter session, held by sum justices of his highnes' peace upon the third day of Ffebruary, $165\frac{8}{9}$, the Laird of Touch being chyrsman :—Upon reading of ane petition given in be Captain Mcgregor, mackand mention that several heritors and inhabitants of the paroches of Campsie, Dennie, Baldernock, Strablane, Killearn, Gargunnock, an uthers, wtin the Schirrefdome of Stirling; did agree with him to oversee and preserve thair houses, goods, and geir frae oppressioun, and accordinglie did pay him, and now that sum persones delay to mack payment according to agreement and use of payment; thairfoir it is ordered that all heritors and inhabitants of the paroches afoirsaid mack payment to the said Captain Mcgregor of their proportionnes for his said service, till the first of Ffebry last past, without delay. All constables in the severall paroches are hereby commandit to see this order put in execution, as they will answer the contrair. It is also hereby declared that all qo have been ingadgit in payment sall be liberat after such time that they goe to Captaine Hew Mcgregor, and declare to him that they are not to expect any service frae him, or he to expect any payment frae them. Just copie, extracted be James Stirling, cl. of the peace, ffor Archibald Edmonstone, bailzie of Duntreath, to be published at ye kirk of Strablane."

Roads.—The roads of the county contain about 116 miles of turnpike. From Linlithgow bridge to Enric bridge, deducting 2 miles intervening in Perthshire, $38\frac{1}{2}$; from the Stirling road by Killearn to near New Kilpatrick, 17; from Kippen to beyond Campsie, $16\frac{1}{2}$; from Stirling to Castlecary, $10\frac{1}{2}$; from the Stirling and Glasgow road to Kirkintilloch, 8; north of Stirling bridge, $9\frac{1}{2}$; Stockiemoor, 6; from above the bridge of Blane to the road leading from Killearn to Strathblane, $2\frac{1}{2}$. Many of the roads are in excellent condition. The basalt, which runs along the middle of the shire, longitudinally, like a back-bone, affords the best possible material. The principal lines, having been originally formed before the most approved engineering had been practised, took, not unfrequently, a direction unfavourable to wheel-carriages. They were, however, propitious to the tourist in search of elevated points whence to view the country. One line, and a meritorious one—the Crow Road—was chalked out in modern times by the liberal genius of Peter Speirs, Esq., of Culcreuch, along the skirt of a precipitous hill above Campsie; and another constructed along the plain from Stirling to Falkirk, so as to avoid Torwood and other eminences.

Woods.—A great forest seems to have anciently covered a country whose modern characteristic, compared with many regions, is a want of wood. In clearing away the peat earth in the vale of Monteith, part of which is in Stirlingshire, the wreck of trees, some of them 60 feet in stem, were found on the surface of the clay which formed the subsoil lying in every direction as if felled. The stools were entire beside them, with their fangs infixed. Five or six have been frequently got within a diameter of twenty yards. The natural oaks of the county, affording a cutting once in twenty-four years, cover 2,900 acres, of which above 2,000 belong to his Grace the Duke of Montrose, who has nearly the same extent in Perthshire. Larch and Scotch fir have also been extensively planted as nurses to the oak, ash, sycamore, and beech. Along the lower skirts of the mountains of Buchanan and on the borders of Lochlomond there is a natural tendency to the growth of oak. On almost every little heathy knoll you meet with stunted stools, which require only to be razed over by the surface of the ground, and preserved from the bite of cattle, to become coppice wood. But to this extension of the woods every attention is and has been paid. Oak now closely covers Craigrostan, the western shoulder of Benlomond, and is rapidly extending over the estate of Buchanan, where, within the last century, heath only grew. We have previously referred to Torwood, which is said to have been "a royal forest;" but for this assertion, repeated by Mr. Nimmo, we can find neither voucher nor authority. Reference has also been made to the woods of Dunmore, and the larger trees which are still in health and growth throughout the county. Dr. Graham mentions an alder tree in the parish of Drymen, near the water of Duchray, which, in 1795, measured $19\frac{1}{2}$ feet round the trunk. An oak in the same neighbourhood, but which was reduced to the stool in 1820, measured 40 in circumference; and another then fresh at Blarquhoish in Strathblane had a girth of 15 feet, while the branches formed the *radii* of a circle of 270. The boar seems to have been a tenant of these forests. A symptom occurs on the neighbouring confine of Perthshire, in the parish of Port. *Choillemuc* is "wood of the boar," and intimates the former existence not only of an animal no longer to be found here, but of a forest where now no forest exists. The old name of Leitchtown, immediately west, was *Blar-choille*, "field of the wood." *Craigmuc*, in the parish of Aberfoyle, and close to Stirlingshire, is "rock of the boar."

MINERALS.—The abundance of minerals in the county has occasioned important manufactures throughout its area which should not else have been thought of. We have already adverted to coal. This valuable mineral runs obliquely along the south-east of the shire, on the south of the Lennox hills, and of the county town. Limestone, in many instances, accompanies coal in two strata, the one above, the other below, and of inferior quality. Freestone, also, in variety, is a frequent accompaniment. That near Kilsyth is of a beautiful white. Timber thrown into a stream above the town is very soon metamorphosed in point of substance, while the organisation remains. The cavity formed by the combined action of the stream and pickaxe contains, also, large masses of flint; and specimens of yellow and red jasper, with nodules of agate and porphyry. Much red freestone is found in many parts of the county, particularly north of the Lennox and Dundaff hills. There is a mineral spring at Boquhan, somewhat resembling that of Pitkaithly. It issues, like the latter, and that also at Dunblane, from sandstone of the burned-brick colour. Such springs are said to be found in other beds of such stones, both in Stirlingshire and elsewhere. At Ballaggan, in the parish of Strathblane, nearly 200 alternate strata of earth and limestone present themselves in the face of a hill, excavated by a lofty and precipitous cataract, subject to vast floods. Copper has been found in the parish of Kilsyth. The York Building Company had wrought it about 170 years ago; and it is said to have been rashly relinquished. A copper mine in the parish of Logie was operated upon seventy years ago; but, on the failure of a rich vein, was forsaken. Between 1760 and 1765, about 12 tons of silver ore, valued at £60 per ton, were dug up in the estate of Aithrey; but, by the bankruptcy of the person to whom it was consigned, Dr. Twisse, of London, the work was stopped. About 1700, Sir James Erskine, of Alva, had obtained, from a ravine in his estate of Alva, above £50,000 sterling's worth of silver ore, in about fourteen weeks. The vein had now become exhausted, and symptoms of lead and other inferior metals had appeared, when the work was forsaken. The communion cups of the church of Alva are made of the parochial silver.

RAILWAYS.—It may be said that railways, by their aids to industrial progress, and to the convenience and enjoyments of civilised life, have done more for the public generally than for the original shareholders at whose cost they were constructed. It was only in 1826 that the sanction of parliament was got for the formation of the first public railway worked by locomotives in the kingdom—the Manchester and Liverpool line; and now their extent throughout the country is about 14,500 miles, which leaves few towns of any importance beyond convenient distance of a railway station. Stirlingshire has, for many years, enjoyed close connection with the iron road. The Edinburgh and Glasgow line, now amalgamated with the North British, was commenced to be formed early in 1839, and 1842 brought its completion. It passes through the parish of Falkirk for about 8 miles, entering from Polmont on the east. The operations in this district consisted of works of considerable magnitude. Among these may be mentioned a tunnel which extends to 845 yards, with a width of 26 feet, and a height of 22 feet; while a viaduct of three arches, one of which, being 130 feet span, crosses the Union Canal near to its western termination at "Lock 16." A bridge, also, of seven arches, goes at once over the Redburn at Castlecary, and over the turnpike road there.

The canal just referred to was projected in 1818, and finished in 1822, by Mr. Hugh Baird, C.E., who resided at Kelvinhead, Kilsyth, till his death in 1827. It runs through the parish of Falkirk for about 3 miles, and falls 110 feet, by means of 11 locks, within the compass of half a mile. At the same distance south of Falkirk, it passes through a tunnel, cut out of the solid rock, nearly 1000 yards in length. For twenty years, this canal was used for the conveyance of both passengers and goods between Edinburgh and Lock 16 of the Forth and Clyde Canal, but now its occupation is gone. Coal and manure, and even little of these commodities, form its only traffic at the present day. Were it, however, continued on from the "Ladies' Cut" at Glenfuir to Wyndford, so as to avoid the locks, it might yet have a considerable trade.

Originally the Edinburgh and Glasgow Railway, which cost about a million of money, extended only to Haymarket on the east, and, for a time, the trains left each end hourly, calling at all the intermediate stations. Mr. Eadie, engineer for the company, was also manager, the agents, as a body, acting as superintendents of the line. But eventually a general manager and passenger superintendent were appointed, when the stationmasters were relieved of that responsibility and position. And it must have been severely trying work for the guards of those days. Their seats, with the break, were outside, at the top of the carriages, and we have heard some of them, now "gone over to the majority," tell of frequently reaching the terminus with their clothes frozen as stiff as boards from the severity of the weather.

The line from lower Greenhill to Stirling was opened for traffic on 1st March, 1848; the South

Alloa branch in 1850; the Polmont Junction, in 1852; the Denny branch, on 1st April, 1858; and the Grangemouth branch, in October, 1861. The other public railways wholly or in part, in the county, are the Forth and Clyde Junction, the Milngavie branch, and the Blane Valley, and Stirling and Dunfermline—all of which are owned or leased by the Caledonian and North British Companies. The mileage of the latter company is the longest in Scotland, measuring over all 735 miles. It extends from Perth and Dundee on the north, to Carlisle, Silloth, and Newcastle on the south, and passes across the country from Helensburgh to Berwick, running out into numerous branches and loops. The railway originally consisted of a line from Edinburgh to Berwick, measuring 58 miles, with a branch to Haddington 4 miles in length. By the opening of the bridge over the Tay, on 1st June, 1878, Glasgow and Edinburgh traffic, to and from Aberdeen and other places north of Dundee, had the *route via* Stirling and Fife opened to it as an alternative *route* to that *via* Perth. The new *route*, as a whole, was North British, but portions of it, namely the portion north of Dundee (part of the Scottish North-Eastern lines), and the portion (part of the Scottish Central line) between Stirling and Larbert for Edinburgh traffic, and between Stirling and Greenhill for Glasgow traffic, belong to the Caledonian Company. The North British, however, exercise running powers over the Scottish Central, now merged in the Caledonian, between Stirling and Greenhill. The junction for their Edinburgh traffic is at Larbert.

The total length of the Caledonian Railway is now 673 miles. But the original line, of which the estimated cost was £2,100,000, measured only 137¼ miles. It comprised a great fork from Edinburgh to Carnwath, another from the north side of Glasgow to Carnwath, a branch from the Glasgow fork at Motherwell to the south side of Glasgow, with a subordinate branch to Hamilton, a branch from the same fork in the vicinity of Gartsherrie to the Scottish Central Railway near Castlecary, and a main trunk extending from Carnwath to Carlisle. The Scottish Central, Scottish Midland, Scottish North Eastern, and several other railways, have been amalgamated with the Caledonian. The company further hold in lease the Alyth and the Arbroath and Forfar railways, while the Bushby, Crieff, and Methven Junction, Greenock and Wemyss Bay, Montrose and Bervie, Portpatrick, and Callendar, and Oban railways are worked by them. Powers were obtained in 1865 for the construction of the last mentioned line, which was opened from Tyndrum to Oban in May last—its full length being 70¾ miles.

It has come out in court in connection with accidents on several English lines, that some of the subordinates have been kept on constant duty for even eighteen hours a-day, but the employés on Scotch railways are not worse off, as a rule, with regard to their working-time than men engaged in other departments of labour. Station-masters receive a salary of from £50 to £130 per annum with free house, coal, and light; drivers a pay of from 27s. to 42s. a-week, according to the nature of their work; stokers, from 16s. to 20s.; guards, from 18s. to 30s.; brakesmen, from 21s. to 25s.; signalmen and pointsmen, 18s.; porters, from 15s. to 19s.; platelayers, from 15s. to 18s.; while booking-clerks are paid at the rate of from £20 to £70 a year. With few exceptions, the agent is responsible both for the office and outside work of the station, and it is only at the more important junctions where he is relieved of the oversight of the books, returns, and cash.

AIRTHREY MINERAL SPRING.—The mineral spring now so celebrated, and so much resorted to by invalids, rises on the Airthrey estate, on the high grounds above the village of Bridge of Allan. It was discovered in the course of working the Airthrey copper mine, from the sole of which it springs. The miners, conceiving it to be a common salt spring, made use of it for culinary purposes, and gave it a decided preference to all other water. There are four springs in all, and of these Nos. 1 and 2, commonly called the Weak Water, are conveyed into the same reservoir and used together; No. 3, the Strong Water, is used alone; and No. 4, which issues from the rock on the western wall of the mine, is not used. It is a scanty spring, termed the Black Spring, in consequence of its depositing into the natural basin, into which it is received, a black substance, which has not been examined. The following is a copy of the results of Dr. Thomson's analysis:—

Springs Nos. 1 and 2; specific gravity, 1.00714. 1000 grains contain—

Common salt, - - - -	5·1 grains.
Muriate of lime, - - -	4·674 ,,
Sulphate of lime, - - -	0·26 ,,
	10·034 grains.

One pint contains—

Common salt, - - - -	37·45 grains.
Muriate of lime, - - -	34·32 ,,
Sulphate of lime, - - -	1·19 ,,
	72·96 grains.

The average quantity of water delivered by these springs in twenty-four hours is about 400 imperial gallons. The weak water, like the strong, is transparent and colourless, and destitute of smell. Its taste, though rather bitter, is by no means unpleasant.

Spring No. 3; specific gravity, 1·00915. 1000 grains contain—

Common salt, - - - -	6·746 grains.
Muriate of lime, - - -	5·826 ,,
Sulphate of lime, - - -	0·716 ,,
Muriate of Magnesia, - -	0·086 ,,
	13·374 grains.

A wine pint contains—

Common salt,	47·534 grains.
Muriate of lime,	38·461 ,,
Sulphate of lime,	4·715 ,,
Muriate of magnesia,	0·450 ,,
	91·160 grains.

The quantity of water delivered by this spring in twenty-four hours is, in round numbers, 1,260 imperial gallons, and the supply is not affected by the seasons. This water is bitter and disagreeable to the taste.

Spring No. 4; specific gravity, 1·00984; contains—

Common salt,	537·567 grains.
Muriate of lime,	282·769 ,,
Sulphate of lime,	26·084 ,,
Muriate of magnesia,	2·438 ,,
	848·858 grains.

The value of these springs, in a medicinal point of view, is unquestioned. Considered as a saline aperient, the Airthrey waters far surpass those of Pitcaithly and Dunblane; and are only inferior in the amount of their impregnation to some of the springs at Cheltenham and Leamington.

THE GLASGOW STIRLINGSHIRE AND SONS OF THE ROCK SOCIETY.—The first dinner of this charitable institution took place on "Auld Hansel Monday," 1809. The gathering on that occasion of upwards of sixty sons of Stirlingshire must have given encouraging hopes of the success of the scheme of brotherly kindness then inaugurated. By another year the society had increased to 160 members. From that time onwards the progress of the institution must have fulfilled the highest expectations formed by those who planted it and first gave it life. From the report of the secretary, Mr. James Low, at the annual business meeting and dinner in January last (1880), it appeared that the funds amounted to £8,243, 11s. 5d., of which £7,699, 3s. was for charitable, and £544, 8s. 5d. for educational purposes. Last year's report gave the amount as £8,189, 15s. 7d. —showing an increase on the year of £53, 15s. 10d. The bounty dispensed by this society is in direct opposition to what is termed indiscriminate charity; and it has now an additional object in view, namely, the encouragement of education. When the society was invigorated by the fresh new blood of the Sons of the Rock, a capital sum was laid aside for the purpose of aiding higher education—a matter which has recently fallen with its administration. There was not a sufficiently large sum to constitute what might be considered a satisfactory bursary; but one of the members, Mr. J. C. Bolton, of Carbrook, kindly made up what was deficient, so as to afford a bursary during five years. The other members of the society include Admiral Sir William Edmonstone, Bart., ex-M.P.; Lieut.-General Sir James E. Alexander, K.C.B., of

Westerton; Mr. James King, Levernholm; Mr. Michael Connal, Parkhall; Mr. John Guthrie Smith, Mugdock Castle; Mr. Charles M. King, Antermony; Mr. James B. Macarthur; Mr. William Connal, treasurer, &c.

BOARD SCHOOLS.—Administration of Elementary Education Acts, in 1879-80.—The heading "rate" is the rate per £ on the rateable value of the district, of the amounts paid to the treasurer by the rating authority :—

	No. of Schools.	Average Attendance.	Rate.	Annual Grants.		
Airth,	4	262	5d	£196	16	1
Alva,	3	822	$5\frac{1}{2}$d	640	11	7
Baldernock,	1	60	9d	66	15	0
Balfron,	1	180	1s $0\frac{1}{4}$d	168	2	0
Bothkennar,	1	208	$4\frac{1}{4}$d	180	18	0
Buchanan,	2	37	$3\frac{1}{4}$d	58	15	0
Campsie,	6	803	$4\frac{1}{2}$d	664	15	7
Denny,	4	640	$5\frac{3}{4}$d	560	1	8
Drymen,	1	18	$3\frac{1}{2}$d	29	2	0
Dunipace,	2	172	$2\frac{9}{10}$d	140	7	0
Falkirk (Burgh),	6	1,402	8d	1,293	17	0
Do. (Landward),	5	920	$2\frac{1}{4}$d & 5d	851	0	0
Fintry,	2	87	$8\frac{1}{2}$d	107	16	1
Gargunnock,	1	55	$4\frac{1}{2}$d	44	6	0
Grangemouth,	2	510	6d	437	3	0
Killearn,	1	142	6d	135	1	0
Kilsyth (Town),	2	619	1s 5d	523	2	6
Do. (Landward),	3	360	$7\frac{1}{2}$d	310	5	5
Kippen,	2	175	$7\frac{1}{2}$d	150	2	1
Larbert,	5	887	$4\frac{3}{4}$d	801	2	0
Lecropt,	1	79	$5\frac{3}{4}$d	68	6	0
Logie,	1	178	—	142	15	0
Carried forward,	56	8,616		£7,571	0	0

	No. of Schools.	Average Attendance.	Rate.	Annual Grants.		
Brought forward,	56	8,616	—	£7,571	0	0
Muiravonside, -	3	317	5d	304	14	4
Polmont, -	6	792	$\left\{ \begin{array}{l} 2\frac{1}{4}d, 3\frac{1}{4}d, \\ 4\frac{1}{4}d, 8d \end{array} \right\}$	789	19	0
St. Ninians, -	9	835	4d	800	1	8
Slamannan, -	5	748	6d	551	12	2
Stirling (Burgh),	10	1,743	5d	1,302	4	0
Do. (Landward),	1	38	5d	31	10	0
Strathblane, -	1	159	7½d	128	4	0
	91	13,248		£11,479	5	2

Stirling High School, of which Mr. A. F. Hutchison, M.A., is rector, is one of the higher class secondary public schools of Scotland. Pupils are prepared both for the University and public service. The attendance this year is about 150.

COUNTY VOTERS' ROLL.—Mr. Musgrave, Assessor, has made up the roll of voters for 1880-81. Appended are the numbers for the various parishes :—

Parishes.	Voters on Roll. 1879-80.	Dead or Disqualified.	New Voters.	Increase.	Decrease.
Airth, -	47	4	3	0	1
Baldernock,	51	4	3	0	1
Balfron,	83	10	10	0	0
Bothkennar, -	120	16	25	9	0
Buchanan,	31	4	4	0	0
Campsie,	232	21	16	0	5
Denny, -	275	29	29	0	0
Drymen,	118	9	9	0	0
Dunipace,	63	9	7	0	2
Falkirk,	431	43	68	25	0
Carried forward,	1,451	149	174	34	9

Parishes.	Voters on Roll. 1879-80.	Dead or Disqualified.	New Voters.	Increase.	Decrease.
Brought forward,	1,451	149	174	34	9
Fintry,	28	7	3	0	4
Gargunnock,	47	5	8	3	0
Killearn,	74	8	8	0	0
Kilsyth,	275	30	37	7	0
Kippen,	100	5	7	2	0
Larbert,	191	11	28	17	0
Lecropt,	12	1	1	0	0
Logie,	217	22	26	4	0
Muiravonside,	104	3	8	5	0
New Kilpatrick,	100	22	19	0	3
Polmont,	134	15	21	6	0
St. Ninians	350	40	46	6	0
Slamannan,	165	11	17	6	0
Strathblane,	56	12	9	0	3
Stirling,	17	3	1	0	2
	3,321	344	413	90	21

Nett increase, - - - 69.

At the last general election (in April, 1880), Mr. J. C. Bolton was returned M.P. for the county by a majority of 360—1,246 voting for Sir W. Edmonstone (C.), and 1,606 for Mr. Bolton (L.). At Falkirk, where the largest number of voters polled, and where the Liberal party received a large measure of support, the election excited great interest. In the shape of electioneering literature, there were posters, informing the electors that to vote for Sir W. Edmonstone was to support Lord Beaconsfield, "conspicuous for his brag, bluster, and bungling;" while, on the other hand, it was proclaimed that to vote for

Mr. Bolton was to secure "British honour and British interests." The Liberals issued the following acrostic :—

B rothers, be brave ; bid blundering boors begone !
O ff out of office occupied too long,
L et Liberal legislators lead our land ;
T remendous issues by your verdict stand.
O n, then ! three ons in Glasgow won the poll,
N ow vote for Bolt-on, too, with heart and soul !

CHAPTER XXV.

EMINENT MEN.

TAKING the distinguished persons of the county alphabetically, the good and brave Sir Ralph Abercromby, K.B., hero of Aboukir, stands first on the illustrious roll. Son of Mr. George Abercromby, by Mary, daughter of Mr. Ralph Dundas of Manor, he was born at the family seat of Menstrie in October, 1734. After a liberal education, he became cornet in the 3rd regiment of Dragoon Guards. His commission is dated 23rd March, 1756. In February, 1760, he obtained a lieutenancy in the regiment, and soon rose to the rank of lieut.-colonel. He was made a brevet-colonel, November, 1780; and in the following year, colonel of the 103rd, or King's Irish infantry. He attained the rank of major-general, 29th September, 1787. In the Continental war, 1793, he had the local rank of lieut.-general. He commanded the advanced guards on the heights of Cateau, and was wounded at Nimeguen. His bravery and skill commanded the warmest praise of the commander-in-chief and army. In the unfortunate retreat from Holland, in the winter of 1794, he particularly distinguished himself by his fortitude, patience, and perseverance. He was created knight of the bath, and, in 1795, appointed to the chief military command in the West Indies; where, in the course of two years, he captured several of the enemy's settlements—Grenada, Demerara, Essiquibo, St. Lucia, St. Vincent's, and Trinidad. Having been raised to the permanent rank of lieut.-general, and returning to Europe in 1797, he obtained the command of the 2nd, or North British Dragoons, and was made lieut.-governor of the Isle of Wight. He was then appointed commander-in-chief in Ireland, and there exerted himself to suppress that rebellion which the French emissaries had endeavoured to excite amongst the disaffected and the ignorant in that country. He was, meanwhile, made governor of Forts Augustus and George in Scotland. When, on a principle of expediency, the civil and military command in Ireland had come to be vested in one distinguished person, the late Marquis Cornwallis, Sir Ralph obtained the chief command in Scotland. He afterwards held a principal command under his royal highness the Duke of York in Holland; when the want of success was owing, not to any want of skill in the arrangements made by the British Government, nor of exertions on the part of the British troops, but partly to the Russian allies, and chiefly to the Dutch themselves, deluded by the French. The memorable expedition to Egypt in 1801 afforded him an opportunity of immortalizing the name of Abercromby. The landing of the British army at Aboukir 8th March, in the face of the most formidable opposition by the French, was one of the most gallant acts of heroism on record, and one of the most successful. The French were afterwards foiled in two general attacks on our army at Alexandria; but Sir Ralph had fallen in the second great victory on the 21st. With a mortal wound in the thigh, received during the heat of battle, he continued in the field, giving his orders with that coolness and perspicuity which had ever marked his character, until the enemy had been totally routed, when he fell from his horse through weakness and loss of blood. Being conveyed on board the admiral's ship, he died on the 28th; and was interred under the castle of St. Elmo, in La Valetta, in the island of Malta. In private life, Sir Ralph was one of the most amiable of men. His mind was contemplative, and his studies general. It is a somewhat remarkable trait that, when called to the Continent in 1793, he had been daily attending the admirable lectures of Dr. Hardy, regius professor of Church history in the University of Edinburgh. To his memory, the House of Commons unanimously voted a monument in St. Paul's cathedral; and settled £2,000 a year on his family. His wife, Mary Ann, daughter of John Menzies of Farnton, was created Baroness Abercromby of Aboukir and Tullibody, with remainder to her sons by her late husband.

Henry Belfrage, D.D., was a native of Falkirk, and a son of the Rev. John Belfrage, minister of the Associate Congregation, now called the East U.P., or Erskine church. He was ordained successor and colleague to his father in 1794, and died in 1835. He published several volumes of sermons, and other theological works, which had a large local circulation.

Mr. James Bell, the celebrated geographer, who was born at Jedburgh in 1769, spent his last years in the parish of Campsie. In 1777, Mr. Bell removed with his father to Glasgow, where, after receiving a liberal education, he served an apprenticeship to the weaving business, and, in 1790, he commenced business as a manufacturer of cotton goods. In the universal depression, occasioned by the shock of the French Revolution, Mr. Bell having a large stock on hand, in common with many others, lost his all, and for a number of years, was employed as a common warper in the warehouses of different manufacturers. It has been said, while Mr. Bell occupied this situation, he was frequently more intent on the metres of Horace, the delineations of Mela and Strabo, and the glowing narratives of Xenophon and Thucydides, than upon the porters and splits into which his baskets of bobbins were to be adjusted upon the warping-mill, in consequence of which his chains, when they came into the hands of the workmen, were found to be inextricably entangled. About the year 1806, Mr. Bell relinquished this uncongenial occupation, and betook himself to a more laborious mode of earning his subsistence, but one for which he was better qualified, viz. teaching the classics to young men attending the University. This he pursued for some years with diligence and success, being at the same time himself a most indefatigible and arduous student, especially in history, systematic theology, and above all in geography, which he followed out with unwearied enthusiasm. Mr. Bell made his first appearance as an author in 1815, when he was engaged to improve the Glasgow Geography, a work in four volumes, which had been well received by the public, and was now, by the labours of Mr. Bell, extended to five volumes. It formed the basis of his principal work. Some years after this, he again appeared as an author in conjunction with a young gentleman (the late Mr. John Bell of Glasgow), in a small volume of Chinese geography and Oriental philology. This work is now rare, but is said to display a considerable amount of talent. Mr. Bell had long been subject to severe attacks of asthma. These gradually assumed a more alarming character, and compelled him to leave Glasgow for a country residence. The place he selected for his retirement was Lukeston, Campsie, where he spent the last twelve years of his life. While he resided at Lukeston, he published an elegant edition of *Rollin's Ancient History*, interspersed with copious and interesting notes. Here he also published his principal work, *A System of Popular and Scientific Geography*, in six volumes. He was engaged preparing for publication, *A General Gazeteer*, when death put an end to his labours on the 3rd May, 1833, in the sixty-fourth year of his age.

Lieut.-Colonel John Blackadder, son of a faithful minister, who, during the time of persecution, after the restoration of Charles II., suffered long for his adherence to Presbytery, and endured a distressing imprisonment on the Bass rock, falls here to be mentioned. He was not more distinguished for his personal bravery and military accomplishments than for his private worth and devoted piety. After serving many years on the Continent, under the Duke of Marlborough, in command of the celebrated Cameronian regiment of infantry, he was appointed deputy-governor of Stirling castle, where he died in August, 1729, at the age of sixty-five.

Robert Bruce, of Kinnaird, was born in 1556. He was the second son of Sir Alexander Bruce, of Airth, by Janet, daughter of Alexander, 5th Lord Livingston, and the Lady Agnes Douglas, daughter of John 2nd Earl of Morton. Sir Alexander had embraced the Reformation. Robert, destined for the law, was sent to study at Paris. On his return, he practised in the Court of Session. Theology, however, was his bent—the grand subject, or, rather let us say, master-passion, that had full possession of his mind; and which, as his manhood ripened, was to keep him ever in heroic action. A man this, evidently, who, once realising his main mission on earth, was resolved that it should be divinely fulfilled at whatever personal sacrifice and cost. The sincerity of that apostolic voice, as it "spoke in thunder to the soul that slept in sin," could not for a moment be questioned. But what an ordeal lay in the future for his faith! And the bitter persecution first emanated from the preacher's home. His mother, chagrined at the great gulf-leap from the bar to the pulpit, compelled him to resign his pretensions to the estate of Kinnaird, in which, as an *appanage* of Airth, he had been enfeoffed. Stripping off his scarlet and gold, he put himself under the tuition of a person more properly the father of Presbytery than Knox—Andrew Melville, then professor of Divinity at St. Andrews. In 1587, Bruce debated on the comparative merits of Episcopacy and Presbytery, which, to his auditors, seemed to decide in favour of the existing *regime*. On the 20th of June, he was presented to the General Assembly by Andrew Melville, as a pupil of great promise; and, in July, ascended the pulpit of John Knox, now dead fifteen years, and of Lawson, recently deceased. He had already dispensed the Lord's Supper without having received the imposition of hands; a ceremony to which, as not being, in his opinion, essential to the sacred function, he never would submit. In the following February, this voluntary exile from civic and baronial honours, was elected moderator of the supreme ecclesiastical court. In 1589, he was a confidential servant of the king during his Majesty's voyage to Denmark; and, on the arrival of the royal pair, in their kingdom, acted the part of primate of the church, by placing the crown on the head of Queen Anne. Both in church and state, indeed, such was his influence amongst all classes, that Bruce may be said to have been regent of the kingdom. On the 6th June, 1590, he married Margaret, daughter of James Douglas, Lord Fotherald, senator of the College of Justice. Along with Melville, Bruce was active in obtaining that Act of the civil legislature, by which, in 1592, Presbytery was established as the ecclesiastical government of Scotland. Although Presbytery had banished all parliamentary representation of the functionaries of religion; yet by private meetings, and *touches* from the pulpit *on the times*, it possessed, in civil as well as ecclesiastical matters, a control bordering on tyranny. As a counterbalance, James secretly encouraged "*the Popish faction.*" Popish domestics occupied the palace. "*The ministers*," having remonstrated, were insulted. Melville and Bruce, having waited upon the queen, were told that her Majesty could not see them, being engaged at a dance. The anniversary of the queen's birth was celebrated with great rejoicings on a day set apart by the church for a solemn fast. The commissioners of the church, having resolved on a grave expostulation with royalty, were, by the royal authority, ordered to quit the city within forty-eight hours. Bruce, from the pulpit, exhorted such as disapproved of the tyrannical mandate, to defend the present religious order of things against all opposers whatsoever; but was obliged, with a brother minister, Balcanqual, to retire into England.

Having in April, 1597, returned to Edinburgh, he obtained the royal pardon; but, not being restored to his charge, confined his instructions to a private circle. He resolutely declined having hands laid on him; and, at length, on the 19th of May, after much discussion. was replaced in his charge without the solemn ceremony. In 1600, Bruce, for refusing to profess his belief in the existence of an alleged conspiracy against his Majesty, by the Earl of Gowrie and brother, who had been suddenly put to death as the actors, was imprisoned in Airth castle, and ordered to quit the kingdom on the 11th November. Embarking at Queensferry on the 5th, he landed, five days after, at Dieppe. Having, by the intercession of Lord Kinloss and the Earl of Marr, been allowed to return to Scotland, he was ordered to remain in ward in his house of Kinnaird. On the 14th January, 1601, he had an audience of the king at Craigmillar; but still withheld his belief of "the Gowrie Conspiracy." On the 25th of February, 1603, the commissioners of the church declared his pulpit vacant. When, in March, James had succeeded to the English crown, Bruce, in person, congratulated his Majesty, but was not restored. He had remained at rest a twelvemonth after the king's departure, when he was summoned to witness his formal deposition from the office of the ministry, by the General Assembly. In July, the chancellor informed him that the king had prohibited him from preaching. Bruce fell, as was believed from agitation of spirits, into a fever. Construing it into a divine judgment for his having ceased to proclaim the truth, he resolved never more to obey human authority in sacred matters. In August, as the head of a faction which met at Kinnaird, he was ordered, under pain of outlawry, to enter into prison in Inverness. Here he remained a year, preaching to great multitudes twice a week. After eight years spent in the north, he returned, with permission, to Kinnaird, in August, 1613. Here, however, he met with much vexation from the clergy in the presbyteries of Linlithgow and Stirling. He, therefore, with leave asked and given, retired, with his family, to Monkland, one of his country seats. The Archbishop of Glasgow, offended, as was alleged, by the resort of people to Mr. Bruce's sermons, obliged him to return to Kinnaird. In 1621, he went to Edinburgh without permission, and was committed to the castle, for having transgressed the verge of his confinement. On the 3rd of January, 1622, he received a royal mandate to return to Kinnaird, remain there till April, and then banish himself, during his Majesty's pleasure, to Inverness. He continued in the north till 1625, when the king died. Charles allowed him to live at Kinnaird. He now preached at home, and even in some of the pulpits around Edinburgh. In 1629, the king wrote to the Privy Council, to confine him within two miles of Kinnaird. He had, at his own expense, repaired the church of Larbert, which had long lain neglected; and held services there regularly, converting, amongst others, Alexander Henderson, minister of Leuchars, about to make a conspicuous figure in the annals of presbytery. That his sentiments possessed not all the moderation which future times have attained, was the fault of the age. Less violent than Melville, more enlightened than

Knox, he viewed with a brighter and milder eye the united interests of the church and nation. To the spirit of a baron, descended of the nobles and warriors of his country, he joined the authority of a minister of Jesus Christ. Of his sermons, eleven were printed in his lifetime; and these display a boldness of expression, regularity of style, and force of argument, seldom found in the Scottish writers of the nineteenth century. In one of his sentences he thus applies the verb *To fotch,* or change one's situation:—" Look in what maner wee see the sheepheards tents flitted and fotched, efter the same maner I see my life to be flitted and fotched."

> " Hasten, O car of light!
> Roll on from realm to realm,
> From shore to farthest shore."

We come now to the intrepid and enterprising traveller who succeeded to the name and estate of Kinnaird through his paternal grandmother. He was, by her, descended of the barons of Clackmannan, representatives till the death of Henry the 13th baron of the family of Bruce of whom the Earl of Elgin is now chief. By his paternal grandfather, James traced his ancestry to the Errol family; which, in the beginning of the fourteenth century, had given birth to the Hays of Lochloy; whence, about the end of the sixteenth, came the Hays of Woodcockdale. In 1687, John Hay of

Woodcockdale and Alexander Bruce of Kinnaird concluded a marriage between David Hay, eldest son of the former, and Helen Bruce, eldest daughter and heiress of the latter. It was contracted that their lineal descendant should enjoy the estate of Kinnaird, and bear the name and arms of Bruce. In February, 1729, Mr. Bruce of Kinnaird, son of this marriage, married Marion Graham daughter of James Graham of Airth, dean of the Faculty of Advocates, and judge of the High Court of Admiralty in Scotland. By her, on the 14th December, 1730, he had a second child James, the celebrated Abyssinian traveller—a man of herculean *physique*, and more than ordinary strength of mind. James received his school education at Harrow, along with his half-uncle, William Graham of Airth, and his cousin, William Hamilton. Quitting the academy, he began life as a student for the English bar; but, in 1754, he retired from the profession on his marriage with Adriana Allan, the beautiful and amiable daughter of a wealthy London wine merchant; and was, at the same time, taken as an active partner into the father-in-law's business. The young wife, however, died shortly after the matrimonial union, while on a trip to the south of France for the benefit of declining health. By this sad bereavement Bruce's attention was directed to the study of foreign languages, with a view to trading, and he soon became an accomplished linguist.

In addition to the ordinary European tongues, he could speak Arabian and Ethiopian with the greatest fluency. Having formed an acquaintance with Pitt (the elder), then at the head of affairs, he proposed to him a scheme of making a descent upon Spain, against which country Britain was expected to declare war. Though this project came to nothing, Lord Halifax, noting his enterprising genius, proposed to him to signalise the beginning of the new reign by making discoveries in Africa; and for this end he was, in 1762, appointed British Consul at Algiers. In an interview with George III., before setting out, his Majesty requested him to take drawings of whatever ancient architecture he might discover in the course of his travels. On his way to Algiers, which he reached in March, 1763, he spent some time in Italy, visiting Rome, Naples, and Florence; thus fitting himself, by surveying the works of ancient art, for the observations he was to make upon kindred subjects in Africa. Here he formed an acquaintance with one Luigi Balugani, a native of Bologna, whom he engaged in the capacity of artist, to assist him in his drawings. These were generally finished on the spot in a *camera obscura*, a hexagon of six feet diamater, and a cone at top, the contrivance of Mr. Bruce. Disliking his situation at Algiers, he asked and obtained leave of the Dey, in 1765, to travel through the interior provinces. Having made his proposed excursion, he took the opportunity of visiting Balbec and Palmyra. But there was a country still beyond, of which the world was as yet comparatively ignorant, that he meant to explore. That country was Abyssinia. Perilous dangers were undoubtedly to be encountered; but Bruce, like the noble Livingstone, was just the man to face and overcome the obstacles of such a splendid enterprise : his was

"A frame of adamant, a soul of fire ;
No dangers fright him, and no labours tire."

Shaping his course to Abyssinia, he carried with him a set of mathematical instruments; and having resolved to personate a physician—a welcome guest in the countries he was about to visit—he obtained medical books and instructions from Dr. Russell at Aleppo. From Cairo, on the 12th of December, 1768, he sailed up the Nile, and on the 17th of February, 1769, joined the caravan to Cosseir on the Red Sea. He crossed to Jidda, and explored part of the Arabian coast. Recrossing to Massowah, the only entrance to Abyssinia in that quarter, encountering many dangers, and going through many strange adventures, he at length, on the 4th of November, 1770, arrived at the object of his ambition. Before departing he received the title of Lord of Geesh. But the difficulty now was to return. How to extricate himself from the natives, who had taken a great liking to him, and were averse to part with him, was the first question. Having obtained leave, he set out from Abyssinia on the 26th of December, 1771. Recollecting the dangers to which he had been exposed at Massowah, he resolved to go by Sennaar. After unparalleled toil and peril, he at length reached Syene. Here he stayed till the 11th of December, when he proceeded to Cairo, where he arrived on the 10th of January, 1773—four years and twenty-nine days since he had left it. Reaching France, he spent some time in the south for the recovery of his health, now greatly impaired. Here he was much with the celebrated Count de Buffon, who acknowledges his obligations to "*M. Bruce*" for several important communications in natural history. He visited Bologna and Rome. He returned to Britain in the summer of 1774, and towards the end of '75 settled on his paternal estate. Like any other later hero of the year, wherever he went he had to speak of what he had seen and suffered in the course of his adventurous wanderings through the "dark continent." He related anecdotes of the Abyssinian and Nubian tribes, and gave descriptions of localities and natural objects which certainly appeared wonderful to a civilised people. "Come, now," said an impertinent intruder into Bruce's study in the house near Loch Lubnaig, "I want to know about those Abyssinians eating beefsteaks raw." Having heard the facts, he went on, "Come, now, you must eat a beefsteak raw; you must indeed. You say you have; I can't believe you, you know, unless you prove it." Bruce rang the bell, and ordered up some raw beef, salt, and pepper. His visitor looked on with delight while Bruce slashed the meat and seasoned it. "Now, then," said Bruce, rising and motioning his guest to his seat, "you eat that." "I! Why, I want you to eat it, and I mean you to eat it." "You come here, a stranger, to insult me in my own house, and I must prove my statements in my own way. You shall find that raw beefsteak can be eaten. You see my staircase; if you do not completely empty that plate, I shall fling you from the top to the bottom." No ordinary man could argue physically to his own advantage with the stalwart Bruce, and the sceptical intruder had quietly to obey. His host stood over him, and made him swallow enough to be able to aver that raw beef is eatable, and then turned him out.

Regarded by press and public as an imaginative liar, Bruce in his mind shrunk from the meanness of his fellows. He retired indignant and disappointed to Kinnaird, where for some time he busied himself in rebuilding his house and arranging the concerns of his estate. On 20th May, 1776, he again married—his second wife being Mary, daughter of Mr. Thomas Dundas of Fingask by Lady Janet Maitland, daughter of the Earl of Lauderdale. For nine years Bruce made little progress in the preparation of his journals for the press. They appeared ultimately, however, in 1790, and consisted of five large quarto volumes, with a volume of drawings dedicated to the king. We need scarcely repeat here the well-known story of his death. After having run the gauntlet with so many hair-breadth escapes in his courageous ramblings as an African explorer, he had his neck broken by taking a false step on the stair outside the drawing-room at Kinnaird. And the gallant Speke—for whom was reserved the still more splendid discovery of the great Lake Nyanza—also meets death, shortly after a return from his heroic and exploratory adventures, by the stone of a dyke he was crossing striking the trigger of his gun, when the contents of the barrel went right through his heart. He had crossed the Continent of Africa from Zanzibar to Cairo, and had travelled between Mtesa's country and Kamrasi's vast lake, out of which he had seen the Nile rushing over the Karuma falls, in a land far beyond the ken of civilised man; from thence he had come northward, striking the Nile at its then highest known point, Gondokoro, and returned home to fame and to a disastrous death. Doubtless, if either of those renowned heroes of geographical research had had to choose where and how they should die, they would much rather have fallen by the axe of some savage Zulu tribe on the wild waste of equatorial Africa. It is so unlike the traditional end of the brave and adventurous explorer, the simple yet fatal mishap at Kinnaird; or even to meet

> " A cadger-pownie's daith
> At some dyke-back."

We assume that the general reader is familiar with the principal discoveries in the Nile country, from the time of Herodotus down to that of the intrepid Stanley himself, and have only to add that, notwithstanding all that has lately been told us of the outlet of Lake Tanganika, and of Lake Victoria, the grand secret of the great Egyptian river's sources has not yet been revealed. Bruce made forty observations as to the exact geographical site of its fountain, and found it to be in north latitude 10° 59′ 25″, and 36° 55′ 30″ east longitude, whilst its position was supposed, from the barometer, to be 2 miles above the level of the sea. But this was the Blue Nile, through whose countries he had, with indomitable courage, wandered all alone away up to Abyssinia. There can be no doubt that the mountains of Lockinga and Bisa on the west, or Killimarjora on the east, give birth to the infant Nile, although it has not yet been determined where those waters actually take their rise.

David Doig, LL.D., to whom the grammar

school of Stirling was originally indebted for much of its fame, was son of a small farmer in Angus. He was born in 1719. His father died while he was an infant, and his mother married a second time. The step-father, however, treated him kindly. From a defect of eye-sight, David did not learn to read till his twelfth year, but such was his quickness and power of application, that, in three years, he was successful in a Latin composition for a bursary at St. Andrews. He studied there with great credit, and became bachelor of arts, and student of theology. But certain scruples regarding the Westminster Confession of Faith, deterred him from the church. He had, for several years, taught, in succession, the parochial schools of Monifieth, Kennoway, and Falkland, when his growing reputation gained for him, from the magistrates of Stirling, the rectorship of the grammar school. This office he held, with great credit, for upwards of forty years, in the course of which period the University of Glasgow had conferred upon him the degree of doctor of laws, and the Royal and Antiquarian Societies of Edinburgh had made him a fellow. He was intimately acquainted with Latin and Greek, and, in addition to a profound treatise on the ancient *Hellenes*, wrote a work entitled *Letters on the Savage State*. His articles on "Mythology," "Mysteries," and "Philology," in the *Encyclopædia Britannica* show that he had also made great progress in

Oriental literature. He died on the 15th of March, 1800, in his eighty-second year.

A native of Stirling of the name of Edmond, the son of a baker, born, it would appear, towards the end of the sixteenth century, having run away from his parents, and enlisted in the service of Maurice, Prince of Orange, so greatly distinguished himself as to rise to the rank of colonel. Having acquired considerable wealth, he returned, as a benefactor, to reside in the place of his birth. A plate, in addition to that which received the usual weekly collections for the poor, was for some time placed at the church door, that such as were able, and willing, might put into it their contributions towards the erection of a manse for the minister. A donation was given by Colonel Edmond so munificent, that it seems to have been equal to, if not greater than all the rest of the amount obtained by this collection. The manse thus built, stood at the junction of Church Street and St. John's Street, not many yards from the south-east corner of the church, the site being still plainly indicated by the state of the ground. It was taken down in 1824, and contained till that time some books, of which Mr. Guthrie had been the custodier, and his chair, both of which had been carefully preserved by his successors in the first charge. The chair is now in the library of the School of Arts. The following anecdote is told of the colonel. When on the Continent, being on the parade with several brother officers, he was accosted by a stranger, who professed to have newly come from Scotland, and left the colonel's relations well, enumerating several of high rank. Edmond, turning from him indignantly, informed the circle, that, however this unknown person might flatter his vanity, he must in candour tell them, that he had the honour, of which he should ever be proud, to be the son of an honest baker and freeman of the ancient burgh of Stirling. He then ordered the abashed impostor out of his sight. He would not visit in Stirling, unless his father and mother were invited. The Earl of Marr, son to the regent, and himself lord high treasurer of the kingdom, asked him to dine or sup. Edmond agreed on the forementioned condition, and, thus happily escorted by the aged pair, did the gallant colonel wait upon his illustrious entertainer.

John Erskine, sixth Earl of Mar, was distinguished both as a statesman and warrior. By James V., he was appointed commendator of Cambuskenneth and Inchmahome; while, by Mary, he was invested with the hereditary prefecture, or captainship, of Stirling castle. His name and seal appeared at the deed of Mary's resignation of the kingdom. On that event, he was entrusted with the keeping of the young prince.

Rev. Ebenezer Erskine, whose name is associated with the rise of the Secession from the Established Church, was for several years minister of the third charge of Stirling. His grandfather, Ralph Erskine, who was a descendant of the family of Marr, had thirty-three children, of whom Ebenezer's father, Henry, was the youngest.

Rev. Henry Guthrie, author of "Memoirs of Scottish Affairs," from 1627 to the death of Charles I., in 1649, was minister of Stirling about the period to which his work relates. Having conformed to prelacy, he afterwards became bishop of Dunkeld.

Rev. James Guthrie, the martyr, son of Guthrie of Guthrie, in Forfarshire, was educated at the University of St. Andrews, in which he afterwards, for some time, taught philosophy. As the reputed author of *The Causes of God's Wrath*, he was seized, imprisoned, and brought to trial before the Parliament in Edinburgh. He defended himself with such eloquence, knowledge of law, and strength of argument, as utterly astonished his friends and confounded his enemies. But he was found guilty of high treason; and condemned to death. His execution took place at the cross of Edinburgh on 1st June, 1661. In pursuance of the sentence, his head, having been separated from his body, was fixed up at the Nether Bow Port, where it remained a public spectacle for about twenty-seven years.

Sir George Harvey, the famous painter of historical pictures, was born at St. Ninians in 1805. At a very early age he displayed a taste for drawing; but, having been apprenticed to a bookbinder, found few opportunities as a lad to cultivate his talent. In his eighteenth year, however, he entered the school of the Trustees' Academy in Edinburgh, where he studied two years with such success as to attract attention. In 1826, when the Scottish artists resolved to establish an academy of their own, framed on the model of the Royal Academy of London, Harvey, though only in his twenty-first year, was invited to become an associate. In 1829, that rank was exchanged for academician. Incidents from the history of the Covenanters supplied the subjects of the pictures by which he first got a name. There were the "Covenanters' Preaching," the "Battle of Drumclog," and the "Covenanters' Communion." But he was also great in *tableaux de genre*. "The Curlers," "The Bowlers," and "The Penny Bank," are only a few of his masterly works in grouping. His paintings, too, have ever a Scotch vigour and fervour. In his faces we have the glow of life and of reality; his style is eloquent; his drawing bold; his light and shade emphatic; and his colour deep and luminous.

Dr. Robert Henry was son of James Henry, farmer in Muirtown, by Jean Galloway, of Burrowmeadow. He was born 18th February, 1718, educated under Mr. John Nicolson, parochial schoolmaster of St. Ninians, and afterwards sent to the grammar school of Stirling. Having completed his academical course at Edinburgh, he became rector of the grammar school at Annan. He was licensed to preach on the 27th March, 1746; and settled minister of a dissenting congregation at Carlisle in 1748. On the 13th August, 1760, he was translated to a meeting-house of the same sort at Berwick-upon-Tweed. In 1763, he married Anne, daughter of Thomas Balderston, surgeon there. He never had any children by his wife; but he out-lived her. In 1768, partly through the friendly intents of Mr. Gilbert Laurie, provost of Edinburgh, he was appointed minister of the New Greyfriars in Edinburgh, and, in November, 1776, became collegiate minister of the old church there. He continued in this charge till his death. In 1770, the University of Edinburgh conferred upon him the degree of doctor in divinity; and, in 1774, being then, for the first time, a member of the General Assembly of the Church of Scotland, he was chosen moderator. He devised, and carried into effect, a plan for the benefit of the widows and orphans of dissenting ministers in the north of England. This beneficent institution commenced in 1762, soon after he had published his scheme of it; and was superintended by him for several years.

It was in 1763, as is conjectured, that he first conceived the idea of his *History of Great Britain, written on a new plan*, and which, in every respective period, arranges, under separate chapters, the civil and military history of the country; the history of religion; of our constitution, government, laws, and courts of justice; of learning, learned men, and the chief seminaries of learning; of the arts; of commerce, shipping, money, and the prices of commodities; of manners, virtues, vices, customs, language, dress, diet, amusements. He begins at the invasion of Julius Cæsar, and comes down to the accession of Edward VI. As a collection of facts, supported by documents, and conjoining the provinces of historian and antiquary, it is very interesting. At its first publication it was much abused, particularly by one Gilbert Stuart. Its merits, however, attracted Lord Mansfield, at whose suggestion his Majesty, on the 28th May, 1781, granted to Dr. Henry a pension of £100, to commence from the preceding 5th of April. The 8vo edition of his history, published in 1788, is inscribed to the Earl of Mansfield. Till 1781, he had printed on his own account. He now sold his literary property to Messrs. Caddell and Strachan, and received from them the sum of £1,400. His profits from the outset amounted, according to his calculation, to £3,300. He had persevered in his literary labours till the summer of 1790. He died that year, on the 24th of November; and was buried in the churchyard of Polmont. He had had a country house in the parish. A monument to his memory has been erected above his remains.

The first volume of Dr. Henry's history was published in 1771, the second in 1774, the third in 1777, the fourth in 1781, and the fifth (which terminates with the accession of Henry VII.) in 1785. A few days before his death, he had executed a deed, by which he bequeathed his books to the magistrates, town council and presbytery of Linlithgow, as the foundation of a public library; and laid down certain specified regulations, by means of which a larger library might, as he hoped, be erected, and knowledge diffused.

The celebrated Sir Thomas Hope, Bart., of Craigiehall, king's advocate, purchased, in 1638, from Sir William Livingston, of Kilsyth, the lands of Kerse, and gave them to his second son, Sir Thomas Hope, Bart., of Kerse, one of the lords of session. Sir Thomas's great grandfather, John de Hope, by birth a Frenchman, and said to be of the H'oublons of Picardy, settled in Scotland with Magdalene, Queen of James V. Sir Thomas's father went from Scotland to Holland as a merchant, and married Jacque de Tott, a French lady, Sir Thomas's mother. Mr. Thomas Hope was an eminent lawyer. He was an able counsel for those of the Presbyterians who, in

1605, were indicted for denying the king's authority in ecclesiastical matters. He was, towards 1725, appointed king's advocate. On the breaking out of the war under Charles I., he joined the Covenanters. They had revived the doctrine held by the Church of Scotland before the Reformation, and still maintained by the remains of the Romish church, but subversive of all government, that the ecclesiastical establishment is independent of the civil. A meeting of the estates of parliament at Edinburgh, on the 20th February, 1639, having resolved, according to the language of the times, "*to act conscientiously,*" took the opinion of eminent lawyers and divines "concerning the legality of raising defensive war;" when Sir Thomas Hope, and others, decided in the affirmative. It is, indeed, to be lamented that he abused his great talents, even in his riper years, by assisting in those cabals by which his royal master's ruin was effected. He had two daughters, Mary, married to Sir Charles Erskine, of Alva; and Anne, the first lady of David second Lord Cardross. To these and to his four sons, Sir Thomas gave fortunes; to his eldest son, Sir John, Craigiehall; to his second, Sir Thomas, Kerse; to his third, Sir Alexander, Grantham; to his fourth, Sir James, Hopeton. The last was ancestor of the Earls of Hopeton. Sir Alexander was cupbearer to Charles I. The rest were senators of the College of Justice; two of them, Sir John and Sir Thomas, during their father's lifetime. As it was deemed indecorous that the father should, as king's advocate, plead uncovered before his sons, he was requested to wear his hat. Hence the privilege, though not claimed, which the king's advocate now enjoys when addressing the Courts of Session and Justiciary. Sir James did not ascend the bench till after his father's decease. Sir Thomas Hope, of Kerse, was subsequently advanced to the high post of lord justice general. The father's jurisprudential writings are highly esteemed.

Alexander Hume appears among the early Scottish poets. He was the second son of Patrick Hume, of Polwarth, from whom the noble family of Marchmont derived its lineage, and is supposed to have been born about the year 1560. Appointed minister of Logie in 1598, he remained there until his death on 4th December, 1609. His pieces, though superior to most of the pious effusions of that age, scarcely merit the name of poems. The description he gives of "The Day of Estival"—a composition which may be found in Campbell's *Specimens of the British Poets*, is rather equable and pleasing, than vivid or striking; while the same may be said of his "Spanish Armada."

Dr. James Jeffray, professor of anatomy in the old University of Glasgow, and who published a valuable medical work, was born in the parish of

Kilsyth. The Rev. Dr. R. Rennie, author of several essays on peat moss, was also a native of that town, and its minister from 1789 to 1820. Sir Archibald Edmonstone, Bart., of Duntreath, chief proprietor in the same district, contributed to literature a well-written and interesting account of his travels in Egypt; while Mr. W. A. Cadell, of Banton, published two very readable volumes, entitled *Travels in Italy*.

The Rev. Duncan M'Farlane, who was parish minister of Drymen from 1743 to 1791, was a man of great shrewdness and vigour of mind. He was also of large stature, and of a bold and intrepid character. During the time of his ministrations in Drymen, there were regularly immense gatherings at the annual markets and feeing fairs, when the various classes of the district banded together for party fights, some occasionally of a very serious character, dirks and bludgeons being freely used. The worthy clergyman was often appalled at such disgraceful scenes, and, being a muscular Christian, as well as a persuasive and powerful preacher, he was in the habit of visiting the markets, and by his presence endeavoured to keep matters quiet. His custom was to walk about the parish with a huge stick, which he carried by the middle. When a quarrel seemed imminent, and his persuasive words of no avail, he seized his " rung " by both hands, and laid about him unmercifully;

and what his advice failed to do, his strength soon accomplished. On account of this, he was locally called "Duncan Rungs." There are many incidents told of his prowess and courage, but it will be sufficient to note the following:— Immediately after his appointment at Drymen, he was preaching at Chapelarroch, near Gartmore, when the famous Glengyle presented a child for baptism. The clan M'Gregor being under prescription, ministers were debarred from baptizing them in that name. The proud Glengyle, thinking to overawe his reverence, told him to baptize the child M'Gregor. M'Farlane, raising himself to his full height, and striking the desk before him, exclaimed, " Neither Glengyle nor all his clan will make the minister of Drymen break the laws of this land." The child was baptized in the name of Graham. Mr. M'Farlane kept for a long series of years a very correct weather report, which was of considerable interest.

The late Very Rev. Principal M'Farlan, of the Glasgow University, was born at Drymen, where both he and his father were, at one time, ministers.

John Moore, M.D.—a well-known author, as well as physician—was son of the Rev. Charles Moore, one of the ministers of Stirling. Dr. Moore was born in 1730, and educated at Glasgow. In 1747, he was surgeon's mate in the army in Flanders, and remained there till the general peace. He then studied at London and Paris. In the latter city, he was appointed surgeon to the household of the Earl of Albemarle, the English ambassador. Returning to Scotland, he became partner with Dr. Gordon, an eminent practitioner in Glasgow. In 1773, he went as travelling preceptor to the young Duke of Hamilton. After spending five years abroad, Dr. Moore settled in London, and, in 1779, published part of the fruits of his travels, *A View of Society and Manners in France, Switzerland, and Germany.* The work was so well received, that, in 1781, he produced two similar volumes on Italy. He published, in 1785, *Medical Sketches*, which, however, gave offence to the "Faculty," by betraying certain professional secrets. His next literary effort was *Zeluco, a Novel*, in two volumes. The principal character is represented as a perfect demon, whose atrocities hold her, by the reader, in utter horror; but all that black-painting was intended to demonstrate the natural and deplorable effect of a wicked or careless education; and how a single vicious indulgence brings a hundred others in its train. In 1792, Dr. Moore accompanied the Earl of Lauderdale to Paris; and, having witnessed some of the principal scenes in the French Revolution, applied his masterly pen to a description of them. The result was given to the world in 1795. His novel, *Edward*, intended as the counterpart of *Zeluco*, came out in 1796, but did not excite the same heart-rending interest. In 1800, Dr. Moore produced *Mordaunt: or Sketches of Life, Characters, and Manners, in various Countries*. A nondescript in literature, it contains many amusing and instructive observations. This once popular author died in London in 1802. He was father of the distinguished soldier, Sir John Moore, K.B., who fell at Corunna in January, 1809.

John de Napier, whose family comes now to be spoken of, had, along with several other leading men of his day, engaged to deliver Stirling castle to Edward I., in 1304. His representative in the sixth generation, Sir John Napier of Merchiston, married Elizabeth, younger daughter and co-heiress of Sir Murdoch Menteth of Rusky, and thus acquired, along with Sir John Haldane of Gleneiglis, who had married the sister, a fourth part of the great domain of the ancient Earls of Levenax. The eleventh representative of the family of Napier from the first mentioned, was John of Merchiston, the inventor of logarithms, of whom Hume says that he was " the person to whom the title of *great man* is more justly due, than to any other whom his country ever produced." He was born in 1550. Local tradition had named Gartness castle, in the parish of Drymen, as his birthplace, when the Earl of Buchan shewed, by an inscription on Napier's portrait, engraved by Cooper from an original painting, that he was born at Edinburgh. That he had begun his arithmetical enquiries in 1593 is proved by a letter of Kepler's in 1624. This philosopher had so greatly admired Napier's genius, that, in 1617, he had dedicated to him one of his publications; and five years after, writing one of his correspondents, he says of his *Canon Mirificus*, "Nothing, in my mind, can exceed Napier's method; though in epistles to Tycho, in 1594, he had expressed a hope of the canon." Mr. Henry Briggs, Gresham, professor of mathematics, availing himself of Napier's communications, carried on those calculations from which Napier had, in 1617, been called off by death. Briggs' discoveries were followed, after his demise in 1630, by Mr. Henry Gellibrand, Gresham, professor of astronomy. They were assisted by Kepler, and improved upon by Sherwin, Schulze, Vega, Callet, and Hutton. Napier, who had inherited a fourth part of the estate of the old Earls of Levanax, married, first, Margaret, daughter of Sir James Stirling of Keir, one of the oldest and most respectable families in Scotland. By her he had Sir Archibald, his successor and the first Lord Napier. He married, secondly, Agnes, daughter of Sir James Chisholme, of Dundorn and Cromlix. By her he had five sons, the second of whom was ancestor of the Napiers of Culreuch. The third was ancestor of the Napiers of Ardmore and Craigannet; and the fifth of the Napiers of Blackstone. He was interred in the church of St. Giles, Edinburgh. A stone east of the northern entrance indicates the spot. No public monument, however, has been erected to his memory, but his invention is a monument *ære perennius*.

The Napiers of Ballikenrain were an ancient family. The late Mr. John Napier of Ballikenrain was the sixteenth of the name and family of Napier, who, in succession, had possessed the estate. The male line is now extinct. The late heiress married Mr. Robert Dunmore, who, though not of the clan, erected the obelisk above-mentioned to the *maximus gentilis*. His second son, Mr. John Dunmore Napier, inherited his mother's estate.

Vice-Admiral Sir Charles Napier, K.C.B., &c., was the eldest son of the Hon. Charles Napier of Merchiston Hall, Falkirk, and grandson of Francis, fifth Lord Napier. He was born on the 6th March, 1786, at he above-mentioned house, and entered the Royal Navy in 1790 as a first-class volunteer, on board the 'Martin' sloop of war. Sir Charles is renowned for the part he acted in the brilliant affair of St. Jean D'Acre, and for other martial achievements which need not here be particularised. In later life, as an M.P., he occasionally attempted war personally, in the House of Commons; but in that battle-field he invariably forgot to keep his powder dry. At times, too, he fired his small-shot through the columns of the press at certain heads of the government; and the last time we saw the plucky old hero was in an editorial room in Glasgow, where, with his hands locked behind, he stood giving the back part of his body the benefit of a rousing fire.

Professor Richardson of Glasgow, author of *Anecdotes of the Russian Empire*, and perhaps more particularly known as a tasteful and philosophical critic of Shakespeare's dramas, was proprietor of Croy-Leckie, where he spent his vacations for above twenty years. He died in November, 1814.

George Ridpath was born in Stirlingshire in 1663. Being at the University of Edinburgh in 1686, when James VII. was attempting to establish Popery, he was chosen by his fellow students as their leader in a pantomime intended to burlesque the Pope. A carver was employed to furnish the figure of a man in wood and hollowed inside. They filled him with gunpowder; dressed him in the papal habit, triple crown, &c., and marched, with his holiness, from the Divinity Hall. They had intended to burn him at the Cross, but found it necessary to adjourn for this purpose to an obscure lane. For this exhibition, unbecoming the character of students, Ridpath was obliged to abscond; but, returning from his hiding place at the Revolution, he was appointed a clerk of session. He translated Sir Thomas Craig's *Treatise on Scotland's Sovereignty.* He died in 1717.

Robert Rollock, son of David Rollo of Powhouse, in the neighbourhood of Bannockburn, born in 1560, had studied at St. Andrews, and, when very young, been elected regent of St. Salvator's College. He was, in 1583, when only in his twenty-fourth year, appointed principal of Edinburgh College, which had been erected the year before. He was a minister in Edinburgh. He was moderator of the General Assembly in Dundee, 1597. He died in 1601, in his forty-first year. His intense study had brought on premature disease. He published admired commentaries in Latin, on Ephesians, Revelations, St. John's gospel, and Daniel; besides sermons.

William Symington, of the Wanlockhead mines, and inventor of the first steam-vessel, lived for many years at Falkirk.

The first Earl of Stirling, Sir William Alexander, Bart., of Menstrie, was not only an eminent scholar, but a true poet as well. His first poetical effusions were founded on an unsuccessful passion for an inexorable fair one, whom he fancifully calls "Aurora." She had married a much older person; and Alexander, like another Petrarch, continued to address her in lachrymatory sonnets. He, at length, consoled himself by marrying another. Next, as poet, he set himself to write tragedies. They were to hold the mirror up to princes, and are hence called "Monarchic." They had, indeed, another title, "Elegiac Dialogues for the Instruction of the Great." Had he checked the intemperate ambition and cruel rapacity of his noble pupil, armed with royal letters of fire and sword, however a negative benefit might have passed unperceived and unpraised, he had rendered a service to humanity. The point of the "Monarchic Tragedies" is to illustrate the superiority of Merit to Dignity,

> "More than a crown true worth should be esteemed.
> One Fortune gives, the other is our own;
> By which the mind from anguish is redeemed,
> When Fortune's goods are by herself o'erthrown." Crœsus.

> "Who would the title of true worth were his,
> Must vanquish vice, and no base thoughts conceive.
> The bravest trophy ever man obtained
> Is that which o'er himself himself hath gained." Darius.

One of these plays, called the "the Alexandrœan," gave rise to an epigram by Arthur Johnson, editor of his "Whole Works."

> "Confer Alexandros; Macedo victricibus armis
> Magnus erat, Scotus carmine Major uter?"

Sir William likewise wrote what he calls "Parænesis, or Exhortation to Government," addressed to Prince Henry, a very noble poem, and said to be the poet's master piece. We quote a specimen.

> "O heavenly Knowledge! which the best sort loves,
>   Life of the soul! reformer of the will!
>   Clear light! which from the mind each cloud removes,
>   Pure spring of vertue, physick for each ill!
>   Which, in prosperity a bridle proves,
>   And, in adversity, a pillar still.
>   Of thee the more men get, the more they crave,
>   And think, the more they get, the lesse they have."

This poem must bear date, of course, before 1612, the year of the prince's death. He finished his large sacred poem, "Doomsday," in 1614; and his "Supplement" to complete the 3rd part of Sir Philip Sydney's *Arcadia*, in 1621. He also wrote "Jonathan," a heroic poem; besides minor productions, some of them in prose, and connected with his transatlantic possessions. Addison said of the "Whole Works" of the poetical peer, "I have read them over with the greatest satisfaction."

John Walker, LL.D., the distinguished engineer of London, was born and educated in Falkirk. His father was a respectable merchant in the town; and likewise proprietor and occupier of an extensive farm in the neighbourhood.

James Wilson, D.D., who died in 1829, was translated from Mid-Calder to Falkirk in 1794. In 1801, he published a *History of Egypt* in three volumes; and in 1819, *Prayers for Families and Individuals.* Besides these works, he was the author of several smaller publications. A son who survived him, became minister of Irvine, and also published various theological books of some note.

CHAPTER XXVI.

OLD COUNTY FAMILIES.

JAMES, the first Earl of Callendar, was a staunch adherent of King Charles, and became a commander in the army which marched to relieve him when a prisoner in the Isle of Wight, being attended by a body of his Falkirk retainers. His army having been discomfited, the earl retired to Holland; but his Falkirk troops valiantly forced their way through the victorious republicans. Alexander, the second earl, was a zealous covenanter, and a copy of the Solemn League is still preserved, bearing his signature, with that of many others. On two different occasions, the troops of government took possession of his house; but, in the last of these, in 1678, a mob from Falkirk put the intruders to flight. The other branch of the Livingstone family adhered to the royal cause, and members of it were engaged at the battle of Bothwell Bridge, and otherwise against the covenanters.

The powerful race of Seton was the parent stock of the Edmonstone family. In the middle of the fourteenth century, Sir John Edmonstone of Edmonstone appears a person of considerable importance, and was appointed by David II. coroner to the shire of Edinburgh in fee, accompanied by grants of lands in the county of Banff. His son, of the same name, was a person of still greater eminence, and was named a commissioner for negotiating with England, on three different occasions, during the captivity of James I. in 1407. He married the Lady Isabel, daughter of Robert II., and widow of James, Earl of Douglas and Mar, who was killed at the battle of Otterburne. By the marriage he had two sons, Sir David, who succeeded him, and Sir William Culloden, ancestor of the family of Duntreath. Sir David left two sons, of whom Sir James, the elder, died without male issue, and John, the younger, in whom the elder line of the family was continued, till the middle of the last century, when it became extinct by the death of the last male heir. This branch of the family continued in possession of Edmonstone, in Mid-Lothian, till late in the seventeenth century, when it was sold to the family of Wauchope; it resided, likewise, at Ednam, in Roxburghshire, a grant of Robert III.

To revert to the family of Duntreath, Sir William Edmonstone of Culloden, second son of Sir John, as above, married the Lady Mary, daughter of King Robert III., who had been married three times previously; first, to George Douglas, Earl of Angus; secondly, to Sir James Kennedy of Dunure, ancestor to the Earls of Cassilis; thirdly, to Sir William Graham of Kincardine, ancestor to the Duke of Montrose; and, lastly, to Sir William Edmonstone. By all four marriages she had issue; and, from the last, the present family of Duntreath are lineally descended. For the next century, the house of Duntreath continued in the highest degree prosperous. Its wealth and possessions had considerably increased, and appanages were bestowed on many of its junior branches, nearly all of which are now extinct. A succession of honourable alliances, too, had greatly tended to keep up its respectability. Sir William (the fourth in descent from the first Sir William of Duntreath), who was killed at the battle of Flodden, with James IV., and the flower of the Scottish nobility and gentry, had been appointed steward of Menteith, and constable of the castle of Doune. His son, of the same name, was continued in the same offices by the Regent, John Duke of Albany, which he held for eighteen years; but an heritable grant of them having been conferred by James V. on Sir James Stewart (ancestor of the Earl of Moray), Sir William and his brother Archibald were much irritated at being thus deprived of what had now for so many years been in possession of their family, and a fray ensued in the High Street of

Dunblane, in which Sir James was killed. This event occurred on Whitsunday, 1543. A pardon for this offence was afterwards granted to the two brothers under the Great Seal by the Regent, Duke of Chatelherault, and being connected with the royal family, in consequence of his marriage with Lady Agnes Stewart, daughter to Matthew Earl of Lennox (grandfather to Henry Lord Darnley, the unfortunate husband of Queen Mary), Sir William was made one of the Privy Council during the queen's minority.

His son, Sir James, was appointed justice-deputy under the Earl of Argyll, justice-general, and in 1582 was named one of the assessors on the trial of the Earl of Gowrie, for the celebrated conspiracy against the liberty of James VI., called the Raid of Ruthven; but he appears himself implicated in a similar plot soon after. He was accused, together with three others of the names of Douglas, Cunningham, and Hamilton, of a design to convey the king to some place of confinement, till those lords who had left the country in consequence of their concern in the above conspiracy should be advertised. It was believed to have been little more than an idle conversation; however, the four were seized and indicted for high treason. Sir James pleaded guilty, and threw himself on the king's mercy. The others convicted of having held this treasonable design were executed. Sir James seems to have acted an unworthy part in this business; and, being pardoned, he retired to Duntreath, which he considerably enlarged. A stone with his arms and cypher, but without a date, mark this. The estate, however, was mortgaged by his son and successor, William, to Sir William Livingstone of Kilsyth, and considerable estates purchased in the counties of Down and Antrim, in the north of Ireland. But, fortunately, his next successor, Archibald, resold part of the Irish purchases and redeemed the estate of Duntreath, though the family residence continued to be, for above a century, chiefly at Red Hall, in a district called Broadisland, in the county of Antrim. This Archibald was a strict Presbyterian, and being returned member for the county of Stirling in the parliament which met at Edinburgh in 1633, in presence of Charles I., he strongly opposed every effort made by that monarch for the establishment of Episcopacy in Scotland. He had two sons, William and Archibald. Of these the elder, known as the Dumb Laird of Duntreath, was disinherited, and put under the tutelage of his brother, on account of having been born deaf and dumb. He was, however, a person of great vivacity and cheerfulness, with a very retentive memory; and, according to a portrait which exists of him, of a handsome and intelligent countenance. It is recorded, moreover, that he had a strong sense of religion; and a tradition is preserved that he was endowed with the faculty of second-sight. He lived to a very advanced age. A tower at Duntreath, which he is said to have occupied, still preserves his name. The inheritance, in consequence of the infirmity of the elder, devolved upon the younger brother, Archibald. This gentleman followed the same line as his father, in opposing the tyrannical acts of the government in their endeavour to establish Episcopal jurisdiction, and was fined and imprisoned for holding a conventicle in the private chapel of his house at Duntreath. After his release he retired to Ireland, and died in consequence of his exertions in defending the fort of Culmore, contiguous to Londonderry, at the famous siege of that city by James II., in 1689. He was succeeded by his son and namesake, who appears to have resided chiefly at Red Hall, so that Duntreath fell into decay. He married, first, the Honourable Anne Erskine, daughter to David, Lord Cardross, ancestor to the Earl of Buchan, by whom he had one daughter; and secondly, Anne, daughter of the Honourable John Campbell of Mammore, second son of the unfortunate Earl of Argyll who was beheaded in 1685. Her brother, John, succeeded to the dukedom of Argyle, on the death of his cousin, Archibald. By this marriage he had three sons and three daughters, and was succeeded by his eldest son.

Sir Archibald, created a baronet in 1774, married, first, Susanna, daughter to Roger Harenc, of Footscray Place, in Kent, by whom he had five sons and three daughters; and secondly, Hester, daughter to Sir John Heathcote of Normanton, in Rutlandshire, by whom he had no issue. Sir Archibald sat for above twenty years in Parliament for the county of Dumbarton and the Ayr and Irvine district of burghs. He very judiciously sold the estate in Ireland, and purchased that of Kilsyth, in 1783, which had been forfeited by the Livingstons, Viscounts of Kilsyth, in 1715, and thus established and concentrated the family in their native country. He likewise began a liberal system of improvement upon his estates, which was carried on to a greater extent and completed by his successor. Sir Archibald died at the advanced age of eighty-nine, in 1807, and was succeeded by his eldest surviving son, Sir Charles, who married, first, Emma, daughter of Richard Wilbraham Booth, Esq. of Lathorn House, in the county of Lancaster. By her he had a son and daughter. His second marriage was with the Honourable Louisa Hotham, daughter to Beaumont, second Lord Hotham, by whom he had four sons and two daughters. Sir Charles represented the county of Stirling in parliament for several years previous to his death, which took place on the 1st April, 1821, in the fifty-eighth year of his age.

He was succeeded by his eldest son, Sir Archibald, the late baronet, who married, in October, 1832, his cousin Emma, daughter of Randle Wilbraham, Esq. of Red Hall. Sir William, the present baronet, to whom we have already referred, is thirteenth in lineal descent from Sir William of Culloden, the first of the branch of Duntreath.

The founder of the family of Buchanan was Anselan, a native of Ireland, who is said to have arrived in the eleventh century. His descendants originally bore the name of M'Aslan, a corruption of Anselan, and were chamberlains to the Earls of Lennox. At an early period, they obtained a grant of part of the lands of Buchanan, which afterwards became the family name. In 1225, they received from Maldwin, Earl of Lennox, a charter for Clarinch, an islet in Lochlomond, which was adopted as the war-cry of the clan. In 1296, "Malcolm de Boughcanian" appears in the list of proprietors in Stirlingshire who swore fealty to Edward I. of England. In 1482, a younger son founded the house of Drumnahill, from which sprung, in 1506, the celebrated George Buchanan. In 1519, "Walterus Bucquhanan de eodem" conveyed to his son, Walter, the lands of Spittal. In 1682, the direct line of male succession became extinct; and, in the absence of other competitors, the late Dr. H. Buchanan, of Spittal and Lenny, claimed, in 1826, to be chief of the family. The Buchanans are a numerous clan in the Lennox and adjacent counties. Besides the M'Aslans, already mentioned, they recognize as clansmen some other branches, whose names are common in the district, particularly the Zuils and the Risks—originally soubriquets of individuals, but afterwards surnames of their descendants. The one was so called from the day of his birth, Yule (Christmas); the other from the place of his residence, the Risk (a bare knoll) of Drymen. Many of the Buchanans have settled and prospered in Glasgow, where they have established a charitable society for the poor members of the clan, which distributes the interest of their capital, amounting to upwards of £500 per annum, among all their branches, whatever be their name. The family of Buchanan, though it flourished for upwards of 500 years, while Scotland remained a separate kingdom, was never distinguished in political transactions. One evident cause was the smallness of the family estate, which included only the lower part of the present parish. Their fame rests on their literary eminence. Besides the classical Buchanan, they can boast of Dr. Buchanan, already mentioned, celebrated for his valuable works on the civil and natural history of India (obiit 15th June, 1829); and Dr. Claudius Buchanan, who is entitled to respect and gratitude for having, by his writings and labours, excited the British nation to send the blessings of education and religion to their Indian empire. Dr. Claudius died 9th February, 1815.

At the death of the last Buchanan of that ilk, in 1682, the estate was sold by his creditors, and purchased by the family of Montrose. They, too, claim high antiquity. Without asserting the existence of the Caledonian who, in the fifth century, is said to have broken down the wall of Antoninus, and to have given it his own name of Graham's Dyke, it may be stated that the present Duke of Montrose is the twenty-first lineal descendant from Sir Patrick de Graham, who fell, regretted by friend and foe, at the battle of Dunbar, in 1296. This family, unlike their predecessor, is famed for their military achievements; and numbers among their sons, Sir John de Graham, the companion of Wallace; the Marquis of Montrose, who flourished in the civil wars; the Viscount Dundee, who fell bravely, though vainly, attempting to support the tottering throne of James II.; and the late Lord Lynedoch, who distinguished himself by his chivalrous exertions in the wars of the French Revolution. The late duke, who died 30th December, 1836, must be mentioned as an able and persevering patron of agriculture. During a long life, he was unwearied in embellishing his residence at Buchanan, in improving and extending his plantations, and in introducing superior breeds of farm stock.

According to tradition, the founder of the ancient and noble house of Drummond was a Hungarian, named Maurice, who came over from Hungary in the train of Margaret, queen of Malcolm Canmore, and obtained, in reward of his services, a grant of certain lands, and, among others, of Drymen, in Stirlingshire. It is not certainly known in what part of that parish the Drummonds had their residence, but it was probably somewhere near the Endrick. It is equally uncertain how, or at what period, the family ceased to be connected with the county. In the year 1360, in consequence of a feud which had long subsisted between them and the Earls of Menteith, a compact was entered into at a meeting on the banks of the Forth, in presence of the justiciaries of Scotland, by which Sir John Drummond resigned certain lands in the Lennox, and obtained in lieu of them others of greater value in Perthshire. Shortly after this, and probably in consequence of it, their residence seems to have been transferred to Stobhall, in Perthshire, which, along with other extensive estates in that county, had some years before come into possession of the family by marriage. Previous to this change of residence, however, Annabella, daughter of Sir John Drummond, married Robert, Earl of Carrick, high steward of Scotland, who afterwards succeeded to the throne by the title of Robert III. The fruit of this marriage was two sons, one of whom afterwards became James I. Thus Drymen parish may lay claim to the honour of having produced a lady from whom descended the royal House of Stuart; and who was not more distinguished for rank and station, than for the many virtues which adorned her character.

The estate of Alva was anciently possessed by the Stirlings of Calder in Clydesdale. According to Nisbet, in his first volume of *Heraldry*, "Sir J. Menteith, son of Sir Walter Menteith, of Rusky, married Marion Stirling, daughter and co-heir to Sir John Stirling, of Calder in Clydesdale, and with her he got ye lands of Kerse and Alveth (Alva), for which ye family carried ye buckler for the name of Stirling, and flourished for many years." Sir William Menteth or Menteath, of Alva, married Helen Bruce, daughter to the laird of Airth, and his son, Sir William Menteth, married Agnes Erskine, daughter to Alexander, Lord Erskine, whose successors afterwards, through right of their mother, inherited the earldom of Mar. The Countess of Mar and Kelly is a descendant of the family of Menteth of Rusky. By the intermarriage before alluded to, it is highly probable that the Alva property went to the Bruce, and afterwards to the Erskine family. In 1620 it went to Sir Charles Erskine, fifth son of John, sixth Earl of Mar. His great grandson, Sir Henry Erskine of Alva, father to the late Earl of Rosslyn, sold it in 1759 to his uncle, lord justice clerk, called Lord Tinwald, whose son, James Erskine, a senator of the College of Justice, inherited it, with the title of Lord Alva. He was one of the most energetic proprietors, with the exception of the Bruces, who founded the present mansion and church. Lord Alva sold the estate in 1775 to John Johnstone, Esq., son of Sir James Johnstone, Bart. of Westerhall, Dumfriesshire, brother to Sir William Pulteney. Sir John and Sir Charles Erskine, two of the Alva proprietors, were both killed when abroad in 1746.

There are several very old families in Campsie parish, the principal of which are the Lennoxes of Woodhead, the Kincaids of Kincaid, the Stirlings of Craigbarnet, the Stirlings of Glorat, and the M'Farlans of Kirkton, who are derived, by the female line, from the same stock from which the Lennoxes of Woodhead claim descent. M'Farlan of Kirkton, or Bancleroche, came into possession of that estate in 1624. Antermony was purchased by Captain John Lennox, a younger son of the Woodhead family. The claim of this family to the Lennox peerage has been brought down to her own time by Margaret Lennox, late of Woodhead; from which case it appears that Askill, a powerful Northumbrian baron of the age of William the Conqueror, having found it necessary, with many other northern barons, to flee into Scotland, was kindly received by Malcolm III., and his son, Alwyne, was by Malcolm VI. created Earl of Lennox, the name being derived from the river Leven, and the estate extending over Dumbartonshire, great part of Stirlingshire, and parts of the counties of Perth and Renfrew. The earldom continued in this family down to the time of Earl Duncan, who, with the Duke of Albany and his two sons, was executed at Stirling, May 1425. After this, Isabella, his eldest daughter, enjoyed it many years, and she having died without issue in 1459, the earldom, without any forfeiture having taken place, but by reason of the feudal incident of non-entry, fell into the hands of the sovereign as superior. Donald, son of Earl Duncan, by a second marriage, was the ancestor of the Lennoxes of Ballcorach. John, the sixth of Ballcorach, came into possession of the lands of Woodhead about 1520.

The Kincaids were in possession of Kincaid in 1280, as is proved by a charter extant. In 1421, Duncan, Earl of Levenax, conveyed to his son, Donald, ancestor of the Woodhead family, the lands of Balcorrach, Balgrochyr, Bencloich, Thombay, and others in the parish of Campsie. His son, John, was served heir of his father in said lands in 1454, and seems to have been also proprietor of the estates of Kilmordining and Caillie. The estate of Bencloich was sold to

Edmonstone of Duntreath in 1660, and was by Sir Archibald Edmonstone sold to Charles Macintosh, Esq., and William Macfarlan, Esq., in 1834. Glorat was a part of the earldom of Levenax, and Isabella, Duchess of Albany, eldest daughter of the last earl of the old line, was in possession of it, as appears from the Exchequer Rolls, in 1456. John, Earl of Lennox, in the Darnley line, gave a grant of the lands of Inchinnan in Renfrewshire, "delecto consanguineo suo Gulielmo Stirling de Glorat et Margaretæ Houstoun sposæ suæ," in 1525, which is the first trace to be found of the family; but very probably Glorat was acquired by the Stirlings about 1470, after the death of Isabella. In 1550, George Stirling of Glorat was captain and governor-in-chief of Dumbarton castle. The arms and motto, "semper fidelis," were granted to the family for their loyalty to their sovereigns Charles I. and II., and in the year 1666, the family was honoured with the dignity of knight baronet. Both the Glorat family and the Stirlings of Craigbarnet are descended from the Stirlings of Calder or Cadder, whose name appears in the Ragman's Roll, 1279. John Striveling or Stirling of Craigbernard (Craigbarnet) is witness to a deed in 1468. Kincaid, "Laird of Kincaid of Stirlingshire," for his valiant services in recovering Edinburgh Castle from the English, in the time of Edward I., was made constable of the said castle, and his posterity enjoyed that office for a long period, carrying the castle in their armorial bearings. There is an old broad sword belonging to a branch of the family, upon which are the arms, *gules* on a fesse *ermine*, between two mullets-in-chief *or*, and a castle triple towered in base *argent*, with these words,—

> " Wha will pursew, I will defend
> My life and honour to the end."

The ancestor of the Macfarlanes of Kirkton was George Macfarlane of Markinch, second son to Andrew Macfarlane of that ilk, in the reign of James V. George having sold the foresaid lands of Markinch, went afterwards and settled in the north Highlands amongst his namesakes the Macfarlanes, promiscuously called in the Irish language, M'Allans, Allanich, or Clan-Allan— *i.e.*, the posterity of Allan, because of their descent from Allan Macfarlane, younger son to one of the lairds of Macfarlane, who settled in Strathdown, Aberdeenshire, several centuries ago. From him are descended the families of Auchorrachan, Balnengown, Lismurdie, &c., as also several others in Braemar and Strathspey. His posterity continued in the north for several generations, until the time of Patrick Macfarlane, the fourth descendant in a direct line, who, returning again to the south, purchased the lands of Kirkton. He married Christian Blair, daughter to —— Blair, commissary of Glasgow, who was younger son to —— Blair of that ilk, an ancient family in the shire of Ayr, by whom he had James Macfarlane of Kirkton, his successor, and a daughter, Christian, married to Sir Hugh Wallace of Wolmet. James married Mary Keith, daughter to John Keith, younger son to the Earl Marischal, by whom he had Hugh, his successor, who married Elizabeth Doig, daughter, and ultimately sole heiress to Paul Doig of Ballingrew, a very ancient Perthshire family. Hugh, by this marriage, had, besides William his heir, a numerous issue both of sons and daughters. The armorial bearing of the family is quarterly—first and fourth, *argent*, a saltier wavey, cantoned with four roses, *gules*, as a cadet of Macfarlane of that ilk; second and third, *gules*, a cheveron between two cinquefoils in chief and a sword pale-ways, *argent*, hilted and pommelled, or, in base, for Doig of Ballingrew; crest, a demi-savage proper, holding in his right hand a sheaf of arrows, and pointing with his left hand to an imperial crown, *or*. Motto—"This I'll defend."

The Dunmore family is a branch of the house of Athole, springing from John, first Marquess of Athole, and his wife Ameliana-Sophia, daughter of James, seventh Earl of Derby, through their second son, Lord Charles Murray, master of the horse to Queen Mary II. of England, who was elevated to the peerage of Scotland 16th August, 1686, in the dignities of Lord Murray, of Blair, Monlin, and Tellymot, Viscount Fincastle, and Earl of Dunmore. His lordship married Katherine, daughter of Robert Watts, Esq., and had three sons and three daughters. He died in 1710, and was succeeded by his eldest surviving son, John, one of the representative peers in 1713, and colonel of the 3rd regiment of foot-guards, a general officer in the army, and governor of Plymouth. His lordship died unmarried, 18th April, 1752, when the honours devolved upon his brother, William. This nobleman married Catherine, daughter of his uncle, Lord William Murray (who became Lord Nairne by marrying the heiress of that family), by whom he had two sons and two daughters. His lordship having been involved in the rebellion of 1745, was arraigned at the court held at Southwark for high treason, in 1746, and pleaded guilty, but obtained the king's most gracious pardon. He died in December, 1756, and was succeeded by his eldest son, John, one of the representative peers from 1761 to 1784. His lordship married, 21st February, 1759, Lady Charlotte Stewart, daughter of Alexander, sixth Earl of Galloway, by whom he had two sons. We have referred in a following chapter to the later members of this noble family, the fifth Earl of which was created Baron of the United Kingdom in 1831. Their motto is "Furth fortune and fill the fetters." The present earl, in addition to his excellent qualities as a landlord and country gentleman, is a man of distinguished gallantry and bravery. A year ago near Harris he, at great risk, when a very heavy gale was blowing, put out in a boat, which other three men and himself pulled for eight hours, and rescued the crew of a yacht. Nobody would face the storm but the earl and the three men who went out along with him, and but for their heroic assistance the ladies, gentlemen, and children in the yacht must have perished. For this act of bravery, the noble earl was awarded the medal of the Royal Humane Society; while a sum of money was distributed amongst the three men who courageously accompanied him. His lordship is also well known as an accomplished musician, both in theory and practice. His concerts in London attract great attention. The Prince of Wales is generally present, and the earl conducts the music himself. These concerts are the most select gatherings that society furnishes. They are, moreover, the only respectable ones at which smoking is permitted, and where good wine is given to the audience free of charge. They usually break up about two o'clock; and are, of course, the occasion of all the gossip of the week.

The Bruce family of Stenhouse claims a common ancestor with the noble house of Elgin. Sir Alexander Bruce, of Airth, lineally descended from Sir Robert Bruce, Knt., of Clackmannan, married Janet, daughter of Alexander, the fifth Lord Livingstone, and had several sons, of whom the eldest, William, was ancestor of the Bruces of Airth, now extinct. Robert, the youngest, became progenitor of the Bruces of Kinnaird; and William, the second son, obtained from his father the lands of Stenhouse, &c., in a charter, dated 28th June, 1611. This gentleman, who was created a baronet of Nova Scotia, with remainder to his heirs male whatsoever, 26th June, 1629, married, first, the heiress of Lothian, by whom he had an only daughter; and secondly, Rachael, daughter of Joseph Johnston Esq., of Hiltoun, by whom he had two sons, and was succeeded at his decease, in 1630, by the elder, William. As we have stated elsewhere, the present representative of this house is Sir William Cunningham Bruce.

The family of Livingston has figured in the history of Scotland. Sir Alexander Livingston of Callendar became governor to James II. on the death of the late king. Sir Alexander and the Chancellor Crichton are accused of confining the queen mother, for the sake of usurping the power committed to her by her deceased lord. Both were concerned in that act of cruelty to which, in the presence of the youthful monarch, William sixth Earl of Douglas fell a victim in Edinburgh castle; by which James was trained to the assassination of another of the Douglasses; and which brought down on the two principal actors the vengeance of the house of Douglas. Livingston was, afterwards, at the instigation of the eighth Earl of Douglas, impeached, sentenced to the loss of his estate, and imprisoned in Dumbarton castle. He was afterwards restored to the royal favour, recovered his estate, was a member of the Privy Council, ambassador to England, and justice general. His son and successor, James, was created Lord Livingston, was master of the household, and, afterwards, lord great chamberlain. Sir Alexander's younger brother, Sir William, had founded the house of Kilsyth, having got the estate from his father. His representative in the sixth generation, Sir William of Darnchester, who, at Prince Henry's baptism, had been knighted during his father's lifetime, was eminent as a lawyer; and, in 1609, was appointed a senator of the College of Justice, and, afterwards, a member of the Privy Council and Vice-Chancellor. He died in 1627, and was succeeded by his son and grandson, but at length, in 1647, by his brother, Sir James Livingston of Barncleugh, who, having maintained his loyalty during the civil wars and usurpation, was, on the restoration of the House of Stuart, created Viscount Kilsyth, Lord Campsie, &c. His second son, William third Viscount Kilsyth, having engaged in the insurrection of 1715, was forfeited. He married first, Jean, daughter of William Lord Cochran, and widow of the Viscount Dundee, who brought him a son; secondly, Barbara, daughter of Macdougal of Mackerston, by whom he had a daughter. Both children died early, and were buried in the family mausoleum at Kilsyth.

Neither the Airths or the Mores have attained to the dignity of the peerage. The first had the baronies of Airth, Carnock, and Plean; which, in the reign of James I, came to heirs female, and, by marriage, to the Bruces, Drummonds, and Somervilles.

The Napiers of Ballikenrain were an ancient family; but the male line is now extinct. They are treated under the head of Eminent Men.

CHAPTER XXVII.

TITLED AND UNTITLED ARISTOCRACY.

IN a general history of this kind, our treatment of the "upper ten thousand" of the county must necessarily be of Spartan brevity.

Lord Abercromby, George Campbell Abercromby of Tullibody, is the eldest son of the third lord, by Louisa Penuel, daughter of the late Hon. John Hay Forbes; who, as Lord Medwyn, was a Scotch judge of session. His lordship was born in 1838; succeeded to the title in 1852; and married, in 1858, Lady Julia Janet Georgiana, daughter of Adam, second Earl of Camperdown.

Sir James Edward Alexander, C.B., of Westerton, who was created a knight in 1838, is the eldest son of the late Edward Alexander, Esquire, of Powis, by his second wife Catherine, daughter of John Glas, Esquire, provost of Stirling. He was born in 1807; and, in 1837, married Eveline Marie, third daughter of Lieut.-Col. Charles Cornwallis Michell, K.H.; and has, with other issue, Edward Mayne, born 1846. Sir James, who is a major-general in the army, was educated at the

Universities of Edinburgh and Glasgow, and at the Royal Military College, Sandhurst.

John Blackburn, Esquire, of Killearn, is son of the late Peter Blackburn, Esquire, by Jean Wedderburn, second daughter of James Wedderburn, Esquire, formerly solicitor-general of Scotland. His father for some time represented the county in Parliament; but, at a general election, was defeated by Admiral Erskine of Cardross (Liberal), who headed the poll with a majority of 34. The Tory was highly esteemed on all hands for his shrewd, energetic, and practical parts. His impolitic antecedents, however, with reference to the commercial treaty, the county franchise, and game laws, sealed his doom with the Stirlingshire electors. Mr. Blackburn, senr., was also chairman of the old E. & G. railway, when the late Mr. Richard Hodgson cleverly, though by no means creditably, clutched it as one solvent spoke at least for the wheels of the North British. But Mr. Hodgson, notwithstanding all his alarming intrepidity and "go" as a railway chief, simply lived a few years before his time. It, perhaps, cannot be said that he had the Tay Bridge in view, but he certainly had the Forth Bridge; and all that the North British company have done and are doing, since his retirement and death, was only what he aimed at achieving. John Blackburn, Esquire, was born in 1843; and succeeded to the estate, with its elegant mansion, on the banks of the Blane, in 1870. The property was purchased in 1814 by his paternal grandfather, who had made a fortune in Jamaica.

J. C. Bolton, Esquire, of Carbrook, sits at present in parliament for the county. He might almost have been ranked as one of the eminent men. His career, which has been exceptionally prosperous, shows what business ability, keen insight, sound judgment, and force of character, can do for success in life. Having had his way to make in the world, he started on fortune's track as a sailor boy; but, in his fifteenth year, entered the British office of an East Indian house, in which he rose from junior clerk to the position of senior partner, and is now the only representative of the well-known Glasgow firm of Messrs. Ker, Bolton & Co. For some years, he was chairman of the Chamber of Commerce, and is still a director of the Caledonian Railway, and chairman of the Callendar & Oban line. Mr. Bolton married a Miss Higginbotham, daughter of the late Samuel Higginbotham, Esquire, Glasgow, but that lady died about a quarter of a century ago.

Sir William Cunningham Bruce, Baronet, of Stenhouse, is the eldest son of the late William Cunningham Bruce, Esquire, of the Bombay Civil Service, by Jane, daughter of William Clarke, Esquire, of London. He was born in 1825; and succeeded his uncle, Sir Michael, as eighth baronet, in 1862. In 1850, he married Charlotte

Isabella, daughter of the Hon. Walter O'Grady, Q.C., and grand-daughter of Standish, first Guillamore. She died in 1873. Sir William was formerly captain of the 74th Foot. The heir, his son Michael, was born 1853.

The Right Hon. Sir Andrew Buchanan, G.C.B., of Craigend, is the only son of the late James Buchanan, Esquire, by the Lady Janet Sinclair, eldest daughter of James, twelfth Earl of Caithness. He was born in 1807; and married, first, in 1839, Frances Catherine, only daughter of the late Very Rev. Edward Mellish, of Rushall Hall, Staffordshire, formerly dean of Hereford. She died in 1854. In 1857, Sir Andrew married, second, the Hon. Georgina third daughter of Robert Walter eleventh Lord Blantyre, and has by the former wife, with other issue, James, commander in the Royal Navy, who was born in 1840; and married, in 1873, Arabella Catherine, youngest daughter of G. C. Colquitt-Craven, Esquire, of Brockhampton, Gloucestershire. Sir Andrew, who entered the diplomatic service in 1825, was sworn a member of the Privy Council in 1863; appointed ambassador at Berlin in 1862, at St. Petersburg in 1864, and at Vienna in 1871.

Henry Ritchie Cooper, Esquire, of Ballindalloch, is the second son of the late Samuel Cooper, Esquire, of Failford and Ballindalloch, by Janet, daughter of Henry Ritchie, Esquire. He was born in 1816; succeeded in 1842; and, in 1846, married Mary Jane, only surviving child of Gerald Butler, Esquire, of Wexfordshire. With other issue, he has Henry, born in 1852.

Thomas George Dundas, Esquire, of Carronhall and Fingask, is the eldest son of the late Joseph Dundas, Esquire (who died at Carronhall in 1872), by Margaret Isabella, youngest daughter of George Moir, Esquire, of Denmore, Aberdeenshire. He was born in 1853, and is lieutenant in the 52nd Foot. The surname of Dundas is very ancient and justly celebrated. It may be traced to Cospatrick, first Earl of March. Sir John Dundas of Fingask, in Perthshire, who flourished about the middle of the sixteenth century, was descended of Alexander, eldest son, by a second marriage, of James Dundas, Esquire, of Dundas, eleventh from Earl Cospatrick, with Christian Stewart, daughter of John *Dominus de Innermeath et Lorn*. This lady was aunt to the Black Knight of Lorn, who married Jane, Queen of Scotland, daughter of John, Duke of Lancaster, son of Edward III., and relict of James I.

The noble house of Murray, Earl of Dunmore, is descended of Sir John de Moravia, high sheriff of Perthshire under the Lion and Alexander II. His son, Malcolm de Moravia, also high sheriff of Perthshire, is witness to a charter by Malise Earl of Strathern, to his sister Annabella, on her marriage with Sir David de Graham, of the lands of

Kincardine in Strathearn. By this lady, daughter and heiress of Sir Gilbert de Gask, he acquired the lands of Gask in Strathearn. His second son, Sir William, who succeeded to the representative of the family, married Adda, daughter of Malise, steward of Strathearn, in right of Muriel his wife, daughter and heiress of Congal de Mar de Tullibardine, son of Duncan Earl of Mar. By Adda, Sir William de Moravia acquired Tullibardine, and, from her brother Henry, steward of Strathearn, obtained a charter of confirmation in 1284. The writ is dated *apud Duffaly*, a place now called Duchally, near the entrance of Gleneglis. He was one of the great barons of Scotland who submitted to Edward I.'s determination in favour of Baliol. His son, Sir Andrew Murray, second of Tullibardine, favouring the Baliol party, paid the forfeit with his life at Perth in 1332. His great grandson, Sir Walter, fifth of Tullibardine, was surety for Sir John de Drummond, in the well-known treaty with the Menteths of Rusky on the banks of the Forth near Stirling 17th May, 1360, and appended his seal, with those of Sir John and Sir Maurice de Drummond, on the one part. His son and heir, Sir David, first styled of Gask, and afterwards of Tullibardine, founded, and largely endowed, the collegiate church of Tullibardine, for a provost and four prebendaries, in 1446. His daughter Christian married Sir Murdoch Menteth of Rusky, and was mother of the two co-heiresses of the Rusky estate and fourth part of the Levenax, who married, the one Sir John Haldane of Gleneglis, and the other Sir John Napier of Merchiston. His eldest son, Sir William, seventh of Tullibardine, was sheriff of Perth and Banff shires, and married Margaret, daughter of Sir John Colquhoun of Luss, lord high chamberlain of Scotland. He had by her seventeen sons, of whom many of the Murrays are descended. His eldest son, Sir William, obtained from James III., in 1782, a charter of the stewartry of Strathearn and lordship of Balquhidder. It was ratified by parliament under the following reign. The ninth of Tullibardine, William, whose mother was a daughter of Lord Gray, married Lady Margaret Stewart, daughter of John Earl of Athole. The tenth of Tullibardine, William, married Catherine, daughter of Sir John Campbell of Glenurchy. The eleventh, Sir William, notwithstanding he had taken an active part in the Reformation, was a favourite of Queen Mary, and had the honour of repeated visits from her Majesty at Tullibardine. He was made one of her privy council and comptroller of the kingdom in 1565. His eldest sister, Annabella, was countess of the Regent Mar, and, when a widow, entrusted with the infant person of James VI., "his hieness continuing under her noriture, as towards his mouthe and ordering of his person." Sir William Murray of Tullibardine, had, with his nephew, the Earl of Mar, afterwards lord high treasurer, the keeping &c. of Stirling castle, and of the infant king, whose residence it was. By Lady Agnes Graham, daughter of William second Earl of Montrose, he had his eldest son, Sir John, twelfth of Tullibardine, who, with his cousin Mar, had been the intimate friend of James VI., was, in 1592, appointed master of the king's household; on the 15th of April, 1604, created Lord Murray of Tullibardine; and on the 10th of July, 1606, Earl of Tullibardine. John first Earl of Tullibardine had, by Dame Catherine Drummond, daughter of David second Lord Drummond, William second Earl of Tullibardine; John Patrick, afterwards third earl; Mungo, afterwards Viscount Stormont; Lady Anne, married to the Earl of Kinghorn; Lady Lillias, to Sir John Grant of Grant; Lady Margaret, to Haldane of Gleneglis; Lady Catherine, to Ross of Balnagowan; and a fifth daughter to John M'Gregor. William second Earl of Tullibardine married Lady Dorothea Stewart, eldest daughter and heiress of John fifth Earl of Athole; had by her John sixth Earl of Athole, father, by Lady Jean, daughter of Sir Duncan Campbell of Glenurchie, of the first Marquis of Athole, and, through him, by Lady Emilia Stanley, daughter of James Earl of Derby, grandfather of Charles, the second son of this marriage, created by James VII. Earl of Dunmore, Viscount Fincastle, Baron Murray of Blair, 16th August, 1686. By Catherine, daughter of Robert Watts, Esquire, of the county of Hereford, the Earl of Dunmore had five sons, three of whom, James, John, and William, became successively his representatives in the peerage; and three daughters married, to Lord Kinnaird, the Earl of Dundonald, and John Lord Nairn. William had by Catherine, daughter of William Lord Nairn, three sons, and four daughters. Lady Catherine married John Drummond, Esquire, of Logie-Almond. His eldest son, John, became fifth Earl of Dunmore. By Lady Charlotte Stewart, daughter of Alexander Earl of Galloway, he had the sixth earl, who succeeded him in 1809, and, by Lady Susan Hamilton, daughter of Archibald Duke of Hamilton and Brandon, had male issue. The first Earl of Dunmore's elder brother, John second Marquis of Athole, was, on the 30th of June, 1703, created Duke of Athole, to the heirs male of his body; whom failing, to the heirs male of his father's body. The Earl of Dunmore and male descendants are thus capable of contingently succeeding to the dukedom of Athole. By Lady Catherine Hamilton, eldest daughter of William Duke of Hamilton, the Duke of Athole had six sons and one daughter. John Marquis of Tullibardine was killed at the battle of Mons in 1709. His next brother, William, having embarked in the insurrection of 1715, was attainted of high treason. Escaping to France, he returned in company with Charles Edward Stuart, in 1745; was made prisoner in 1746; and died in the Tower of

London in 1747. The duke procured the settlement of his estates and honours on his third son James; who, on the death of his father in 1724, became second Duke of Athole. On the death of the Earl of Derby, in 1735, without issue, while the estates and honours of Derby went to his male heir Sir Edward Stanley, the title of Lord Strange, and the lordship of Mann and the Isles came to the Duke of Athole, as heir of line and at law. By Jean, daughter of Sir John Frederick of Westminster, Bart., his grace had one son, who died young, and two daughters, Lady Jean, Countess of Crawfurd, who died without issue, and Lady Charlotte, married to her cousin, Mr. John Murray, eldest son of Lord George Murray, younger brother of her father. Mr. Murray succeeded his uncle and his father-in-law in the dukedom of Athole, and Lady Charlotte preserved in the family the honours and estates which had otherwise gone out of it. They were the parents of a late duke; who, in 1786, was created Earl Strange. The sovereignty of Mann was, in 1765, purchased by the parliament, and annexed to the crown of Great Britain. The lords of Mann, though they waved the title of king, had the powers. Mann was a royal fief of the English crown, and the only one; so that the Dukes of Athole had latterly united the characters of subject and sovereign, and the Earls of Dunmore might, contingently, have been in the same situation. Charles Adolphus

Murray, the present earl, is the only son of Alexander Edward sixth earl, by Lady Katherine, daughter of George Augustus eleventh Earl of Pembroke. He was born in 1841; succeeded in 1845; and, in 1866, married Lady Gertrude, daughter of Thomas second Earl of Leicester. The heir, his son Alexander Edward, Viscount Fincastle, was born in 1871. Lady Susan Catherine Murray, the earl's eldest sister, became, in 1860, the second wife of James Carnegie, K.T., Earl of Southesk, who married, first, Lady Catherine Hamilton, daughter of Charles first Earl of Gainsborough. His lordship, who was educated at Eton, is a skilled musician both in theory and practice. Of late years he has devoted his attention and means chiefly to the breeding and rearing of prize cattle. He is lord-lieutenant of the county, and a lord in waiting to the Queen.

The surname Edmonston is certainly as old as Alexander II. Sir John de Edmonston *Miles* was a person of note under David Bruce on the 17th of March, 1499, who bestowed upon him the barony of Boyne, in Banffshire. Sir John had Edmonston in Mid-Lothian; and was, by the same monarch, appointed hereditary coroner of that county, with a power of assignment. He was proprietor also of Culloden in Inverness-shire. He married the Princess Isabel Stewart, relict of James Earl of Douglas, slain at the battle of Otterburn 1388, and daughter of Robert II., king of Scotland. During the reign of his brother-in-law, Robert III., Sir John de Edmonston was employed as plenipotentiary in different treaties with England, and had the same dignified function in three successive treaties with the same nation under the regency of his other brother-in-law, Robert Duke of Albany. By Lady Isabel he had two sons, Sir David de Edmonston, who died without male issue, and Sir William Edmonston of Culloden. The latter was the direct and immediate ancestor of the Edmonstons of Duntreath. He married the Princess Mary Stewart, eldest daughter of Robert III. and Queen Annabella Drummond; and, from his lady's nephew, James II., obtained the lands of Duntreath. By the princess, Sir William Edmonston had a son, Sir William, and a daughter, Matilda, married to Sir Adam Cunninghame of Caprington. Sir William Edmonston of Culloden and Duntreath, who, by the death of his uncle without male issue, succeeded to the representation of the family of Edmonston, fixed his residence at Duntreath, and dropped the addition of Culloden. By Lady Matilda Stewart, daughter of Lord James, son of Murdoch, Duke of Albany and Regent, by Lady Isabel, Countess of Levenax in her own right, he had two sons, Sir Archibald, his heir, and William, who, by royal grant, obtained the lands of Buchynhadrick in the stewartry of Monteith. Sir William had, by the same lady, a daughter,

Mary, married to Sir William Cunninghame of Glengarnock. He was, under James III., in 1472, one of the senators of the College of Justice. Sir Archibald Edmonston of Duntreath was, by James IV., made captain of Doune castle, and steward of Monteith and Strathgartney. By Janet, daughter of Sir James Shaw of Sauchie, comptroller of Scotland, and governor of Stirling castle under James III., he had three sons, Sir William, his heir, James, ancestor of the Edmonstons of Broich in Stirlingshire, Jacob, of the Edmonstons of Balinton in Perthshire; and five daughters, Janet, married to William first Earl of Montrose, Catherine, to John second Earl of Eglinton, Christian, to John second Lord Ross, Margaret, to George Buchanan of Buchanan, Beatrix, to James Muschet of Burnbank in Perthshire. Sir William Edmonston of Duntreath, after his father's death in 1502, was, by James IV., appointed captain of Doune castle and steward of Monteith. He sold Culloden to Strachan of Scotstown. He fell on Flodden field 9th September, 1513. By Sybilla, daughter of Sir William Baillie of Lamington, he left, Sir William, his heir, Archibald, ancestor of the Edmonstons of Spittal, James, ancestor of the Edmonstons of Newton and of Cambuswallace, and several daughters, the eldest of whom, Marion, was married to John Campbell of Glenurchy, paternal ancestor of the Earls of Breadalbane. Sir William Edmonston of Duntreath, and his brother Archibald Edmonston of Spittal, were, in 1516, made, by royal charter, joint captains of Doune castle and stewards of Menteith and Strathgartney. He was a privy councillor in 1565. By Margaret, daughter of Sir James Campbell of Lawers, and ancestor of the Earls of Loudon, he had, besides five daughters, all respectably married, Sir James, who married Helen, daughter of Sir James Stirling of Keir, and had, by her, William, his heir, and three daughters. William Edmonston of Duntreath married Isabel, daughter of Sir John Haldane of Gleneglis; and had, by her, Archibald, his heir, James, and John. The last married the sole heiress of Edmonston of Broich. The eldest was a member of the parliament met at Edinburgh in 1633, when Charles I. presided in person. By Jean, daughter and heiress of Hamilton of Halcraig, brother of Viscount Clandeboy, he had two sons, William, who, being dumb, did not succeed his father, and Archibald, his father's successor. By Anna Helena, daughter of Scot of Harlwood-burn, he had, besides two daughters, both respectably married, Archibald, who married Miss Campbell, daughter, by the Honourable Miss Elphinston, of John Campbell of Mamore, son of Archibald ninth Earl of Argyll, and father of the late duke; and, by her, had Sir Charles Edmonston, created a baronet of Great Britain in 1774, and father, by

Miss Harren, of the late Sir Charles Edmonston, Bart. of Duntreath. Sir William, ex-M.P. for the county, is the present representative of this noble family. We have referred to the Duntreath estate in an earlier chapter.

The first of the family of Elphinston who appears on record, John de Elphinston, flourished under Alexanders II. and III., and possessed the barony of Elphinston, in Mid-Lothian. His grandson and representative, Sir John de Elphinston, is forward with his younger brothers, Aleyn and Duncan, among the involuntary subjects of the English monarch, in 1296. By Margaret de Seton, niece of King Robert Bruce, he had Alexander de Elphinston, who by marriage with Agnes de Airth, acquired Airth-Beg, and several other lands in Stirlingshire; and by exchange of part of Airth-Beg, Kirkunbar in this county. Alexander's great-grandson and representative, Sir Alexander Elphinston, *dominus de Elphinston*, was succeeded in the barony of Elphinston in Mid-Lothian, by his only child Agnes, who carried, by marriage, that estate into the family of Johnston. Her uncle, Henry Elphinston, Esquire, of Pittendreich, succeeded his brother in the Stirlingshire property; which, also, with some lands in Perth and Aberdeen shires, was subsequently called the barony of Elphinston. Henry's great-grandson and representative, Sir Alexander Elphinston of Elphinston, a man of good parts, great honour, and unimpeachable integrity, was, at the baptism of Prince Arthur, in 1509, raised by James IV. to the peerage, by the title of Lord Elphinston. In 1510, Lord Elphinston, as he was now diplomatically styled, obtained a charter under the great seal of the lands of Gargunnock and Carnock. In 1512, he obtained a royal charter of Quarrol and other lands in the county. He accompanied his royal friend and patron to Flodden, in 1513, and, having a great likeness of that elegant monarch, fell a victim to his personating him in a battle fatal to James and many of his nobles. His only son, Alexander, second Lord Elphinston, was slain in the battle of Pinkey 1547. By the Hon. Catherine Erskine, daughter of John, Lord Erskine, or, more properly, Earl of Mar, he had five sons and three daughters. The eldest son, Robert third Lord Elphinston, was, by Margaret, daughter of Sir John Drummond of Inverpaffrey, ancestor, through his third son, Sir James (a lord of the treasury, a secretary of state, and president of the court of session, in Scotland), of the noble house of Balmerinoch, forfeited, on account of its attachment to the House of Stuart, in 1746. His eldest son, Alexander fourth Lord Elphinston, was, in 1599, when Master of Elphinston, appointed one of the senators of the College of Justice, and lord high treasurer of Scotland. He was, in 1604, appointed, by the Scottish parliament, a commissioner to treat with the English regarding a more complete union of the sister kingdoms. He obtained many charters under the great seal at different times, particularly of Bothkennar in 1608. He lived till 1648. By the Hon. Jean Livingston, daughter of Lord Livingston, he had four sons and five daughters. His representative, Alexander fifth Lord Elphinston, married Elizabeth, daughter of Patrick, Lord Drummond, and sister of James first Earl of Perth, and had only one daughter. She married her cousin, Alexander, eldest son of James, her father's next brother, and the male representative of the family; and was, by him, the mother of Alexander, seventh Lord Elphinston, and of John the eighth lord. The latter nobleman married Lady Isabella Maitland, daughter of the Earl of Lauderdale, and had by her three sons and three daughters. The eldest daughter, Elizabeth, was by the Hon. John Campbell of Mamore, mother of the Duke of Argyll. The eldest son, Charles ninth Lord Elphinston, had, by Elizabeth, daughter of Sir William Primrose, Bart., and sister of James first Viscount Primrose, four sons and two daughters. The youngest of the daughters, Primrose, married Alexander ninth Earl of Home, and brought him his son and heir. The third son, Charles, succeeded as tenth Lord Elphinston. He married Lady Clementina Fleming, only surviving child and heiress of John sixth Earl of

Wigton, by Lady Mary Keith, eldest daughter of William ninth Earl Mareschal. He had by her four sons and four daughters. One of the sons was the Hon. William Elphinston, chairman of the India-House. Another was George Keith Elphinston, Lord Viscount Keith, a British peer, Lord Keith of Stonehaven Mareschal, K.G.C.B., admiral of the Red, commander of the Channel Fleet, and knight of the Turkish order of the Crescent. The eldest brother was John eleventh Lord Elphinston. He married the Hon. Miss Ruthven, daughter of James third Lord Ruthven, by Lady Anne Stewart, daughter of James second Earl of Bute, by Lady Anne Campbell, daughter of Archibald first Duke of Argyll. By her he had Lord Elphinston, who was, till his decease, lord-lieutenant of Dumbartonshire; and to whom his lady, Janet Elliot, daughter of Cornelius Elliot, Esquire, and relict of Sir Thomas Carmichael of Skirling, Bart., had the late lord. Another brother was the Hon. Charles Elphinston Fleming of Cumbernauld, rear-admiral of the White, and some time M.P. for Stirlingshire. A third brother, the Hon. Mountstewart Elphinston, in the Indian service, produced a most interesting statistical work on the kingdom of Cabul.

Archibald Orr-Ewing, Esquire, of Ballikinrain, is the seventh son of the late William Ewing, Esquire, of Ardvullin, Dunoon, by Susan, daughter of John Orr, Esquire, of Underwood, Paisley. He was born in 1819; and, in 1847, married Elizabeth Lindsay, daughter of James Reid, Esquire, of Berriedale and Caldercruix. He has, with other issue, William, born in 1848; and educated at Pembroke College, Cambridge. Mr. Orr-Ewing was elected M.P. for Dumbartonshire in 1868.

William Forbes, Esquire, of Callendar, is the eldest son of the late William Forbes, Esquire, by Lady Louisa, daughter of Francis seventh Earl of Wemyss. He was born in 1833; succeeded his father, who for some time represented the county in parliament in 1855; and in 1868, married, second, Edith Marian, third daughter of the Rev. Lord Charles Harvey. He has, with other issue by his first wife, who died in 1866, William Francis, born in 1860.

The Hon. Charles Spencer Bateman, Hanbury-Kincaid-Lennox, is the second son of William first, Lord Bateman, by Elizabeth, daughter of the late Lord Spencer Stanley, Chichester. He was born in 1827; and educated at Eton and Brasenose College, Oxford. In 1847, he took the degree of B.A.; and in the following year, that of M.A. In 1861, he married Margaret, eldest daughter and heiress of the late John Lennox Kincaid-Lennox, Esquire, of Lennox castle, and widow of George seventh Viscount of Strangford, when he assumed the surnames and arms of Kincaid-Lennox by royal licence.

Thomas Fenton Livingstone, Esquire, of Westquarter, is the only son of John Thomas Fenton, Esquire, by Selina, younger daughter of the late Sir John Edensor Heathcote, Knt., of Longton Hall, Staffordshire. He was born in 1829; succeeded his grand-uncle, Admiral Sir Thomas Livingstone, Bart., of that ilk, in 1853, when he took the additional name of Livingstone; and in 1855, married Christian Margaret, only daughter and heiress of William Waddell, Esquire, D.L., of Moffat House, Lanark. Mr. Livingstone has, with other surviving issue, John Nigel Edensor, born in 1859.

John Mangles Lowis, Esquire, of Plean, is a son of John Lowis, Esquire, who had been a member of the Supreme Court of India, and died in 1870. His mother was Louisa, daughter of John Fendall, Esquire. Born in 1827, he married in 1854, Ellen, daughter of Ross Donnelly Mangles, Esquire, of Stoke, Surrey; and has, with other issue, John, born in 1855. Mr. Lowis, who was educated at Hayleybury, is in the Bengal Civil Service.

John Warden M'Farlane, Esquire, of Ballencleroch House, Campsie, is the eldest son of John M'Farlan, Esquire, by Janet Buchanan, daughter of Robert Ewing, Esquire, of Glasgow. He was born in 1824; succeeded his father in 1852; and in 1857, married Elizabeth, daughter of Duncan Gibb, Esq., of Liverpool. Mr. M'Farlan, who is a captain in the 5th Lancers, was educated at Edinburgh.

Douglas Beresford Malise Ronald Graham, Duke of Montrose, is the eldest son of James fourth duke, by the Hon. Caroline Agnes, daughter of John second Lord Decies. He was born in 1852; succeeded as fifth duke in 1874; and, in 1876, married Violet, daughter of Sir Frederick Graham, Bart. His education was got at Eton. In the House of Lords he sits as Earl Graham, G.B. He is also hereditary sheriff of Dumbartonshire; lieut. of the 5th Lancers; hon. colonel of the Highland Borderers Light Infantry Militia; and late of the Coldstream Guards. The heir presumptive is the duke's uncle, Lord Montagu William of Worsted Park, Suffolk, who was born in 1807; and married, in 1867, the Hon. Harriet Anne, daughter of William first Lord Bateman. His lordship was formerly captain in the Coldstream Guards; was M.P. for Grantham, 1852-57; and for Herefordshire, 1859-65. Buchanan house is the seat of the Montrose family. At the death of the last Buchanan of that ilk, in 1682, the estate was sold by his creditors, and purchased by James the third marquis. The family of Graham, which attained to rank under the titular distinction of Montrose, is said to have been settled in Scotland in the reign of David I., about the middle of the twelfth century. Brave and useful at a time when personal bravery was of importance, the Grahams for various services had grants of land from the crown, and gradually rose to eminence. The first notable member of the family was Sir John Græme of Dundaff, who, during the wars of the succession, fell at the battle of Falkirk in 1298. Then early in the fifteenth century Sir William Graham married, for his second wife, a daughter of Robert III.; and Robert, the eldest son of this branch, was the ancestor of the Grahams of Claverhouse. We can only briefly refer here to the attempt made by the great Marquis of Montrose, in May, 1650, in favour of Charles II. His army, consisting of 500 foreigners, was soon defeated, and their gallant leader taken. He was carried on the 18th to Edinburgh, and there treated with extreme indignity. The magistrates, with the city guard and executioner, met him at the Watergate. The prisoners walked, bound two and two, except Montrose, who followed, mounted on a new cart made on purpose, with a high seat, to which he was bound with cords. The hangman rode before, in his livery coat and bonnet, while Montrose sat uncovered. Thus was his fate, before his trial, pantomimically announced. The Earl of Argyll was, in 1685, similarly insulted after his trial, escape, and apprehension. Mr. Fox, while he relates with appropriate indignation the hard fate of Argyll, might, without quitting his subject, have adverted to the indignities offered to Montrose under the auspices of Argyll's father. Such facts, properly grouped in the historic page, afford a useful lesson to partizans. Tranquil as on a birthday, the marquis bore with equanimity the reproaches with which the chancellor accompanied the sentence of death, and maintained that superiority over his iniquitous judges, to which the greatness of his mind, the fame of his exploits, and the justice of his cause entitled him. On the scaffold, while the executioner, having brought a book reciting his gallant exploits, was tying it round his neck, he smiled, thanked him, and added that he wore this testimony of his bravery and loyalty with more satisfaction than the garter had ever given him. After life was extinct his body was dismembered on the scaffold, his head stuck on a pike at the west end of the prison or tolbooth of Edinburgh, and other parts of his person placed over the gateways of different towns, while the trunk was buried underneath the gallows.

Andrew de Moravia, in David II.'s time, and by that monarch called "our dear blood-relation," is the undoubted progenitor of the Murrays of Touchadam and Polmaise. Kepmad was his first estate in the county, as appears from a royal charter of 10th May, 1365. About this time Laurence Killebrand had obtained a royal charter of Touchmaler and Toulcheadame. On the 28th July, 1369, Andrew Murray received from David a grant of these lands. His great-grandson and representative, William Murray of Touchadam, had been *scutifer* to James II., and was appointed constable of Stirling castle under James III. The seventh representative of the founder of the family, William, about 1568, married Agnes, one of the daughters and coheiresses of James Cunninghame of Polmaise, in Stirlingshire. He and his descendants have since been promiscuously known as Murrays of Touchadam and Polmaise. His son and heir, Sir John Murray *Miles*, got a charter under the great seal of the lands and barony of Polmaise, 8th April, 1588. A late representative of the family, William Murray, Esquire, was designed of Touchadam and Pitlochie. The latter property is in Fife. The present representative is Lieut.-Colonel John Murray, late of the Grenadier Guards. His father was John Murray, Esquire, of Polmaise, and his mother, Elizabeth Bryce of Edinburgh. Born in 1831, he succeeded to the estates in 1862; and in 1859 married Lady Agnes Caroline Graham, daughter of James fourth Duke of Montrose, who died in 1873. The heir presumptive is Mr. Murray's brother, James, born in 1834.

Alexander Henry Murray-Menzies, Esquire, of Avondale, is the eldest son of the late Gilbert James Murray-Menzies, Esquire, by his first wife Anne Matilda, only child of the late Alexander Murray, Esquire, of Pitlochie. He was born in

1854. His father, who died in 1874, was formerly an officer in the Black Watch.

John Bell Sherriff, Esquire, of Carronvale, is the youngest son of the late George Sherriff, Esquire, of St. Petersburg, by Margaret, daughter of John Bell, Esquire, of Lyon Thorn, Stirlingshire. He was born in 1821; and, in 1854, married Flora Taylor of Islay, who died in 1876. With other issue, he has George, born in 1856, and educated at Rugby and Glasgow University. Mr. Sherriff purchased Carronvale from the Robertsons in 1857.

Alexander Graham Spiers, Esquire, of Culcreugh, Fintry, is the eldest son of Peter Spiers, Esquire, by Martha Harriet, second daughter of Robert Cunningham-Graham, Esquire, of Gartmore, Perthshire. He was born in 1793; succeeded to the estate in 1829; and, in 1828, married Mary, second daughter of William Murray, Esquire, of Polmaise. Mr. Spiers, who was educated at the Royal Military College, Marlow, was formerly an officer in the army. He was also M.P. for Paisley 1835-6. The heir of entail is his niece Anne, born in 1833. In 1858, she married Sir George Home, Bart.; and has, with other issue, James, born in 1861.

David Stewart, Esquire, of Stewarthall, is the only son of Robert Stewart, Esquire, by Helen, daughter of Walter Buchanan, Esquire. He was born in 1830; and, in 1861, married Dorothy

Emily, only daughter of the Rev. John Cox, rector of Fairstead, Essex; and has, with other issue, Robert John Archibald, born 1863. Mr. Stewart was formerly a captain in the 34th Foot.

Sir Henry James Seton-Stewart, Bart., of Touch House, is the eldest son of Sir Reginald Macdonald Seton-Stewart, Bart., of Staffa, by Elizabeth, daughter and heiress of Sir Henry Stewart, Bart., F.R.S., of Allanton. He was born in 1812; succeeded, as third baronet, in 1838; and, in 1852, married Elizabeth, daughter of Robert Montgomery, Esquire. Sir Henry is hereditary armour-bearer and squire of the royal body in Scotland. The heir presumptive is his nephew, Alan Henry, elder son of the late Archibald Seton-Stewart, Esquire, by Catherine, daughter of Robert Stein, Esquire. He was born in 1856.

Andrew Stirling, Esquire, of Muiravonside, is the eldest son of Charles Stirling, Esquire, by Charlotte Dorothea, only daughter of the late vice-admiral Charles Stirling of Woburn Farm, Chertsey, Surrey. He was born in 1829; succeeded to the estate in 1867; and, in 1864, married Georgina Louisa, second daughter of Sir Henry Martin Blackwood.

Sir Charles Elphinstone Fleming Stirling of Glorat House is the third and only surviving son of Captain George Stirling, by his first wife, Anne, daughter of William Gray, Esquire, of Oxgang, and grandson of the late Sir John Stirling, Bart., of Glorat. He was born in 1832; succeeded his brother in 1861; and in 1867, married Anne Georgina, eldest daughter of James Murray, Esquire. In 1550, George Stirling of Glorat was captain and governor-in-chief of Dumbarton castle. The arms and motto, "semper fidelis," was granted to the family for their loyalty to their sovereigns Charles I. and II.; and in 1666, they were further honoured with the dignity of knight and baronet. Both the Glorat family and the Stirlings of Craigbarnet are descended from the Stirlings of Cadder, whose name appears in the Ragman's Roll, 1279.

Major Charles Campbell Graham-Stirling of Craigbarnet is the only son of John Graham, Esquire, of Feddal, by Isabella, daughter of Captain Campbell, late 88th Regiment. He was born in 1827, succeeded his cousin in 1852, and, in 1856, married Elizabeth Agnes, eldest daughter of Robert Dunmore Napier, Esquire, of Ballikinrain.

James Stirling, Esquire of Garden, Kippen, is the eldest son of James Stirling, Esquire, by Isabella, daughter of William Monteith, Esquire. He was born in 1844; and, in 1875, married Anna Selina Gartside, daughter of Gartside Gartside Tipping, Esquire, of Ross-ferry, county Fermanagh. Mr. Stirling was educated at Rugby, and Christ Church, Oxford.

John Stirling Stirling, Esquire of Gargunnock,

is the only son of Charles Stirling, Esquire, by Christian, daughter of John Hamilton, Esquire, of Sundrum, Ayrshire. He was born in 1832, succeeded his father in 1839, and, in 1871, married Henrietta Charlotte, youngest daughter of John Buchanan, Esquire, of Carbeth, by whom he has Louisa Christian, born in 1872.

William Stirling, Esquire, of Tarduf, is the third son of the late William Stirling, Esquire, by Elizabeth, daughter of Henry Barrett, Esquire, of Cinnamon Hill, Jamaica, and grandson of John Stirling, Esquire, of Kippendavie, to whose estates in Jamaica he has succeeded. He was born in 1822; and, in 1855, married his cousin, Mary Katherine, daughter of the late Sylvester Douglas Stirling, Esquire, of Glenbervie, and has, with other issue, William George Hay, born in 1861. Mr. Stirling is colonel of the 31st Lanark Rifle Volunteers.

Nathaniel William John Strode, Esquire, of Candie, is only son of Nathaniel Nugent Strode, Esquire, an officer in the 16th Regiment of Foot, who died in 1831. His mother was Caroline, daughter of Captain Kirk, 47th Regiment. He was born in 1816; and, in 1872, married Eleanor Margaret, third daughter of the late W. C. Courtney, Esquire, and has had with other issue Louis Edward Maitland, born in 1874.

Lawrence Dundas, Earl of Zetland, is eldest son of the Hon. John Charles Dundas of Wood

Hall, Wetherby, Yorkshire, who died in 1866. His mother was Margaret Matilda, eldest daughter of James Talbot, Esquire, of Maryville, Wexfordshire. He was born in 1845; succeeded his uncle, Thomas, second earl, K.G., in 1873; and, in 1871, married Lady Lilian Elizabeth Selina, daughter of Richard ninth Earl of Scarborough. His lordship was educated at Harrow and Trinity College, Cambridge; was M.P. for Richmond for two years, and formerly served as lieutenant in the Royal Horse Guards.

CHAPTER XXVIII.

ROBERT ROY MACGREGOR.

ROBERT MACGREGOR having, from the redness of his hair and complexion, the descriptive name of "Roy," was, by a daughter of Campbell of Glenlyon, the younger son of Lieut.-Colonel Donald Macgregor, between whom, "for himself, and for all those descended of his family, commonly called *Clan Duill Chere*," on the one part, and John Buchanan of Arnprior, "for himself, and all those descended of his family of Mochaster," on the other, a contract of friendship, founded partly on relationship, took place at Buchanan and Glengyle, on the 23rd and 24th of May, 1693. *Clan Duill Chere* is clan or family of Dougald of the mouse-coloured hair, a branch of the Macgregors. Mr. Penant's remark regarding the general redness of their hair is unworthy of the natural historian. Of their "mischievous dispositions," and their having committed "a horrible massacre," it is impossible for any one acquainted with facts not to smile at the tourist's ignorance and credulity.

Colonel Macgregor's second son, Robert, assumed the surname of his noble friend and patron, John, second Duke of Argyll, and military commander on the side of Government in 1715; who, also, from his golden locks and florid complexion, was celtically denominated "Roy." Robert Roy's portrait, executed by no mean artist, and representing him with his blue bonnet, is still in possession of the Argyll family, and had a narrow escape from the fire which, in May, 1802, destroyed Rosneath castle, where it had occupied a conspicuous place in the principal dining-room. Robert Roy Macgregor is styled, "Robert Campbell of Inversnait, and one of the curators of James Graham of Glengyle," his fraternal nephew (whose real name was Gregor Macgregor, with the descriptive addition of *Ghlun-Dhu*, from a black mole on one of his knees) in a marriage contract of the said James Graham and "Mrs. Mary Hamilton, lawful daughter of James Hamilton of Bardowie, with consent of her father," dated at Buchanan and Bardowie, the 28th and 29th of November, 1703.

Craigrostan, which is generally said to have been Robert Roy's property, belonged, in great part at least, and not long before his day, to the lineal ancestor of John Macgregor, Esq., of Aucharn. Mr. Macgregor, of Craigrostan, had become surety for money borrowed by a friend, and was reduced to sell his estate, which was purchased by the lender, the Marquis of Montrose. Craigrostan's representative takes the name of Gregorson, an English form of Macgregor. Robert Campbell, of Inversnait, had, with one Macdonald, borrowed in 1708, a sum of his grace the Duke of Montrose, for the purchase of cattle. Campbell's partner fled with the money, and Inversnait, with all pertinents, was adjudicated for payment. It does not, however, in any way appear, that the charge of harshness attaches to the then representative of the noble family of Montrose; but his chamberlain, Graham, of Killearn, over-zealous in his master's service, had recourse to a mode of expulsion inconsistent with the rights of humanity, by insulting Mrs. Campbell in her husband's absence. The date of the outrage is not known. It was probably in 1708, or the year following. The fort of Inversnait, intended to check Rob Roy's incursions, was built in 1713, after repeated interruptions by him. Mr. Campbell, on his return, being informed of what had taken place in his absence, withdrew from the scene which he could no longer suffer, and vowed vengeance. He seized part of his grace's rents, as the only way which, as he argued, he could regain any part of those of his own estate. On the unmanly insulter of his wife, he took a personal satisfaction which marks the mildness of his character. Killearn was collecting rents at Chapellaroch, when Robert, arriving with an armed force, demanded his tythe.

The chamberlain attempted to conceal the money by throwing it upon a loft above the room in which he sat. Robert, however, insisted on having what he considered his share; and on the pleasure besides of Mr. Graham's company to the Highlands. Carrying him to Loch Kettern, he confined him three days on a deserted island near Glengyle.

The averment of the statist of Kippen, that " old Rob Roy " was a "robber by profession," is not supported by the instance brought forward, that in 1691, he had headed " the herrship of Kippen," which amounts to nothing more than a military diversion by the *laird* of Inversnait in favour of his legitimate sovereign. He had, it would appear, though we have seen no voucher to that effect, been, subsequently to his expulsion from his lands, a contractor for aiding the police of the country, and in the habit of receiving what, in allusion to earlier times, when contracts for this purpose had not received the countenance of law, was called " black maill." He asserted an alleged claim on this score somewhat differently from his accustomed urbanity. Mr. Stirling had, with his lady, gone in 1710 on a visit from Garden castle, which stood on an eminence forming an island in what was once a lake, but what is now a fertile meadow. On their return, they found the fortalice occupied by a party under Robert Roy Macgregor, and the drawbridge up. Robert, appearing at a window, thus accosted the outed owner :—" You have hitherto withheld the reward of protection, Garden, but must render it now." Garden firmly refused, stating reasons more satisfactory to himself than to the other party; when the latter, bringing a child from the nursery, held it out of the window. The father, partly by the entreaties of the mother, was induced to comply.

The following are two anecdotes connected with what has been said of his personal prowess. He had been overnight in an alehouse at Arnprior, in Perthshire, in company with Cunningham of Boquhan. They had quarrelled; and the latter having no sword, sent home for one, which, however, his family, suspecting a foolish broil, did not forward. He and Robert had remained till break of day; when Boquhan, spying a rapier in a corner, insisted on fighting. Robert engaged; but instantly dropped his blade's point, and yielded to one who, he found, was too expert a swordsman. He is also said to have been worsted, when very old, by Stewart of Appin, between the church and manse of Balquhidder. The duel took place about sunrise, when the rays shone in Robert's face, while his antagonist enjoyed the advantage of having his back to them. Robert's eyesight had, not improbably, been decayed. Another anecdote told of him reminds us of the death-bed scene of Rhoderick Dhu. Robert was bedfast, when he was told that a person, with whom, in the days of his strength, he had had a quarrel, wished to see him. "Bring me," said Robert, "my clothes and sword. It shall never be said that an enemy saw me on a sick-bed." In this guise the host received his guest. When the latter had departed—"It is now," said the exhausted veteran, "all over with me;" and desired to be put to bed, and to hear, from his piper, one of his favourite airs.

"Rob" died in the braes of Balquhidder. He is interred in the churchyard of the parish, a few paces due east of the church. His grave is marked by a blue slate stone, rudely sculptured, and without inscription. He left four sons— Coll, the eldest, of a high character for every manly virtue; James, called *Mor*, or "Large," who assumed the name of Drummond, and fought bravely as a captain of the Macgregor regiment at Preston; Ronald; and lastly, Robert, vulgarly, amongst lowlanders, called "Roy," though of a dark complexion, but by the Highlanders Rob Og, viz., junior, as distinguished from his father. Young Robert is believed to have been born at the farm of Kirkton of Balquhidder, in 1718, and was seventeen years of age at his father's death. He is said to have been a favourite of the old man, who, a short time before his death, bequeathed to him his sword and dirk, counselling the youth never to draw them without cause, or to lay them past without honour.

It would seem that old Rob had been a life-renter in the farm, or that the lease had expired with his life, for an attempt was at once made to oust the family by one of the neighbours offering a rise of rent. At this time the Laurins were pretty strong in the district, and a well-to-do member of that clan had married a younger sister of Mrs. Macgregor. The son, who was in the neighbouring farm of Wester Innernenty, attempted to get his aunt's possession, and a deadly feud at once sprung up between the cousins. The elder Macgregor seems to have taken the matter more cool. Robert, however, swore to be revenged, and Ronald, well knowing his brother's ungovernable nature, warned his friend of the danger he was incurring from the impetuous temper of his brother Rob. At this time Rob Roy's famous gun, now in the Abbotsford collection, was in the hands of Mr. Caddell, the celebrated Doune pistol manufacturer, for repairs. Despatching a messenger for the gun, he had it loaded with powder and slug, and following his cousin, who was ploughing in a field called Drumloch, on his farm, shot him through the thigh so severely that the result was almost instant death. Rob then rushed home to his mother, and exultingly exclaimed—"I have drawn the first blood of the M'Larens;" and thus closed the first act in the life drama of young Macgregor.

This happened in the spring of 1736, and it would appear that the authorities were either very negligent or afraid to take up the case; while the M'Laren family were warned against participating in the matter if more after-ill was to be prevented. But the case was of so flagrant and boastful a nature that it roused the ire of all law-abiding subjects, and when the young desperado found that his conduct was to be made the subject of serious enquiry, he fled to France some time prior to July of the same year. For this crime he and his two brothers, Ronald and James, were summoned to appear before the High Court of Justiciary at Edinburgh. Ronald and James appeared for trial, but Robert, having left the country, was declared an outlaw. The two brothers were found "not guilty" of participating in the murder. The court, however, was not inclined to let them off scot free, and caused them to find bail for £200 against stealing cattle. It is not known whether Robert visited home during his exile, but still retaining the fighting propensities of the family, he joined the English army under George II. in 1743—the last instance of a British sovereign being under the fire of an enemy, that monarch going to aid the Queen of Hungary against the combined forces of Frederick the Great and France. Two years later we find him fighting under the Duke of Cumberland at Fontenoy, where he was wounded and taken prisoner. After obtaining his release he returned to England, when he joined the regiment of General Campbell, afterwards Duke of Argyll; and about this time he "swerved" from the Catholic faith, in which he had been brought up, and became a Protestant. The final conflict at Culloden gave him his colonel's discharge, and he returned to his friends. He then settled as proprietor of the farm of Ballisfirl, and, so far as the murder of his cousin was concerned, remained unmolested. His change of front did him good service, as being under the Duke he escaped the penalties of that Act of Attainder under which his brothers and other leaders of hi clan came.

Young Macgregor was of rather slender build, but tall and handsome in his person, a daring rider and expert swordsman, but vain-glorious in his character, and thus easily made the tool of more cautious rascals. By his ten years' residence in France the young Highlander had acquired considerable accomplishments, and he was admitted into some of the best society in the country. About 1748 he married Miss Graham, daughter of the Laird of Drunkie, and, according to the marriage contract, made "suitable remuneratory settlements out of his own private fortune and estate" to his lady. Mrs. Macgregor unfortunately only survived her marriage some months, and after her death her husband began afresh his reckless and roving life.

The Macgregor brothers, still carrying on the trade of cattle dealers, were secretly suspected of dealing underhand in stolen stock, and one of their neighbours declared they had beasts not rightly come by, and that might be inquired about after. They occasionally associated with Buchanan of Machar, the head of a gang of desperadoes, who made repeated incursions into the Lennox, carrying off cattle and other plunder, and it is believed it was on one of their raids that Rob performed the really clever exploit of galloping off with the Ballikinrain mare in face of the dragoons, who, in small troops, paraded the country, at this time, for the purpose of checking marauding bands. It was after this exploit that Macgregor looked upon the strath as a place to be robbed, and immediately following, his acquaintance with Jean Kay commenced which had such a disastrous termination. The following is the story of the capture of the unfortunate heiress, and its unhappy results:—About 1732, James Kay, a native of Strathendrick, with a fortune of £2000, married a lady of the name of Janet Mitchell. The issue of this marriage was one daughter, Jean, born in October of that year. In 1742, Mr. Kay purchased the property of Edinbelly, for which he paid £1,500, the balance going in stock and furniture. In 1744, Mr. Kay suddenly died intestate, and his daughter, then in her twelfth year, became heiress of the property and effects. After this she was naturally an object of considerable interest in the valley, and, as she advanced in years, she had many suitors, among the number being Mr. John Wright, son of the laird of Easter Glinns, whom she married in 1749, being in her nineteenth year. All now went well for a time, but by Mr. Wright's unexpected death in October, 1750, about a year after their marriage, Jean was again left alone with her mother. Rob got his eye on the young widow shortly after the death of her husband. He called at the public-house in December following, and sent a messenger "desiring leave to visit her." This being refused, the wrath of Macgregor was roused, and he declared if "fair wooing would not do, he should carry her off by force." Mrs. Wright, well-knowing the determined character of the clan, advised her daughter-in-law to be on her guard, and for safety thought she had better remove to Glasgow. Jean, however, treated the matter lightly, and remained at home. Rob, with his three brothers and five retainers, left Balquhidder, in due course, for the capture of the heiress, and to avoid the villages of Aberfoyle and Gartmore, they appear to have taken the old ride track down the west side of Loch Ard and Gartmore, reaching the well-known hostelry at Chapelarroch the same night. The evening being very dark, and a moorland country to be crossed, one of the brothers rode back and got two local brewers to act as guides. Arriving at Edinbelly, they at once seized the object of their search, and placing her on the saddle behind her future husband, rode off in triumph. The horse, however, of one of the Gartmore brewers got bogged, which caused some delay. At the then little inn of Rowardennan, a sham marriage took place, and next morning they crossed Loch Lomond for the house of Mr. Campbell of Glenfalloch, and ultimately landed at Inverorick. Meantime, to prevent Macgregor taking possession of the estate, her friends had the property sequestrated, and warrants were issued for the capture of the offenders.

Rumours soon reached the North that the authorities had the matter in hand, and, deeming it unsafe to remain long in one place, the couple seem to have moved a good deal about the country. They spent their new year in Callendar but in a few days returned to Glendochard, visiting afterwards the village of Killin, and returning to Ronald's house at Balquhidder. The captive heiress was next taken to the manse, and introduced to Mr. Ferguson, the minister of the parish, as the wife of Robert Macgregor. They then moved on to Ackroston, stayed there a week, then rode to the farm of "Hole," on the estate of Torry, and next turned up at Lochend house, lake of Menteith, where they were entertained by the proprietor, Mr. Campbell of Kilport and Lochend. The following morning, James and Jean rode off to Edinburgh, with the view of presenting a bill of suspension regarding the sequestrating of her property. This, however, was bearding the lion in his den, the lady being cared for in a milder way by the authorities, while James returned home.

Jean Kay emitted her declaration on the 20th of May following, and the M'Gregors and their accomplices were summoned to stand their trial at the Justiciary Court at Perth, to be held on the 25th of May, but disregarding with contempt all such forms of law, they were all, nine in number, declared outlaws.

By order of the Court of Session, Mrs. Wright was placed under the care of one "John Wightman" of Maulsley, in the Potter Row, near Edinburgh, who was, along with the magistrates, responsible for her safe keeping. By order of the court she was set at liberty on the 4th of June, and returned to some friends in Glasgow on the 7th of the same month, where she remained till her death by smallpox on the 4th of October, 1751.

James was the first of the brothers who was brought to trial. His capture was effected by the military, while at Fort-William, early in December.

He was brought to Edinburgh on the 18th under military escort, and lodged in the Tolbooth. He was indicted to stand his trial on the 3rd August, 1752, and on the 5th the jury found him guilty of acting part in the forcible abduction of Jean Key, but nothing more. Delay being claimed by his agents to "allow an opportunity to inform upon the debate," the defence was ordered to be heard on the 20th November following. By this date, however, James had made his escape, and sentence was accordingly delayed. Rumours having reached the authorities that a release might be attempted, Macgregor was removed from the jail to the castle, and placed under strict guard. Four nights before his sentence his daughter, Miss Macgregor, planned his escape in the most adroit manner possible.

The *Scots Magazine* for November, 1752, records it as follows:—"James Macgregor, alias Drummond, under trial of carrying off Jean Key of Edinbelly, made his escape from Edinburgh castle on the 16th. The manner of it is thus related. In the evening he dressed himself in an old tattered big coat put over his own clothes, an old night cap, and old leather apron, and old dirty shoes and stockings, so as to personate a cobbler. When he was thus equipped, his daughter, a servant maid who assisted, and who was the only person with him in the room, except two of his young children, scolded the cobbler for having done his work carelessly, and this with such an audible voice as to be heard by the sentinels without the room door. About seven o'clock, while she was scolding, the pretended cobbler opened the room door, and went out with a pair of old shoes in his hand, muttering his discontent for the harsh usage he had received. He passed the guards unsuspected, but was soon missed, and a strict search made in the castle, and also in the city, the gates of which were shut, but all in vain. The serjeant, and some of the soldiers on duty, were put under confinement. On the 20th the Court of Justiciary met to judge the import of the verdict returned against him, and continued the diet until the 18th of December. We are told that the commissioners of the customs, in consequence of an application made to them, despatched orders to their officers for strictly searching all ships outward bound, to prevent his escaping out the kingdom. P.S.—A court-martial sat in the castle, December 8, in consequence, it is said, of orders from above, to inquire into this affair. It consisted of one lieutenant-colonel, two majors, and ten captains. They rose on the 13th. Two lieutenants and four private men were put under arrest; but we have not yet learned what is to be the result of their proceedings." The following note occurs in the same magazine for December :—" A return from London, to the report of the proceedings of the court-martial appointed to inquire into the manner of James Drummond's escape, arrived at Edinburgh, December 30. In consequence of which, two lieutenants, who commanded the guard the night Drummond escaped, are broke, the serjeant who had the charge of locking the prisoner in his room is reduced to a private man; the porter has been whipped, and all the rest are released."

The fate of James was particularly hard. After he escaped from the prison of Edinburgh he fled south to Cumberland, and on the fourth night found himself benighted on a lonely moor. Entering a wood, he stumbled on the camp of a Highland gipsy, whom he had often befriended at home. Here he remained for two days. The gipsy and Macgregor rode to near Whitehaven, where he got a fisherman's boat and went over to the Isle of Man, whence he sailed to France. About the end of September, he died there suddenly, and in great poverty, leaving fourteen children, seven of them in extreme youth.

CHAPTER XXIX.

BLACK MAIL.

IN an abridgement of the Acts of the Scottish parliament (1567) the following passage occurs:—"That none sit under the assurance of thieves, or pay them black-mail under the pain of death, and escheat of their moveables." In 1587, the year of the institution of justices of the peace, "It is statute and ordained that the justice-clerk and his deputes, and the kingis commissioners, constitute to further justice, quietness, and gude rule in all schires, sall diligently enquire and take up dittary of the uptakers and payers of black-maill, and to make rentals of the quantities thereof, and to person alsweill the takers, as payers thereof, at justice aires, and particular diettes, and do justice upon them, according to the lawes, and receive soverty, under great pains, that they sall abstaine in time coming."

Few ancient customs are so generally yet so imperfectly known as that of black mail. It was, however, simply a lawful and beneficial service to the public which now falls to the share of the police, or, in other words, money paid voluntarily by contract, for the protection of property against the depredations of migratory freebooters who lurked in the borders of the Highlands. One of the original documents is still in the possession of the descendants of Mr. Dunmore of Ballikinrain, and as it is not only a literary curiosity, but, perhaps, the only contract of the kind now existing, we subjoin a copy of it verbatim :—

Copy of an original Contract for Keeping a Watch on the Borders of the Highlands, anno 1741.

It is contracted, agreed, and finally ended betwixt the parties underwritten, to witt James and John Graham, elder and younger of Glengyle, on the one part, and the gentlemen, heritors, and tenants within the shires of Perth, Stirling, and Dumbarton, who are hereto subscribing, on the other part, in manner following: Whereas, of late years, several persons within the bounds aforesaid have been very great sufferers through stealing of their cattle, horses, and sheep; for preventing whereof the saids James and John Grahams, with and under the conditions, provisions, and for the causes after specified, hereby bind and oblige them, conjunctly and severally, their heirs, executors, and successors, that the said James Graham shall keep the lands subscribed for, and annexed to the respective subscriptions, skaithless of any loss, to be sustained by the heritors, tenants, or inhabitants thereof, through the stealing and away taking of their cattle, horses, or sheep, and that for the space of seven years complete, from and after the term of Whitsunday next to come; and for that effect, either to return the cattle so stolen from time to time, or otherwayes, within 6 months after the theft committed, to make payment to the persons from whom they were stolen, of their true value, to be ascertained by the oaths of the owners, before any judge-ordinary; providing always, that intimation be made to the said James Graham, at his house in Correilet, or where he shall happen to reside for the time, of the number and marks of the cattle, sheep, or horse stolen, and that within 48 hours from the time that the proprietors thereof shall be able to prove by hable witnesses, or their own or their herds oaths, that the cattle amissing were seen upon their usual pasture within the space of 48 hours previous to the intimation, as said is; and declaring, that it shall be sufficient if the heritors or tenants, be-south or be-east the town of Drymen, make intimation in writing at the house of Archibald Strang, merchant in Drymen, of their losses in the before mentioned, to a person to be appointed by the said James Graham of Glengyle to attend theire for that purpose, and in his absence to the said Archibald. And further, it is specially condescended to and agreed upon, that the said

James Graham shall not be bound for restitution in cases of small pickereys; declaring that an horse or black cattle stolen within or without doors, or any number of sheep above six, shall be constructed to be theft, and not pickerey. And with regard to horses and cattle stolen within the bounds aforesaid, and carried to the south, the said James Graham obliges him, that he shall be as serviceable to the gentlemen subscribers in that case as he possibly can; and if he cannot recover them, he submits himself to the discretion of the heritors on whose ground the theft was committed, whether he shall be liable for their value or not.

And it is hereby expressly provided and declared by both parties, That in case of war within the country, that this present contract shall henceforth cease and become void; for the which causes, and on the other part, the heritors and tenants hereto subscribing, with and under the provisions and declarations above and underwritten, bind and oblige them, their heirs, executors, and successors, to make payment to the said James Graham of Glengyle, or to any persons he shall appoint to receive the same, of the sum of £4 yearly during the space foresaid, for ilk hundred pound of ye valued rent of the lands annexed to their respective subscriptions, and that at two terms of the year, Whitsunday and Martinmas, by equal portions, beginning the first term's payment thereof at the said term of Whitsunday next, for the half year immediately following, and so further, to continue at the said terms during the continuance of these presents: providing always, like as is hereby specially provided and declared, that it shall be leisome and lawful for both parties to quitt and give up this present contract at the end of every year as they think fitt, intimation being always made on the part of the said James Grahame at the respective kirk-doors, with the bounds aforesaid, on a Sabbath day, immediately after the forenoon's sermon, a month before expiration of the year; and on the part of the heritors and other subscribers, by a letter to the said James Grahame from them, and another from him, acknowledging the receipt thereof, or the attestation of two witnesses, that the letter was left at his house, or was delyverred to him two moneths before expyring of the year; it being always understood, that any subscriber may quitt and give up the contract for his own part, whether the rest concur or not, at the end of each year, as said is. And both parties bind and oblidge them and their foresaids to perform the premisses *hinc inde* to others under the penalty of £20 sterling, to be paid by the party failzier to the party observer, or willing to observe their part thereof, attour performance. And moreover for the said James Grahame's farther encouragement, and for the better restraining the evil practices above-mentioned, the subscribers hereby declare, that it is their intention that all such thieves and pickers shall be apprehended by the said James Grahame of Glengyle, or occasionally by any other person within the bounds aforesaid, against whom there is sufficient proof, shall be prosecute according to law, and brought to justice. And for greater security, both the saids parties consent to the registration hereof in the books of council and session, or others competent, that letters of horning on six days, and other executorials needful may pass hereon as effeirs. And to that effect they constitute . . . . . . their procurators, &c. In witness whereof, both the saids parties have subscribed these presents, consisting of this and the preceding sheet, written on stamped paper by Andrew Dick, chyrurgeon in Drymen, at Balglas, the twentyeth day of Aprill Im vije. and fourty-one years, by Robert Bontein of Mildovan, before William MacLea his servant, and Mr. William Johnston, schoolmaster at Balglas, the said Robert Bontein having filled up his first date, and witnesses names and designations. At Ballikinrain the tuintie-first day of foresaid moneth and year, by James Napier of Ballikinrain, before Alexander Yuill his servant, and Gilbert Couan, tenant in Ballikinrain, the said James Napier having filled up this second date, witnesses names and designations. Att Boquhan the tuenty-second day of Aprile, moneth foresaid, and year by Hugh Buchanan of Balquhan, before these witnesses, John Paterson and Robert Duncan both tenants yr. Att Glins, the tuenty-seventh day of moneth and year foresaid, before these witnesses, Walter Monteath of Keyp, and John Buchanan younger of Glins. Att Easter Glins, the tuenty-seventh day of moneth and year foresaid, before these witnesses, Walter Monteath of Keyp, and Thomas Wright younger of Easter Glins, subscribed be Alexander Wright of Pensid. Att Arnmere, the first day of Mey seventin hundred and fortie-one years, befor thees witnes, Arsbelt Leckie of Arnmere, and Walter Menteath younger of Keyp, Walter Monteath, att above place, day, date, year, and witnesses, by James Key portioner of Edinbelly, moneth, date, place, and year aforesaid, before these witnesses, Walter Monteath therein, and Walter Monteath younger of Keyp, and by Robert Galbraith of Fintrie, fourth May, before Robert Farrie of Balgrochan, and James Ure, tenant in Hilltowne of Balgair.

William Johnston, witness.

William M'Lea, witness.

Gilbert Cowan, witness.

ROBERT BONTEIN of Mildovan, for my lands of Balglas in the paroch of Killern, being three hundred and fifty pound of valuation; and lands of Provanstoun in the paroch of Balfron, ninety-seven pound seven shilling valuation.

Alexander Yuill, witness.

John Paterson, witness.

Robert Dunn, witness.

Walter Monteath, witness.

John Buchanan, witness.

Thomas Wright, witness.

Archibald Leckie, witness.

Walter Monteath, witness.

Alexander Wright, witness.

Archibald Leckie, witness.

Walter Monteith, witness.

Walter Monteith, witness.

Robert Farrie, witness.

James Ure, witness.

John Buchanan, witness.

James MacGrime, witness.

JAMES NAPIER of Ballikinrain, for my lands in the paroch of Killern, being two hundred and sixtie pound of valuation. And for my Lord Napier's lands in said paroch, being three hundred and twentie-eight pound of valuation. And for Culcreuch's lands in the paroch of Fintrie, being seven hundred and twentie-seven pound of valuation. And for said Culcreuch's lands in the paroch of Balfrone, being one hundred and ten pound valuation.

HUGH BUCHANAN of Balquhan, for my lands of Boughan and Brunshogle, in the paroch of Killearn, being one hundred and seventy-three pound of valuation.

MOSES BUCHANAN of Glins, two hunder sextie-two pund valuation.

JOHN WRIGHT of Ester Glins, sixtie-six pound valuation.

ALEXANDER WRIGHT of Puside, one hundred and foure pound and six shilling and eightpenny Scot valuation.

WALTER MONTEATH of Kyp, three hundred pounds valuation.

JAMES KEY, portioner of Enblioy, for sextiey-six pond Scots vaiuation.

ROBERT GALBRAITH, portioner of Edinbelly, for thritie-three pound Scots valuation.

ALEXANDER BUCHANAN of Cremanan, for my land of Cremanan, in the paroch of Balfron, and . . . being two hundred and sixty-eight pound of valuation.

And the saids James and John Grahames have subscribed these presents at Buchanan, the eleventh day of June jaj vij and forty-one years, before David Græme of Orchill, and John Smith, writer, in Buchanan: Declareing that notwithstanding of the date of the saids James and John Grahame's subscriptions, yet it shall be understood, that the obligations on both partys by this contract shall and do commence from Whitsunday jaj vij and forty-one, in regard it was agreed betwixt the partys, that the saids obligations should commence at that term. The date, witnesses names, and designations, with this declaration, being wrote by the said John Smith, and declared to be part of this contract.

Da. Græme, witness.
John Smith, witness.

JA. GRAHAME.
JOHN GRAHAM.

It would appear from the following letter, that this contract was not disadvantageous to Mr. Grahame.

"Ballikinrain, May 25, 1743.

Sir,—Notwithstanding of the contract entered into betwixt several gentlemen of the shyres of Stirling and Dumbarton, you, and I, anent keeping of a watch, whereby you was to pay yearly four *per cent.* of valuation; yet I now agree with you for three *per cent.* for the lands you have contracted for; and that the first term of Whitsunday, and in time coming during the standing of the contract. And I am, sir, your most humble servant. JA. GRAHAME."

The following receipt granted by Mr. Grahame of Glengyle, to Mr. Robert Galbraith, for the payment of " watch-money " is, probably, the last of its kind. In the beginning of the following year (1745), the train of the rebellion was laying; in July, Prince Charles had actually embarked for Scotland; and by Martinmas, Glengyle's hands must have been filled with more important concerns:—

"Hill, 12th Dec., 1744.

Then received by me James Grahame of Glengile from Robert Galbraith, portioner of Enbelly fourtie shillings Scots money in full payt. of all bygone watch money due to me out of his portion of Enbelly preceeding Martinmas last as witness my hand place and date above written.

JA. GRAHAME.

(There is marked on the back in the same hand,) "Recit. Glengile to Galbraith."

A contract existed between Rob Roy's father and the heiress of Kilmaronock, known as Lady Cochrane, and for the protection of her property he was to receive sixteen bolls of meal yearly. Contracts of this kind were generally paid by agricultural produce, that commodity being very scarce north of the Forth. For some time Lady Cochrane paid her annual tribute with considerable regularity, and by the stern watchfulness of Macgregor and his clansmen thieving became less and less frequent on her ladyship's property. Thinking herself secure, she refused to pay the impost until she had fallen considerably in arrears. By and by Macgregor led her to understand what would be the result, if her obstinacy continued, but to this message something like a threat of defiance was returned. Macgregor now summoned his retainers, and, assisted by his son-in-law, Macdonald of Glencoe, swept the banks of the Leven of all its valuable stock. Sitting down beside Lady Cochrane in her own parlour, he told her that if she did not feu off her lands to enterprising "tacksmen," he would take the estate from her altogether. Hence the number of small proprietors that once existed in the district. At this time the plundering of stock was not regarded as theft, but simply "liftings"; and, unless the loser could stake his lost cattle or sheep in fair fight, there remained no other alternative than to be content with the loss.

A party of the Macraes, seventeen in number, belonging to Ross-shire, stole fifteen head of cattle from a property in Rob Roy's neighbourhood. He received notice of the lifting two days afterwards. It is said he had some reluctance in pursuing the Macraes, but knowing by his contracts of protection he was bound to restore the lost cattle. if over seven, and also recollecting that it was his first exploit of the kind, that his honour was at stake, and that all his future success as a preserver of the peace depended on the recovery of the cattle, he " selected twelve of his best lads, and they after them." For two days Macgregor and his hardy little band followed on the trail of the lifters. On the second night they reached a deep and dark glen in Badenoch, and here they resolved to rest. There was no sound to break the grim silence, save the gurgling of the mountain streamlet as it pursued its downward course among the rocks, the scream of the eagle as he floated around his mate on her eyrie, the hoarse croak of the raven on the crag, or the mew of the wild cat among the heather. Somewhat wearied, a number of his party fell fast asleep, but to Rob his errand was so exciting that, though

> " He seeks his couch, and down he lies,
> Sweet sleep has fled the chieftain's eyes."

Macgregor had not been long lain down when he saw a fire kindling in the distance, and believing this to be the Macraes, he set out to reconnoitre. The kindlers of the fire turned out to be a band of wandering tinklers, who, at once recognising Macgregor, gave him the best of their fare till morning. Here he was informed that the Macraes were at no great distance, and two of the men promised to point out their place of rendezvous. It was not long ere they heard the calls of the northern banditti to their dogs as they gathered the cattle for a further march, and hastening to the brow of the hill, he saw them about to depart. The place was favourable for attack, and Macgregor gave a loud call on them to surrender.

> " One blast upon his bugle horn
> Was worth a thousand men."

Disregarding this, however, Rob ordered his lads to follow him, and dashing down the hill-side before the robbers could rally, they stretched six of their number dead or dying among the heather. The remaining eleven made a gallant defence, and it was not until other six had been disabled that they gave in. The fierceness of the combat may be judged from the fact that one of Rob's lads was killed, and he and four others severely injured. All the cattle were brought back in triumph and restored to their owner. Macgregor received the greatest praise for his achievement, accomplished under the greatest disadvantages, both from the superior number of his opponents, and the long distance of pursuit. It at once showed his ability to deal firmly and expeditiously in his protection contracts, and many who had hitherto stood aloof from him were now anxious to conclude agreements with him for his services.

CHAPTER XXX.

SMUGGLING.

THE illicit distilling of whisky was never considered a crime, so long as smugglers kept clear of the officers of the law. It was rather regarded as one of the legitimate industries of the country. Men of all shades of character were connected directly or indirectly with the trade—from the lawless ruffian, who would not scruple to commit murder, if need be, to the simple-minded cottar, who was incapable of doing any mischief.

About the beginning of the present century, a small government vessel, called the 'Cutter,' was stationed on Loch Lomond, with the twofold object of searching the small boats which conveyed contraband traffic down the loch from the north, and of assisting the land officers, when occasion required. These excise officials, however, differed materially in their views as to the discharge of their duty. While some were stern and rigorous, and never missed an opportunity of bringing the offenders to justice, others were of opinion that they only deserved to be caught when they did not keep proper hours. The former class were certain sooner or later to meet the reward of their temerity at the hands of the smugglers, by being waylaid and thrashed, and in some instances murdered; whereas the latter class fared sumptuously at their hands in houses kept "het and reekin'," which simply meant fully stored with meat and drink.

Some seventy years ago, there lived in the parish of Killearn a man of the name of James Gilfillan. He belonged to respectable parents, was stout, of a fine appearance, and for his station in life had received a somewhat superior training. James, however, had rather a chequered career. When a young man, he was taken by the "press-gang," and placed on board the 'Loch Lomond Cutter,' and thence conveyed to a training ship on the Clyde. Ultimately he found himself under service with the renowned Nelson; but, disliking the life, he and a companion took the first opportunity of deserting his Majesty's ship. One night, when the vessel was lying about a mile from the English coast, he and his friend slipped overboard, and, being expert swimmers, soon reached the shore. On his way home he made some very narrow escapes, being pursued for a whole day by a sergeant of marines and his men, but eventually reached Killearn in safety. Shortly after this, he set about employing himself at the only "industry" that the country offered, namely, that of smuggling, and as this required a companion, he associated himself with a person called Bryson, and the two certainly made a most formidable pair.

In those days a Mr. Hosie was excise officer in Bucklyvie, who had charge of the ride district. He was somewhat short built, but was of a proud disposition, and waged war against the smugglers with considerable rigour. Having got information against Gilfillan, and not daring to run the risk of apprehending him, he cited him to attend a sheriff court to be held in Drymen with a view to his capture. Hosie called in the assistance of the 'Cutter' men, and had them waiting in an adjoining room. The sheriff duly arrived, accompanied by a number of county gentlemen, among them being the late Captain M'Lachlan of Auchentoig. James attended, not expecting anything serious. But when about to enter the court-room he observed a number of blue jackets through a slit in the door. Turning the key cautiously in the lock, and slipping it into his pocket, he walked into the court-room. The excise officer was sitting near the window, and on the smuggler's entry rose to state the complaint, when James was asked if he had anything to say in his defence. Looking round he observed that two officers had taken their place at the door. He seized the lower sash of the window, pulled it to him, and dashed it with great violence over the officer's head; then vaulting into the road below, walked quietly away, none daring to follow him. The old captain exclaimed—"That's a rare man-of-war's trick," while the other gentlemen indulged in a hearty laugh. Hosie was rather seriously cut, and some difficulty was experienced in getting his head extricated from the pane.

A man of the name of M'Farlane, a cattle-dealer in Aberfoyle, also kept a regular working still. During his absence from home on his dealing business his men carried on the distilling. On one occasion, when absent with lambs, an excise officer of the name of Shortus paid a visit to the domicile. The servant in charge, on seeing the officer approach, fled and left the still at his mercy. Shortus, being a man of a rigorous nature, at once proceeded to demolish the utensils, which he did most effectually. The exciseman, believing the servant who fled to be M'Farlane, had him summoned to appear at the J. P. Court. M'Farlane brought witnesses from Glasgow to prove that he was there on that day, and that his presence at the still was an impossibility. This evidence was overruled in favour of the officer's oath, who swore positively that it was M'Farlane he saw running off, and he was fined £30 sterling. The cattle-dealer paid the fine, but when leaving the court was heard to mutter, " that he would take the worth of it out of his English hide." Shortly after this M'Farlane waylaid and nearly murdered Shortus at the mill of Aberfoyle, but escaped suspicion by hurrying to a neighbour's house, where he joined some friends at card-playing. Shortus was discovered by the miller, who ran for assistance to the house where M'Farlane was, and who assisted to carry in his almost lifeless victim.

Stationed over the country to assist the regular excisemen were officers, with smaller or larger bodies of assistants, as the necessity of the district might require. These were commonly called "rangers," the chief of whom was an officer of the name of Dougal. He was a very quiet and inoffensive man, but powerful and of a self-reliant nature. He was much liked by the smugglers, and often told them that a smuggler deserved to be taken if he did not keep smuggler's hours. Mr. Dougal had been repeatedly warned of the threatening character of one of the most villainous of the class, but treated these warnings lightly, and said he was a match for him at any time. Once when riding between the villages of Arnprior and Fintry, and on looking accidentally round, he observed this wretch priming his pistol behind a dyke on the roadside. Being at the time unarmed, but possessed of considerable presence of mind, he suddenly dashed his hand into his pocket and took out a small spy-glass.

Springing from his horse, he rushed to the place where the ruffian lay concealed, crying, "Come on, I am ready for you, my lad." The would-be assassin, taking the spy-glass for a pistol, fled into the wood, and Mr. Dougal rode on his way to Fintry. Some short time after this the officer went amissing, and dark suspicions floated about that he had been the victim of foul play. Ultimately his body was discovered on the farm of Glins. Traces of a scuffle, and some articles identified as his, were found on the shore of Loch Laggan, and it is believed he was murdered there and his body carried to where it was found, upwards of a mile. Well-grounded suspicion soon fell upon this man, who was afterwards totally rejected by his former companions, and died a wandering outcast.

CHAPTER XXXI.

GEOLOGICAL LANDMARKS.

THE general configuration of the country in Stirlingshire, and the causes which, in bygone ages, may have operated in moulding the land into its present shape, give rise to some very interesting thoughts and speculations. We shall briefly advert to a few of these, which will readily be understood by any one acquainted with the county. Looking at the surrounding coal stratification, and taking it to have been deposited in a more or less horizontal position, we see that great dislocations and changes of level must have been produced by the eruption into it of enormous masses of trap rock, or whinstone. That the trap rock was not, in the first instance, thrown up, and the coal strata afterwards deposited, is evident from the fact that the coal, where it comes in contact with the rock, is found to be singed. And that the condition of the trap when erupted was really molten, is beautifully shown by the strata in the grounds at Castlecary. Connected with the sweet cascade in the "Fairy Dell" there, it is interesting to see the trap, over which the water falls, with the strata on each side running towards it, and likewise the curious alteration of angle which takes place as these strata come close to the rock. The late Mr. Charles Maclaren, of Edinburgh, first suggested, what is, no doubt, the true explanation of this phenomenon, viz.—That the rock, in cooling, contracted, and hence allowed the strata in contact with it to fall in.

Subsequent to the irruption of the trap into the coal measures, we have many evidences in the Falkirk district of the existence of what is called by geologists the drift, or boulder-clay flood, and this appears to have been one of the chief operative agents in giving the land which has been left us its present configuration. The reality of such a flood was clearly shown by Sir James Hall, and no one can doubt its existence and power who will look at the well-known phenomenon—the "Crag-and-tail," so well seen at the castles of Stirling, Edinburgh, and other places, where the solid rock has protected the softer stratifications lying on the south-east side. The natural inference from this is, that the flood set in with its chief force from the north-west, and keeping this in view, let us consider what would be its effect upon the adjacent country when the land, as it evidently then did, stood at a much lower level than at present; and to do this the more effectually let a position be taken on the high ground—on Cannel

Moss, for example, to the south of Falkirk, which is now about 612 feet above the level of the sea. But before commencing this survey, it may be well to notice how peculiarly, even now, this portion of Scotland is situated. Take, for instance, the neck of country through which the Forth and Clyde Canal runs, and we shall find that, its highest point is under 150 feet above our present sea level. If a canal were therefore dug, only 20 fathoms deep, in the same line, we should have a direct communication between the Atlantic Ocean and the German Sea. The extraordinary effects that were produced by this great flood must force themselves upon the mind of any one who will look at the huge rolled boulders that are exposed in almost every field to the south of Falkirk, or have been excavated in the neighbourhood, and these generally from fragments of rock not otherwise found in the district. In the railway cutting between Laurieston and Redding, some large boulders of grey granite were found, portions of which were afterwards converted into elegant curling stones. At the same place, or at Brighton's quarry, above the sandstone may be seen multitudes of boulders, several many tons in weight, embodied in the stiff clay, or "till" as it is sometimes called.

From the elevated position we are supposed to occupy, let us now look towards the west and north-west—the directions from which the flood has come. We perceive at once that there are two great gullies, or valleys, through which this flood must have chiefly set—the one between the Denny hills and other high grounds on the south, and the Ochils on the north, with the trap rock of Stirling castle in the centre; and the other between the Denny hills on the north, and the high ground west from Cannel Moss on the south. These two great currents would naturally meet a few miles to the east of Falkirk, and the more northerly one seems to have struck with great force the land which now forms Bo'ness Bay, and probably was the chief agent in scooping it out. The south current has, apparently, been less intense, most likely from the protection afforded by the Denny hills; but even here we shall find that its effects have been very decided, both upon the strata carried away and those which have been left. Directing our view still further north, we see that it was in all likelihood the same agent which scooped out what must, at one time, have been a bay at the Bridge of Allan; for here, also, the current, no doubt, flowed with great force, striving to get an exit through the Stirling valley.

Generally speaking, it is found that where the currents have been strongest, there the denudation of the strata has been greatest, and a knowledge of this fact might be advantageous to landlords and coal proprietors in their searches for the different kinds of minerals. The survey already taken will show this pretty accurately, for at Bridge of Allan—the most exposed of the localities mentioned—all the upper portions of the stratification have been swept away, and consequently we find not the coal measures of the Falkirk district, but the old red sandstone. At Bo'ness, on which the chief force of the north current seems to have been reflected, only the lowest portion of the coal deposit is formed; while at Bannockburn appears the coarse sandstone which underlies the Shieldhill coal-field. On the south side of the Ochils, however, to the east and south of the Denny Hills, and between the two currents at Kinnaird and Grangemouth, we find some of the higher of the Shieldhill coal strata. At Bonnyside again, which was specially exposed to the influence of the south and less powerful current, all the upper Shieldhill minerals have been removed, and those above the lower Bannockburn series are alone left; while from Glenfuir eastwards only the lower and inferior series of the Shieldhill minerals have been, or are ever likely to be, found. In fact, from the elevated position occupied, it seems to us a simple matter to say generally where coal ought to be got, and where it need scarcely be looked for—the important consideration being as to whether it was protected or otherwise from the operation of the flood. Depth beneath the sea bottom, elevation above the sea level, and the shelter afforded by some solid mass of rock, seem to have been the main circumstances by which this valuable mineral was locally preserved.

Naturally, as the land continued to rise, a period arrived when the communication we have alluded to between the two seas became more and more shallow, and at last closed altogether. The impress left on the surface of the land by the changes which hence followed, is both marked and curious. Above the level previously indicated we have a stiff boulder clay—the former sea-bottom of a pent-up current similar probably to our own Pentland Firth. Below this level we find the natural products of a comparatively quiet sea—gravel, sand, and soft clay. When the sea had become shallow, but with the current still setting from the west through the Falkirk valley, the gravel might possibly preponderate; and this may have some connection with the great deposit of gravel known as the Redding Ridge, which extends from Laurieston on towards Linlithgow bridge, the causes leading to the formation of which, in this and other localities, are still matters of conjecture with scientific men. However this deposit may have been formed, when once brought into existence, and raised above the sea level, it must have given rise to a somewhat extensive loch, or series of lochs, on its south side. One of the passages by which the water has escaped is well seen a short distance to the east of Polmont station; and through this gap the Gilston burn, from the upper grounds to the south, now takes its course.

After the entire stoppage of the current through the southern valley, a quiet, sheltered sea must have existed, into which the various streams—but especially the Carron, whose embouchure would then be above Denny—began and continued to pour down the *debris* of the high grounds which they drained. This process, it is clear, had lasted until a considerable part of the valley left by the former current had been filled up with such fine sand, gravel, and clay, as it at present contains; but still not in its present form, for as the land continued to rise, another agent came into operation which has had much to do in giving character and variety to the picturesque portion of country lying between Falkirk and Denny. As the potter with his handful of clay, and the turner with his rude piece of wood, bring out beautiful forms by a few apparently simple touches; so here nature, working with the sharp cutting edge of the Carron, has shapen this uniform sandy deposit into the lovely valleys lying along the course of the river, and has given us the exquisite rural scenery of Dorrator, Larbert, and Dunipace.

But what of the ancient sea-beaches which are thought to be so well seen on the course of the Carron? At Lock No. 2, on the Forth and Clyde

Canal, and at Carron, we have well marked the 20 feet beach, upon the top of which stands Mungal Mill, as do also parts of Glasgow and Dundee. The same beach is finely seen at the foot of the Red Brae; and from this situation, looking towards Dorrator, may be had an excellent view of the 20, 40, and 53 feet beaches rising in succession above each other, and thus constituting the fine terraces which have long given a character to this part of the Falkirk neighbourhood.

The erosions of the Carron are best observed from the road between Larbert and Dunipace, in the direction of Carmuirs. In fact, the mounds at Dunipace are but evidences of the same eroding action, being composed of stratified sand, part of the original uniform deposit. The river, as we see, formed a passage for itself at Larbert church, and then appears to have been reflected southwards, cutting out at the Red Brae what is said to have been the site of the Roman port of ancient Camelon. Along a higher portion of the deposit, and between the two valleys, runs the Stirlingshire Midland Railway, and an inspection of the ground shows that had the eroding action continued much longer, this ridge would have disappeared, and the two valleys would have been laid into one.

A short time ago, an ancient river channel buried under drift, extending from Kilsyth to

Grangemouth, was discovered through means of borings for minerals. Journals of these operations were collected for the purpose of ascertaining the depth and character of the surface deposits of the country; and it was while examining the same that the incidental discovery was made of a deep pre-glacial, or perhaps inter-glacial, trough or hollow, extending from the Clyde above Bowling, by Kilsyth, to the Forth, near Grangemouth. It is clear that this hollow was due purely to denudation, as the strata which it intersects was found to be intact and unbroken beneath—consequently cut out of the solid rock. It was at first supposed that the denuding agent might be the sea; but be it observed, that however effectually a sea-current might deepen and widen this trough where it was narrowest, or shallowest—that is, in the tract between Kilsyth and Castlecary—it could not have hollowed it out at either end, as these parts must have been, in that case, sunk about 410 feet below sea level, and, consequently far beneath the eroding action of the current. Moreover, it is quite contrary to the ordinary action of sea currents that they should cut out in the comparatively flat bottom they flow over a long narrow channel, the sides of which are everywhere steep, and in some places perpendicular, and even overhanging. For these and other reasons, it may be concluded that this hollow had been cut out by running water in the form of rivers, when the land stood higher than now. These rivers, starting from the present watershed of the district near Kilsyth, would run, the one westward, flowing along the valley of the Kelvin, into the Clyde, near Bowling; and the other eastward, along the present course of the Bonny Water, till it entered the Firth of Forth. The geological state of this ancient river channel is shown by the deepest bore at Grangemouth to be either just before, or shortly after the beginning of the glacial epoch, which conclusion is confirmed by the deepest bore in the western portion of the hollow. The chief geological value of this discovery consists in the evidence it affords, that at the time when water flowed down this ancient river channel into the sea, the land must have stood nearly 300 feet higher than at present. The surface of the land at Grangemouth is only 12 feet above the level of the sea; and as the bottom of this old river channel is 273 feet below the surface, it is evident that the land must have stood about 260 feet higher than now. It is satisfactory thus to find on land a confirmation of what has long been inferred from the mammalian and other remains found in the German Ocean, the English Channel, and other parts, that at a very recent period our island must have stood several hundred feet higher than at present, and formed part of the great eastern continent, which then included in its area the present isolated lands of Great Britain and Ireland.

Several districts of the county offer happy hunting ground for the geologist. Here and there many rare specimens of minerals may be found. We make a running survey, starting from the west. The mountains in Buchanan parish, like the rest of the Grampian range, belong to the primary formation. Roof-slate and lime frequently occur, but schistus is the chief mineral.—The base of the Killearn district is the old red sandstone. In the rising ground a variety of strata is exposed to view by the action of the mountain streams, such as clay, lime, and freestone. In the trap formation, near the south end of the parish, there is a singular chasm called the Wanzie. A transverse section of a hill, running east and west, seems to have slipped off; probably from the partial decay of the subjacent sandstone leaving it without support. The chasm is 346 feet in length, 10 feet in greatest width, and 30 feet in present depth. Attempts have frequently been made to find coal in this neighbourhood. That they have always been unsuccessful is what should be expected from the mineralogy of the district. Coal is never found where the old red sandstone forms the base.—Fintry affords a great variety of minerals. Coal, in small seams, is found in many places; and granite occurs in detached fragments. There are also whinstone, freestone, redstone, jasper, and fine specimens of zeolite. The rocks, which belong to the trap formation, are numerous, and lie in a position very similar to those of Stirling castle, Craigforth, and others in that locality.—The rocks of the Lennox hills are composed chiefly of trap, or whinstone. In the gently sloping lands, between the hills and the carse, strata of red and white sandstone are everywhere found.—The Ochils consist of trap. The beds are of various thickness, nearly vertical, having their dip to the south. The veins, with a few exceptions, run in a northerly direction. The amygdaloid rock is abundant, with agates and calcareous spar. Along the face of the hills, and partially to the westward, is a thick bed of conglomerate rock, or breccia, having a dark brown coloured arenaceous base, in which are embedded fragments of trap rock, chiefly angular. The greenstone, of which the Abbey Craig is for the most part composed, is of felspar and horn-blende, and when broken presents a rough crystallized appearance.—In Baldernock the minerals are coal, lime, ironstone of various kinds, fireclay, pyrites, and alum-ore. Coal and lime have been wrought here for more than 200 years.—The Campsie Fells consist principally of large tubular masses of trap. The minerals of the district also include those of the coal formation—coal, with the usual alternating rocks of freestone, limestone, argillaceous ironstone, aluminous clay, slate, &c., with beds of fossil shells. In the Kirkton glen there is a very fine section of a dyke of compact felspar, about 20 feet in height and 5 feet in breadth, elevating the strata of limestone, slate-clay, and ironstone which bear upon the dyke, and dip on either side of it at a considerable angle.—The greater part of Kilsyth parish is a coal-field, but the mineral is not of so much value as might be anticipated from the broken nature of the strata by dykes and hitches. The principal dyke is known to run into the river Forth, near Airth, and commences here at Tomphin. It varies both in material and thickness. At some places it is 30 feet thick, at others double that number of yards. In one part it consists of the hardest basalts; at another of the softest blaes; and again, it appears as a mass of freestone *debris*, or whinstone interspersed with balls. There are also large ironstone fields at the two baronies and Banton; while limestone is found at Riskend.—At Denny the rocks are whinstone and freestone; but both coal and ironstone mines are wrought in the parish.—The whole of the easter part of Larbert parish is well stored with coal. Five seams have been discovered, and more or less wrought. The lowest of these dips out on the wester part of the Kinnaird and Carronhall estates. The dip is usually to the north-east, and the coalfield is intersected by several dykes. A fine freestone was formerly obtained at Carronhall, situated considerably above the highest seam of coal. This quarry, however, has been filled up. —All the rocks in the parish of Airth are of the coal formation, and form a part of the great coalfield of Scotland. The line of dip varies. Next to the Forth it is southerly, but in the south part of the parish it is towards the north-east. The sandstones are of various shades of yellow and grey, while some approach to white.—Coal is found in the higher districts of Falkirk in great abundance. Also ironstone, limestone, and sandstone.—Polmont contains coal, freestone, ironstone, and fireclay. Freestone, however, is the only rock which extends nearly throughout the whole parish. The dip of the strata is generally to the north-east, except when their position is altered by a dyke which traverses one part of the parish, as exemplified in Brighton's quarry, where the strata, in consequence, dip to the north-west.

We need hardly say that our pen has done little more than skirt the fringe of this interesting subject. But in geological matters we occupy the position of the unlearned.

CHAPTER XXXII.

RIVERS AND LOCHS.

THE Avon takes its course from a moss in the parish of New Monkland, and is augmented by a small tributary from Tannyside Loch, and another stream from Moss Cannel. At the outset it is dull and sluggish, but after cutting the flank of the Bathgate hills, between Carrubber castle and Muiravonside house, its now wooded banks rise nearly 200 feet. Running towards the flood mark of the Forth, scenes still more precipitous and inaccessible are to be found on the river as it bursts through the high-ground of Kinneil into the alluvial carse. Good trout were common in its waters before poisonous pollution came from lint-pools. It forms the south-eastern limit of the county, and was anciently noted for its nunnery of Manuel.

The Blane—*Beulabhuin*, pronounced *Beul-uin*, and signifying "river issuing from the ravine"—rises from the earl's seat in the Lennox hills. The nobles of the old race of Levenax had a castle near, and in sight of, this romantic spot.

Speeding onwards, the stream proceeds in a south-westerly direction for three miles, when, thereafter, it is precipitated over several lofty falls. The lowest, but the most remarkable of these is the Spout of Ballagan, a cascade 70 feet in height. Here a very singular section of the hill is presented. The side of it is cut perpendicularly by the water, and shows no fewer than 192 alternate strata of earth and limestone. Near the bottom of the section are found several thin strata of alabaster of the purest white. Fragments of antimony have also been got, and, when tried by a chemical process, proved to be exceedingly rich specimens. After an additional course of 8 miles, the Blane loses itself in the Endrick, which, in its turn, flows westward to Loch Lomond.

The burn of Boquhan forms the boundary between the parishes of Kippen and Gargunnock. Descending from the rock of Ballochleam, it meets with the red sandstone through which it has opened a passage, and wrought its soft materials into a number of curious forms, resembling the wells and cauldrons of the Devon. After running through a beautiful and well-wooded glen, along which the proprietor of Boquhan has made extensive and agreeable walks, it discharges itself into the Forth at the Bridge of Frew.

The Carron, famed in ancient Celtic song, and of importance in modern trade and manufactures, issues from the Campsie hills near the middle of the isthmus between the firths of Clyde and Forth. Both the source and the place where it discharges itself into the sea, are within the shire of Stirling, which it divides into about two equal parts. The whole length of its course, from west to east, is some 14 miles, the first half of which is spent among bleak hills and rocks, but, when it has reached the low grounds, its banks are fertile and wooded, and, as it advances, the neighbouring soil increases in richness and value till, after passing through the carse of Falkirk, it falls into the Firth of Forth. The stream is small comparatively, yet there is no river in Scotland whose surroundings have been the scene of so many memorable events. Etymological researches are for the most part void of instruction, as they seldom result in certainty. Names of rivers, mountains, and towns have perhaps more frequently had their origin from casual circumstances than from important transactions, or natural peculiarities. Nennius, an author of the ninth century, derives the name of this river from Carausius, who is commonly called the Usurper. The translator of Ossian's poems informs us, that it is of Gaelic origin, and that *Caraon* signifies "Winding River." This fully expresses one characteristic of the stream, which, in former times, before it had forced a new channel for itself in some places, and been straightened by human industry in others, fetched many serpentine sweeps in its passage through the carses. Nevertheless, if we say that the original name was *Caeravon*, that is, river on the *Caers*, or castles, alluding to the Roman fortifications upon its banks, we probably give an etymology just as plausible, though equally uncertain. A short distance from its source, the river enters the Carron Bog. This vast plain and meadow lies partly in the parishes of St. Ninians and Kilsyth, but chiefly in Fintry. Its length is about 4 miles, and its medium breadth 1 mile. Considerably elevated above the ocean, it occupies part of the table-land between the eastern and western coasts. It has, probably, been a lake at no very distant period, and gradually filled by the hill brooks washing down *debris*. Part, indeed, is a swamp scarcely passable at any time, but nearly inundated by every heavy rain. Two miles below Graham's castle, in the division called Temple Denny, the Carron, having worn a hollow channel in the rock, forms a beautiful cascade, by pouring its contracted stream over a precipice above 20 feet in height. This cataract is little known, being situated in a very remote and unfrequented valley, and, were we writing in verse, we would say of it what Horace says of the little town, in which he lodged a night, on his journey from Rome to Brundusium, "*Versu dicere non est.*" It goes by the name of Auchinlilly-linspout—"Field of the overflowing torrent and pool." Spout is an absurd tautology of what has been expressed with emphasis by the reduplication of *ly* in the middle of the compound Celtic name. When the river is in flood, and a triumphant torrent sweeps down the glen, this cascade is unsurpassed among Scottish streams for the grandeur of its storm of spray. The ruins of the Hermitage, too, are to be seen here on the very margin of a deep fissure of rock. The rustic cottage of whin-stone, now utterly desolate—roof fallen, windows gone, and crumbling gables ivy and lichen draped—was built in 1801 by Mr. Robert Hill, W. S., Edinburgh, who had purchased the lands of Forest Hill. It was a thoroughly romantic building, most suitable, in its wild situation and surroundings, for habits inclined to the delights of shrieking solitude. In 1840, a reservoir, near the Carron Bog, broke through its embankments, when the heavy down-rush of water carried away much of the masonry of the deserted house. Strange stories are told of the reasons why men have been influenced to seek seclusion from the world in an eremitical life, and we can readily imagine a powerful combination of circumstances leading thitherward. Sad experiences may have given them a distaste for society, or, possibly, noble aspirations and generous feelings have been cruelly chilled and disappointed. But, in early times, the recluse's cave had often in or near it a rudely carved chapel in the rock for piety and prayer, while the foliage of the trees that surrounded the arched cavern gave a deeper shade of sanctity to the lonely cell. Such, for example, as Bridgenorth Hermitage, in Shropshire, wherein dwelt that royal anchorite, Athelward, the Saxon prince, brother of King Athelstan, or the cave presently occupied by a Welsh hermit, on the estate of the Earl of Powis in Montgomeryshire. Leaving the hermitage ruins, the waters of the Carron rumble and foam through a deep ravine for a spray-wreathed cauldron, from which, with deafening din, they speed on buoyantly in their sea-ward course; where, at many points,

"Grey rock is brown beneath the flow of limpid water."

Over the serpentine road down-hill to Denny the spirit of beauty everywhere prevails. The intervening district, indeed, is famous for its pastoral undulations; and from almost every breezy brae-top a charming view is got of the wooded banks of the river—foliage which, even in the present green-tide, displays all the variety of autumnal richness. The "Lady's Loup," with the romance that hangs over the linn, merits more in passing than a prosaic paragraph. But, here, we must simply refer the reader ignorant of the tragic tradition to the well-known "Douglas" play, in which the heroic incidents of the leap are fully and vigorously told.

"She ran, she flew like lightning up the hill,
  Nor halted till the precipice she gained,
  Beneath whose low'ring top the river falls
  Engulf'd in rifted rocks.

. . . . .

RIVERS AND LOCHS.

> Oh, had you seen her last despairing look!
> Upon the brink she stood, and cast her eyes
> Down on the deep; then lifting up her head
> And her white hands to heaven, seeming to say,
> Why am I forced to this? she plunged herself
> Into the empty air."

Now we tread ground filled with classic memories. What a thrilling and matchless story we should have could the river, as it rolls along, only tell of all it has seen and known! Here Ossian, the ancient Gaelic bard, tuned his lyre; and here also the young Oscar won his brightest laurels in war. In a poem entitled "The War of Caros," and dedicated to Malvina, the daughter of Toscar, the son of Fingal, sang—

> "He (Oscar) came not over the streamy Carun
> The bard returned with his song.
> Grey night grows dim on Crona."

Historians also mention a bloody battle fought upon the banks here between the Romans and the confederate armies of the Scots and Picts, commanded by Fergus II., in the beginning of the fifth century. Probably the two armies disputed the passage of the river at Dunipace. The Romans remained masters of the field; but not without such dreadful slaughter on both sides, that authors, in their description of the combat, have used the extravagant, though trite, hyperbole of the waters running red for miles with blood. From this point to Dorrator and West Carron, the stream runs sinuously in a flattish haugh, which varies in breadth at different places; and is, for the most part, bounded by sloping banks of sand. For lovers of the piscatorial sport merely, the Carron offers little attraction. It was at one time, however, famed alike for the quantity, quality, and size of its trout. The endless variety of alternate pool and stream, and the openness of its banks, rendered it the favourite resort of the angler. But its waters have been polluted; and it is, in fact, nothing now as a fishing river, although a few of the common trout may occasionally be hooked. Many rills, of course, find their way to the Carron. The Bonny, supposed to be the Crona, celebrated by Ossian, falls into it about a mile below the village of Bonnybridge. Near Camelon, it also receives the Light-water-burn, which flows in the centre of what, to all appearance, must at some remote period have formed the bed of a considerable river. The Grange Burn, too, from the upper part of the parish of Polmont, unites with it in the vicinity of Grangemouth.

The Devon is a mere rivulet, which washes a detachment of Stirlingshire, and divides it from Clackmannan. It has its source among the hills in the parish of Blackford, Perthshire; and was written Dovan in a charter granted by Robert III. to the burgh of Inverkeithing. *Dhu-avon*, "black river," seems a not improbable etymon, it being a deep and sable stream, as it lazily creeps along the plain from near the Cauldron Linn, till it falls into the Forth at Cambus, a course, including curves, of a dozen miles. Although the run of the romantic and beautiful little river is peculiarly circuitous and winding in its round of the Ochils, it flows at first almost due east towards Glendevon; but, near the church of Fossaway, it makes a sudden turn westward, and passing through the parishes of Muckhart, Dollar, and Tillicoultry, gently glides along the southern boundary of Alva district. It is somewhat odd, that the stream, after having performed a circular route of about 30 miles, should end its career nearly opposite the point at which it started on the other side of the hills, reaching the Forth exactly where the latter assumes the character of a firth, two miles above Alloa. The first of its principal waterfalls is the Rumbling Bridge, so-called from the hoarse music made by the river in its wonderful passage through arching rocks; but a little further on, amid a series of cascades, we find the water producing the curious excavation of that never empty boiler, the Cauldron Linn.

The number of the lesser streams in the county is legion. The Dualt, which flows through mossy ground in the parish of Killearn, would not be thus particularized, but for a fine cataract it presents in the glen of Dualt, near Killearn house. In a deep, wooded ravine, with many smaller falls, the rivulet rushes over a precipice of 60 feet. In the same neighbourhood, the Carnock has worn a channel 70 feet deep, through red sandstone. The chasm is called Ashdow, a corruption of *Uisk-dhu*, "black water."

The Duchray, which is the southern and most considerable branch of the Forth, rises near the summit of Benlomond, and forms the northern boundary, for some miles, of the parish of Drymen. Leaving it on the south, it joins a tributary from Loch Ard; and now acquiring the name of Forth, it again approaches and skirts the same parish as far as its eastern extremity.

The Endrick—derived from *Auon*, "river," and *eirich*, "to rise"—springs from the Gargunnock hills, north-east of Fintry. It is a bold and rapid stream, subject to sudden "spates," which frequently do serious damage. In September, 1836, twenty score of lambs were swept, by one of its floods, from the lawn of Buchanan into Loch Lomond. After running a short distance east at the start, it takes a southerly course; and, gaining strength by the accession of tributary waters, it separates the parishes of Gargunnock and St. Ninians from that of Fintry, till it reaches the high road leading from the latter village to Denny. It then flows for about 4 miles due west through the northern valley of Fintry, when it becomes the boundary betwixt the parishes of Killearn and Balfron. The Endrick comes down with a deafening noise over its rocky channel; and in the "Loup of Fintry," pours its waters over a rock, nearly perpendicular, of about 60 feet. When the river is much swollen, nothing can exceed the grandeur of this scene. In its usual state there are three breaks in the fall; but, in a flood, the waters dash over the precipitous rock, which is upwards of 90 feet wide, in one unbroken cataract. The stream cannot be supposed to contain a great quantity of water. Yet it is the sole moving power of a considerable weight of machinery in Fintry parish. A reservoir of good depth, covering about 30 acres of land, was constructed on the high ground, and supplied wholly by the Endrick, for driving the Culcreuch cotton factory. At Gartness, there are also cascades of some character. For a quarter of a mile, the channel of the stream is here scooped out of the solid rock, and the vexed waters have to force their way over a series of precipices. In greater part, at least, the Endrick is a clear-running and beautifully-wooded stream, by which anglers can sport, and get rewarded with full baskets of deliciously flavoured trout. After a course of 18 miles, it discharges itself into Loch Lomond, being the largest river which that lake receives.

The Forth, as we have already said, traverses Stirlingshire for 10 miles from its source, under the name of Duchray, or Glenguoi. Augmented as it proceeds, by numberless mountain streams, it then enters Perthshire, where it receives an accession equal to the volume of its own waters, in the river which issues from Loch Ard in Aberfoyle. It is now called Avondow, or "black river," being generally dark and muddy here from the quantity of moss that is floated in it. After a course of about 5 miles, it again joins Stirlingshire below Gartmore house, where it gets the name of Forth, which it retains. By several of the earlier writers, it has been confounded with a much nobler river, the Teath, that flows from the Callander district as a tributary stream, and which is nominally merged about 2 miles above Stirling. Even Mr. Nimmo, living near the eastern extremity of the county he described, fell into this error. Sir William Alexander, first Earl of Stirling, was correct, however, when in his *Parænesis, or Exhortation to Government*, addressed to Prince Henry, he says :—

> " Forth, when she first doth from Benlowmond rinne,
> Is poore of waters, naked of renowne ;
> But Carron, Allan, Teath, and Devon in,
> Doth grow the greater still the further downe ;
> Till that abounding both in power and fame,
> She long doth strive to give the sea her name."

The Romans, adopting the words of the natives, and fitting them to their own pronunciation, called this river " Bodotria." But what was Bodotria ? Probably the Celts, in comparing the much finer stream, the Teath, with the sluggish, moss-banked river which the Forth exhibits from Gartmore to Frew, called the latter *Bao-shruth*, "insignificant stream," or *Bath-shruth*, "smooth slow stream." Still, how came it to be named Forth? *Phorth*, pronounced with the aspirates quiescent, becomes Port; and changing the *Ph* into *F*, we have Forth—a name applicable to a river affording the means of navigation. In point of magnitude, the Forth, as a Scottish river, is only surpassed by the Spey and Tay. The surface which it drains is estimated at 541 square miles. Steamers ply regularly between Granton and the port of Stirling. At neap tides the flow is about $5\frac{1}{2}$ feet in the harbour, at stream tides it rises to 11 feet. At one time, the navigation between this and Alloa—a distance of $10\frac{1}{2}$ miles, though the direct line is only 5—was greatly impeded by seven fords, or shallows, composed of boulders. But it was determined to have two of these at least removed—the town and abbey fords, which were found the greatest obstructions to the free passage of vessels. The works were commenced at the lower end of the abbey ford, where the channel excavated was about 500 yards in length and 175 in breadth; while it was also deepened in some places $3\frac{1}{2}$ feet. Here is a specimen of the wisdom of our ancestors under similar circumstances:—During the reign of Charles II. of

Spain, a company of Dutch contractors offered to render the Mancanares navigable from Madrid to where it falls into the Tagus, and the latter from that point to Lisbon, provided they were allowed to levy a duty for a certain number of years on the goods conveyed by this channel. The Council of Castile took the proposal into their serious consideration, and after maturely weighing it, pronounced the following singular decision:—"That if it had pleased God that these two rivers should have been navigable, He would not have wanted human assistance to have made them such; but, as He had not done it, it was plain He did not think it proper that it should be done. To attempt it, therefore, would be to violate the decree of His providence, and to mend the imperfections which He designedly left in His works." Though the Forth is far from being the most sediment-carrying river in Scotland—the Tay surpassing it in this respect many times over—it has been calculated to bring down more than 5,000,000 cubic feet of sediment per annum; and it is probable that, at one time, when the ice and snow fields were melting from off the country, and the glacial *debris* lay more abundantly on the higher grounds, it brought down much more. Thus was the "fine land" accumulated in the gradually-shallowing waters of the ancient firth. Before any written human history, but not before the human occupation of the island, the land received its most recent elevation of from 30 to 50 feet, and the river then began its slow and winding course over the level tract which it had itself laid down to the now more distant sea. Such, briefly, is the history of the "Bonnie Links o' Forth." In this river there are, besides the regular flows and ebbs, several irregular motions which, betwixt Alloa and Culross, are commonly called the *Leakies*. When the tide flows some time, it intermits and ebbs for a while, and then fills till full sea; and, on the contrary, when the tide is ebbing, it intermits and flows for a period, and, afterwards, ebbs till low water. This extraordinary phenomenon is called the *Lakies* of Forth. A large salmon fishery is still carried on at Stirling, chiefly for exportation. The burgh revenue derived from this source, even in 1816, was £1,200 sterling; but a privilege of the inhabitants to have the fish at 3d. a pound has been, for many years, abolished. Salmon seems to have been a staple article of diet in Lent during the reign of James IV. His Majesty used, especially during this season, to become Franciscan monk here, where he had founded a convent in 1494. The poet Dunbar, to whom it had been recommended, probably by high authority, to be a friar of the king's favourite order; but who, not relishing the proposal, endeavours, in what he calls "Dirigie to the king, bydand our lang in Stirling," to prevail on his Majesty to

> " Cum hame and dwell nae mair in Stirling,
> Quhair fisch to sell at nane but spirrling.
> *Credo gustare statim vinum Edinburgi.*"

The smelt, or sparling, was wont to be caught here in great numbers during the spring months. A specimen of the *Beluga*, or White Whale, was also killed near the town in 1815.

The Garrel, as its name denotes, is a rough, brawling stream. But why blame the poor brook for outrageous behaviour? Similarly situated—a water-child of the mountains with strength to be wild, and a rough road to travel—no stream could conduct itself more circumspectly. To be what it is, and to be capable of what it is capable of becoming, is the true end of even a river's existence. The Garrel rises on one of the Kilsyth range of hills; and, within a mile and a half, falls 1,000 feet, having numerous cataracts in its course. The narrow chasms worn by its rapid and powerful current in winter, are singularly romantic. When it reaches the Burn Green, near the town of Kilsyth, it is joined and augmented by the little Ebroch, which springs from the foot of the Barwood. After flowing half-a-mile further, in the valley westward, it loses itself in the Kelvin at the end of a course of about three miles.

The Glazert, which runs through a considerable part of the parish of Campsie, empties itself into the Kelvin, opposite the town of Kirkintilloch. It is formed by the junction of three burns, near the lodge at the entrance to Lennox castle—the Pu', a small, sleepy streamlet which skirts the base of the South Brae; the Finglen burn, which crosses the valley at the west end of Haughead; and the Kirkton burn, which crosses at the eastern extremity of the same village. No less than nineteen burns are said to discharge themselves into the humble Glazert.

The Kelvin has its source, in a sort of marsh, on the lands of Ruchill; and descends, as a petty rill, to the low ground on the south, where it soon receives an accession from a portion of Shawend burn, and further west from the Garrel. It moves slowly forward; but near Inchterff, and near Inchbelly, it becomes a beautiful stream with banks verdant and wooded. Until the year 1792, it was much choked up with flags, rushes, and water-lilies, and frequently overflowed the adjacent valley. But Sir Archibald Edmonstone, Bart., of Duntreath, who purchased the estate of Kilsyth in 1784, projected and carried into effect a great improvement, under the inspection and according to the plan of Mr. Robert Whitworth, engineer, by straightening, deepening, and embanking the river. In its *route* to the Clyde, the Kelvin passes many sweet bits of scenery; but having left the wooded bend, near the old "Three-tree well," its waters, from industrial pollution, become sickening even to look at, and detract greatly from the healthful amenities of that attractive breathing ground—the West-End Park, so much and so wisely appreciated by the citizens of Glasgow.

The county is not peculiarly rich in its lochs. Several of the islands, however, in Loch Lomond belong to the parish of Buchanan. Inchcaileoch, "old woman's island," once contained a nunnery, and the parish church; but is now without either house or inhabitant, and stands covered with copsewood. Inchfad, "long island"; and Inchcruin, "round island," are arable and inhabited. Inchmurrin, the island of St. Murrin, who was tutelary saint of Paisley, is the largest of the whole, being two miles long and one broad, and remains preserved for fallow deer. Lomond, a corruption of the Gaelic Lomnochd, is literally "naked," a character which cannot apply to the thickly wooded shoulder of the kingly "Ben" on the west. Metaphorically, it signifies "insulated." A pronunciation of the name nearly approaching the Gaelic occurs in a notice of a charter in David II.'s time by Donald Earl of Levenax to Maurice of Bouchcannane, of various lands, and, amongst others, "*illam terram de Sallachy per has similiter divisas, a Sallachy usque Kelg, et sicut descendit in stagno de Lough-*

lomneid." If there be any force in these remarks, they go to show that the loch is named from its mountain. According to Richard of Cirencester, it was anciently called *Lyncalidor*, and certainly it did not receive its present appellation till the fourteenth century. Few there must be who have not heard of its three wonders, " waves without wind, fish without fin, and a floating island." The swell in the widest part, more particularly after a storm, has originated the first. Vipers are said to swim from island to island, and may account for the second. As for a "floating island," such a phenomenon has been heard of elsewhere. Pliny tells us that certain green lands, covered with rushes, float up and down in the lake of Vandimon.

There is in MacFarlan of MacFarlan's papers, now deposited in Advocate's Library, a curious passage, witten in 1724, by Alexander Graham, Esq. of Duchray, in his account of several parishes, and, amongst others, that of Buchanan. "On the north side of Loch Lomond, and about three miles west from the church, upon a point of land which runs into the loch, called Cashel, are the ruins of an old building of a circular shape, and in circumference about 60 paces, built all of prodigious whinstone, without lime or cement. The walls are in some places about 9 or 10 feet high, yet standing; and it is surprising how such big stones could be reared up by the hands of men. This is called the Giant's castle, and the founder thereof said to be Keith MacInDoill, or Keith the son of Doillus, who is reported to have been contemporary with the famous Finmacoill, and consequently to have lived in the fifth century. This Keith, notwithstanding the great number of natural isles in the loch, was, it seems, so curious as to form an artificial island, which is in the loch at a little distance from the point on which the old castle stands, founded on large square joists of oak, firmly mortised in one another; two of which, of a prodigious size (in each of which there are three large mortices), were disjoined from the float in 1714, and made use of by a gentleman in that country who was then building a house." The point on which the castle stands is called at this day Rownafean, i. e. "giant's point." No doubt the buoyancy of an island, in some places, may be ascribed to an accumulated mass of decaying vegetable matter, by which it is surrounded; but, in our opinion, the decrease of the waters of Loch Lomond, at certain particular seasons, affords a simple solution of the anomaly of its so-called "floating island." The length of this queen of Scottish lakes is 24 miles; its greatest breadth, which is nearly opposite Rossdhu, about 8 miles; and its average height above the sea level 22 feet. From lower Inveruglass, up to near its northern point, it is of considerable depth. Opposite Farkin, it is 66 fathoms; a little farther north, 80 fathoms; a mile south of Tarbet, 86 fathoms; and opposite Alt Gary, 100 fathoms, which probably is its greatest depth. South from Luss it seldom reaches 20 fathoms. The chief tributary rivers of the loch are the Endrick on the east, and the Fruin on the west. Its outlet is the river Leven, at Balloch, which, after a course of 5 miles, flows into the Clyde at Dumbarton. In wet seasons, the surface of the lake sometimes rises 6 feet, when much valuable land at the mouth of the Endrick is heavily flooded. In 1782, a late harvest being followed by an early and severe winter, the corn, before it was ripe, was covered with water, and afterwards enveloped in ice. The upper part of the loch, from its great depth, never freezes; but the lower part occasionally bears ice of sufficient strength for the enjoyment of the exhilarating exercise and art of skating. In the beginning of 1838, it was traversed to and from Inchmurrin by horses and vehicles. Its scenery is well known, and has frequently been described both by practical and poetic pens. We touch it not; but leave it with silent admiration. Singularly bold and beautiful, it is, in its aggregation of exquisite forms, unsurpassed by any British lake.

The other lochs which have a place in Stirlingshire need only be summarised. Contiguous to Carron iron-works, there are two reservoirs supplied from the Carron at Larbert, by means of a convex dyke. The wester-dam, which covers 30 acres, is somewhat picturesque, with trees skirting its edge, and a fleet of swans sailing with proudly-arched neck over its surface. But at times we have seen some memorable night effects at the forge dam, into which the belching furnace flames are brightly reflected. More vividly seen in the water than in the air, they seem to dart downwards into a dark abyss, illumining the whole surface of the dam and the row of outlying cottages with all but lime-light brilliance.

At the southern part of Killearn parish, lies an artificial lake, covering about 150 acres, which serves as a reservoir for the supply of water during summer to the Partick mills on the Kelvin. The sources of that river, as many are aware, were taken to form the high summit reservoir of the Forth and Clyde Canal. The latter was called the Townhead Loch, and is situated near Kilsyth. It is of an oval form, full three-quarters of a mile long, and from one-quarter to half-a-mile broad. It covers 75 imperial acres.

On the moor of Kippen, there is a small lake of water, called Lochleggan, about a mile in circumference, and for the most part surrounded with wood. A considerable stream issues from it; which, increasing as it flows, forms the burn of Broich, whose waters, after passing through a beautiful glen close by the house of Broich, are chiefly employed in floating moss from the plain below.

There are two lochs in Slamannan parish—the Little and the Great Black Lochs. The latter is the principal feeder of the reservoir constructed on the lands of Auchingray for supplying the Monkland Canal. Another, called Ellaig Loch, is situated to the north-east of the annexation. Perch and eel are plentiful in all three.

Loch Coulter lies in St. Ninians parish. It is about 2 miles in circumference, shallow to the west, but very deep to the north-east. In 1755, the great earthquake, by which Lisbon was destroyed, greatly agitated this lakelet, and it was then, as is supposed, that a large stone, in weight about a ton, was raised from its bed and carried towards the shore. The shock was particularly severe around Drymen. On that day, Whitefield, the great English divine, was preaching in the adjoining parish of Kilmaronock. The weather was fine, and a large concourse of people assembled to hear the noted southern preacher. The speaker and his hearers occupied the face of an eminence. Instantly the earth heaved, and the people were bent forward as if by a wave.

Strathblane parish contains six lakes; Loch Ardinning, of 60 imperial acres; Craigmaddie and Dunbroch, of 10 each; Carbeth of 8; and Craigallion, of 40 acres. These lie in romantic situations; and with the exception of the first mentioned, are adorned partly with natural wood, and partly with plantations. Mugdock Loch, containing 25 acres, is also ornamented with trees, and is further enhanced by the ruins of the ancient castle which stand on its south-west point.

Milngavie has an irregular and somewhat straggling appearance. In and around the village, on the banks of the Allander, are a number of public works, the most extensive of which are the calico printing and cotton spinning establishments of Messrs. John Black & Company. About a mile north from the railway station there is also the Mugdock reservoir, which is supplied with water from Loch Katrine for the service of the citizens of Glasgow. It is formed in a natural valley, by an embankment on the south side 400 yards long, and 68 feet high; and by another on the east side 240 yards long, and 50 feet high; each with a puddle wall in the centre, and stone pitching 2 feet thick on the front, which is formed to a slope of 3 horizontal to 1 vertical, and covered with soil on the back, which has a slope of 3 horizontal to 1 vertical. The water surface of the reservoir extends to 60 acres, and a small detached portion at the upper end to 2 acres more; the depth is 50 feet, and it contains 548,000,000 gallons, or a supply for the city, at the present rate of consumption, for eighteen days. The water is drawn from the reservoir by pipes laid in a tunnel through the rock which forms the hill-side, there being no pipes through the embankments themselves. These pipes lead into a well, also cut out of the solid rock, 40 feet diameter and 63 feet deep, at the bottom of which are placed the various valves by which the flow of the water is regulated. At the reservoir end of the tunnel, a cast-iron stand-pipe is erected, with sluices to draw off the water; and in the well the water is strained by passing it through copper wire-cloth, fixed in frames of wood, so as to form an inner well of octagonal shape, 25 feet diameter; and from this latter the water finally passes into the mains leading to the city. This work may truly be said to surpass the greatest of the nine famous aqueducts which fed the city of Rome. Of the 26 miles which lie between Loch Katrine and the Mugdock reservoir, 13 miles are tunnelling, $3\frac{3}{4}$ miles are iron-piping, and the remainder, where the ground has been cut open, is an arched aqueduct. There are in the whole work, 70 district tunnels, upon which 44 vertical shafts were sunk for facilitating and expediting the completing of the scheme. In addition to the tunnel at the commencement of the aqueduct at Loch Katrine, and the one at its termination, there are at intermediate places, others of 700, 800, 1,100, and 1,400 yards in length. Not to speak of smaller constructions, there are 26 important iron and masonry aqueducts over rivers and ravines, some 60 feet and 80 feet in height, with arches 30 feet, 50 feet, and 90 feet in span. The number of people employed in constructing the works, exclusive of iron-founders and mechanics, was generally about 3,000; and for the greater part of these, huts and roads, and all other accommodation had to be provided; the country in many districts being of the wildest and most inaccessible character. The works were designed in 1853-4; completed at a total cost of £1,987,548, in 1859; and opened by Her Majesty the Queen on 14th October of the latter year.

CHAPTER XXXIII.

HILLS.

THE Campsie Hills have taken their name from the place where the village of Old Campsie now stands; and, therefore, were probably so called only in the later times of Gaelic dialogue south of the Forth. They are also known as the Campsie Fells. *Fell* is, by Dr. Jamieson, defined "a precipitous rock, a rocky hill." He remarks that Suidas uses the Greek *phelleis* for mountainous places. Hardinge, about 1460, calls Dundaff hill "the fell" above "the foord of Frew," and speaks of

> "the high Ochhilles,
> Which some men call montaignes, and some felles."

The general surface of the Campsie district may, in the strictest language, be described as highly undulated, and these undulations follow each other in regular succession. They are of great length from south to north, and nearly all run in that direction. The general contour of these lengthened hills, individually, although somewhat uncommon, is not peculiar to this part of the country. Each hill has a considerable degree of curvature, the convex of which is uniformly presented to the west; while the central part of that curve forms the highest point of their elevation, and they gradually slope towards the extremity of the segments which their curvatures form. Upon their eastern sides, they rise with an equal acclivity of from 20 to 30 degrees; the rapidity of which, in some measure, diminishes as it approaches the summits, where they are somewhat roundbacked. Their central or highest points seldom or ever exceed an elevation of from 1200 to 1500 feet above the level of the sea; at which height their western faces generally become abrupt and broken, and continue to be precipitous for a considerable depth under the lip of the hill. They seldom show, however, more of the stratification than that of the trap, which in such situations evidently points out its strong tendency towards columnar form. At the bases of these precipices, a long and rapid slope of *debris* succeeds, which is frequently covered by vegetation. The troughs or hollows, between the undulations, generally form narrow dales or glens, but some few of them have a sufficient breadth to entitle them to the denomination of valleys. The most extended of these are the vales of Campsie and Fintry. Most prominent among the heights is a hill of somewhat conic appearance called the Meikle Bin. Situated a little to the south of the road which leads from Fintry to the Vale of Campsie, it towers above all the other heights of the district, and rises superior to them at least 300 feet. From its top, is one of the most extensive, beautiful, and variegated views in the country, part of fourteen, if not of sixteen counties, and perhaps one-half of Scotland, being at once under the eye. At a moderate calculation, the area of the whole view is said to be 12,000 miles.

As far as this tract of country has been dipped into, the geological materials of which it is formed are as follows:—A surface of vegetable soil; trap; sandstone; limestone; shale, or slate clay; blue clays of various tints and of various consistencies; bituminous shales; clay iron-ores, some of which are thinly stratified, and others are embedded in the shale in lenticular form; coal and clay marle; all of which have been arranged by nature in the order here given, from the surface soil downward.

The north side of Ben Lomond, like that of the west, is very steep—in one part, a dreadful precipice of more than 1,800 feet, and firm must be the nerve of him who can look down unmoved. The perpendicular height of the mountain above the surface of the lake is 3,240 feet, and the average height of the lake above the level of the sea 22 feet, which, added to the former height, gives the perpendicular altitude of the Ben, above the level of the sea, 3,262 feet. In height it is surpassed by other mountains; but the difference is more than compensated by the elegance of its insulated situation with regard to the neighbouring hills; its form being that of a huge truncated cone, and its appearance, from whatever part it is viewed, much more noble and magnificent than that of the other neighbouring mountains. Ben Lomond is chiefly composed of gneiss, or granite, interspersed with great quantities of quartz. The latter substance is found near the top, in immense masses, some of which weigh several tons. These appear like patches of snow upon the mountain, even when seen from Luss. Considerable quantities of micaceous schist, shining like silver beautifully undulated, and in some places imbedded with quartz, are also at the top, and many rocks towards the base are entirely composed of this substance. To the south, the ridge continues with the same characters along the eastern side of the loch, but nowhere rises into summits of distinguished height. One of these, which is of some elevation, is called Conic Hill, beyond which appears the Hill of Ardmore, the final termination of the chain.

The ascent to the top of Ben Lomond, directly west, is steep, but from the south it is more gradual, until near the top, and then it becomes more precipitous. The view from the summit is inconceivably interesting and grand. At the bottom is seen the beautiful lake, stretched out like a map, its islands having lost their rugged forms and appearing as flat substances amidst the bright expanse. The banks of the lake are at hand, ornamented with seats and cultivated grounds. Looking towards the east, the rich plains of Lothian and Stirlingshire are distinctly in sight. Casting the eye from thence to the south, and pursuing the view towards the east, the high grounds of Lanarkshire, the vales of Renfrewshire, with the firth of Clyde, and the wide Atlantic, with its islands, are clearly discerned; while the Isle of Man and the coast of Ireland blend as it were with the sky, being scarcely visible. But, to one unaccustomed to Highland scenery, the most striking view is undoubtedly on the north side, which may with truth be termed fearfully sublime. The eye, from where it first discovers the Ochil hills near the east, ranging along the north until it comes near the Western Ocean, sees nothing but mountain upon mountain, elevating their summits in almost every variety of shape.

The Alpine plants are found here. Amongst others, a species of the bramble, the cloud-berry (*rubus chamæmorus*), is got in great profusion. The blossom is a purplish white. The fruit is a bunch of red berries, ripe in July, and well flavoured. The Laplanders store it in the snow, and preserve it from year to year, eating it with the reindeer's milk; and it sometimes graces the festive board of the Scottish Highlander. But there are also the *Silene acaulis*, or moss catchfly; the *Sibbaldia procumbens*, or procumbent silver-weed; the *Rhodiala rosea*, the *Azalea procumbens*, the *Trientalis* (in the weeds overhanging the lake), and the *statice*. Vegetables abounding below, assume here a new habit—the *Epilobium*, the *Alchemilla* or lady's mantle, the saxifrages, and the *Cerastium*. Near the bottom of the mountain two plants are found which catch flies, and kill the insects, by closing their leaves upon them—the *Drosera rotundifolia*, or round-leafed sundew, and the *Drosera angelica*, or great sundew.

On the precipitous side of Ben Lomond, where, ascending from the south, the stranger would imagine there can be no footing, a safe path descends by a deep ravine, leading to the farmhouse of Comar, and thence to Aberfoyle. Along the eastern shore of the loch, and the western side of the Ben, or what is called Craigrostan, a narrow Alpine road conducts through scenery of gigantic features. Here tradition, countenanced by Barbour, has assigned to Robert Bruce a cave, in which he spent a night when passing from Strathfillan after the nearly fatal combat with MacDougal of Lorn. Here, too, a steep shelving rock is pointed out as "Rob Roy's prison," where that Highland *Laird* is reported to have stowed such of his vassals as he had adjudged to durance. North of Craigrostan is what is said to have been his "Cave," in which he rendezvoused with his followers in the exploits attributed to him. Many tales, indeed, have been told of this unfortunate man, for which there is no evidence and no foundation. Of his cage, or prison, an anecdote is mentioned, for the veracity of which we do not pledge ourselves, but which we report as illustrative of the tradition, true or fabulous. One of his tenants had not paid his rent when it had become due. Rob, suspending him on a rope by the shoulders, let him down into the fastness. Having drawn him up at the end of twenty-four hours, he told him that, if he failed to pay by a particular time, he should draw him up by the neck.

That portion of the Ochils which extends into the parish of Alva, when seen at some distance from the south, appears to be one continued range, with little variation in height; but, as the mountain slopes towards the south, it is intersected by exceedingly deep and narrow glens. From this circumstance the foreground is divided into three separate hills, distinguished by the names of Wood Hill, Middle Hill, and West Hill of Alva. Wood Hill rises immediately from its base to the height of 1,620 feet, and continues still rising gradually for about two miles further north, until it reaches the top of Ben-cloch, or Bencleugh, the highest point of the Alva hills; and the summit of all the Ochils being, according to an observation, 2,420 feet above the level of the river Devon, and 2,300 feet above the level of the Forth at Alva. The view from this summit is very extensive; but the Wood hill, the Middle, and the West hills are incomparably the most beautiful of the whole range, from Glen-Devon on the east, to their termination near the bridge of Alva on the west. They are not so steep, rugged, or inaccessible as those immediately westward in the parish of Logie, and they present a more regular, noble, and bold aspect than any of those that lie immediately on the east; besides which they are clothed with the richest verdure at all seasons, and produce grass of the finest quality and in the greatest variety. The summits of the central parts of the Ochils, particularly Bencleugh, are composed of granite, both red and grey, many varieties of which are extremely beautiful, and contain distinct crystals of black schorl.

CHAPTER XXXIV.

BOTANY.

FOR simplicity and intensity of enjoyment, what can excel a country walk? Spring returns, and a new impulse is given to all inward and outward life. The tender green, peculiar to the vernal season, is spread over the leas, hedgerows, and gardens; while the woodside walks are literally paved with flowers—bluebells and violets, and primroses nursed in the recesses of gnarled roots of trees. There are men certainly, like Sir Michael de Fleming, a baronet fashionable in the gay world of Johnson's time, who are not to be ruralised, preferring the smell of a flambeau at the playhouse to the sweet fragrance of nature, with the hum of busy insect life, and the lark rising blithely through the summer air; but with an open door to both theatres of pleasure, our taste inclines to the subtle and vague joyousness produced by the soft fresh breezes, the melody of birds, and

> "The sweet smell
> Of different flowers, in odour and in hue."

In his at-home researches, the experienced botanist knows well to confine himself chiefly to the southern parts of this shire. Throughout the higher grounds of Drymen parish, none of the rarer Scottish plants are found. The common ling (*Erica vulgaris*) and the fine-leaved heath (*Erica cinerea*) prevail; and, in the absence of heath, the *Aira flexuosa, Festuea ovina,* and *vivipara* are the principal grasses. All over the moorland, the cow or red whortle berry (*Vaccinium vitas idœa*) is abundant, and thrives where very few other plants will grow. Its leaves much resemble those of the box, both in texture and colour. Its flowers, which are of a delicate flesh-tint, appear in June; while its berries, of a rich crimson, are ripe in August. This plant is the badge of the clan M'Leod. In the low marshy parts, the *Tofieldia palustris, Carex,* or sedge; and *Parnassia palustris* abound. It is worthy of remark that where the last-mentioned plants are common, the soil is most congenial to the growth of oak coppice, producing bark of the best quality. Upon such ground, however, hard wood never reaches a large size; nor does the *Pinus* there outlive forty or fifty years. The *Pinus larix,* for example, begins to fail or rot in the heart. The vale of Endrick is well-wooded. At the park of Drumquhassle, Dalnair, and near the manse, there are some magnificent oaks and beeches; while at the churchyard gate, there is a noble ash, once the bell-tree, which has weathered at least 200 years. It now measures about 18 feet in circumference at one foot from the ground, and 17 feet 6 inches in the middle of the stem. Clustering round the walls of the castle of Duchray, is some remarkably fine ivy, next, in age and strength, to that at Kenilworth. In the old orchard, there are also some aged filbert trees, that produce a nut of a larger size and higher flavour than the common nut of the wood. They were brought originally from the monastery of Inchmahome, to which they had been conveyed from foreign parts.

Besides the plantations that surround the houses of proprietors in the arable part of the parish of Killearn, every glen and ravine is covered with copsewood. Several ancient yew trees, of remarkable size, are to be seen near the mansion of Ballikinrain; and oaks and silver firs, of equally gigantic proportions, on the estate of Killearn. One berry-bearing yew has a girth of 8 feet 10 inches; and a barren one, of 10 feet 9 inches. The largest oak measures 14 feet 6 inches; and a silver fir, 16 feet 5 inches. From many observations on yew trees, De Candolle, of Geneva, calculates their average annual increase of diameter at one-twelfth of an inch; and, by that rule, the age of the one yew mentioned must be about 440 years, and of the other 530. The oak has probably seen 460 years, and the silver fir 140. Bishop

Watson says that as soon as a tree is worth a guinea, the most profitable plan is to cut it down. This we may suppose to have been an oak of 7 to 8 feet solid measure, and such the bishop, who took pleasure in his woods, deemed ripe for the axe. From want of timely thinning, the larch trees have not thriven. They are remarkable only for extreme height, many of them being 100 feet high. The banks of the lochs and glens, eastward through the Blane valley, furnish fields rich in vegetable productions. There is the white water-lily (*Nymphœa alba*), one of the most beautiful of the British plants. The Germans call it the sea-rose. The flower opens about 7 A.M., and closes at 4 in the afternoon; re-opening the following day. The bud forms below the water, and does not rise to the surface till it is ready to expand. Thus only leaves may be seen on a pond one day, and it may be covered with flowers the next. The water lobelia (*Lobelia Dortmanna*), a perennial plant, also presents itself. The flowers, which bloom in July, are of a pale lilac, and appear above the surface of the water; while the bottom of the lake lies clad with a thick carpet of leaves. On land, we have that splendid perennial, the great snap dragon *Antirrhinum majus*). Although not a true native of this country, it is now very common on all old walls and rocks. The flowers vary much in colour; but they have all the same peculiarity of shape, and can be seen from July to September. Agrimony (*Agrimonia eupatoria*) grows by the roadsides, where it produces its yellow flowers throughout the end of summer. The whole plant is hairy. The stem, which grows erect, to the height of about two feet, has somewhat the appearance of a small vascellum. Its roots are strong and woody. The qualities of the whole plant are tonic; and the flowers, when newly gathered, smell like apricots. Snakeweed (*Polygonum bistorta*) is here, as elsewhere in rich soil, very troublesome. It creeps rapidly underground, and destroys the grass and other crops. The root is a valuable astringent. The giant bell-flower (*Campanula latifolia*) is a coarse plant, 4 or 5 feet high; and has broad, hairy leaves. The blooms, which appear in August, are generally purple, though they occasionally vary to a pale rose-colour, and sometimes to white. The water hemlock, or cowbane (*Cicuta virosa*), is happily scarce. It is a poisonous production, and grows in ditches and about the sides of streams. The cuckoo pint (*Arum maculatum*), one of our most curious plants, is abundant in this district. Its large handsome leaves never fail to attract attention. They all proceed, shiningly, from the base; and are often spotted with black. The flowers rise from the centre, and are formed of a light green spatha. This envelops the parts of fructification, which consist of a ring of germens, and one of anthers, and above them another ring of apparently imperfect pistils. Above these again rises the spadix, which is generally of a pale purple hue. The root is large; and, in England, after proper preparation, is sold and used as a substitute for bread flour. Among the other wild plants around Strathblane are the common celandine (*Chelidonum majus*); the shining crane's-bill (*Genarium lucidum*); and the bladder campion (*Silene inflata*). In Campsie Glen, the *Gymnodenia conopsea* so luxuriates as sometimes to scent the air. The so-called *Weissia tenuirostris* species, which was long supposed to grow exclusively here, has been proved to be simply a curious variety of *Tortula tortuosa*.

Hardwood of every description does well in the lower part of Fintry parish. Larch and spruces thrive in the plantations, all of which were planted by the late Mr. Speirs; who, in 1834, also introduced the *Abies Douglasiæ*. The mountain ranges furnish almost the whole family of ferns, mosses, lichens, and gnaphaliums. On the moor pastures may be found, together with the juniper (*Juniperus communis*), the *Gentiana campestris*, and the *Empetrum nigrum*. The field gentian, while the commonest of all the British species, is never seen on calcareous soils. It is an annual, and flowers in September. Its bitter is so aromatic, that, in Sweden, it is frequently used instead of hops. The crowberry affords abundant food for the moor game. It is a small trailing shrub with curious leaves, the edges curling up till they meet at the back. Its berries, which grow in clusters, are used as a dye. In the woods we find the lily of the valley (*Convallaria majalis*). This beautiful and delightfully-fragrant flower is, however, most abundant in rocky situations, and seldom produces its large crimson berries in any other place. But everywhere it spreads rapidly from its creeping roots.

> " Fair flower that, lapped in lowly glade,
>   Dost hide beneath the greenwood shade ;
>   Than whom the vernal gale
>   None fairer wakes on bank, or spray ;
>   Our Scottish lily of the May,
>   Our lily of the vale."

The sweet woodruff (*Asperula adorata*), likewise in sight, is well known for its fragrance. Though quite destitute of smell when gathered, its sweetness increases as it dries, and remains long permanent. On account of this virtue, it is frequently put into drawers to give an agreeable odour to linen. The name, woodruff, alludes to the leaves, the whole of which are so placed as to look like a series of little ruffs down the stem. In the groves and thickets, nestles the curious and pretty little tuberous moschatell (*Adoxa moschatellina*). Being very delicate, and all green, it is easily overlooked. The leaves spring from the root on very long footstalks, and are divided at three or four parts. Its small yellow flowers have a musky smell in the evening, or in the early morning when the dew is on them. *Adoxa* signifies not showy.

Passing to the parish of Logie, we fall upon several other interesting phœnogamous plants. The scarlet pimpernel (*Anagallis arvensis*), has the name of "poor man's weather-glass," or "shepherd's barometer," from the corolla closing before rain. It, however, always shuts soon after mid-day, though the sun be shining. It produces lovely flowers of a bright scarlet; but these are occasionally found blue, and sometimes white. The leaves are ovate. Most young people are acquainted with the quaking grass (*Briza media*). The spikes of flowers are very elegant; and the thread-like stalks, to each spikelet, get tremulous with the slightest wind: whence its name. Rampant fumitory (*Fumaria capreolata*), has a climbing stem. Its petrioles twine; and the calyx leaves, which are broadly oval, are larger than the seed vessel, or fruit. It is generally to be met with in corn-fields; but may also be seen hanging very gracefully from rocks. The flower is a pale purple. Dwarf furze (*Ulex nanus*), a spiny shrub, usually trailing, is only a variety of the whin or gorse. The yellow ox-eye (*Chrysanthemum segetum*) has peduncles that thicken upwards. The leaves, which clasp the stem, are smooth-cut at the top, and toothed at the base. The flowers are large, and yellow both at the ray and centre. Marsh mallow (*Caltha palustris*), has an erect stem. Its lower leaves are large, heart-shaped, and of a deep glossy green. It is a handsome plant; but is not considered good for cattle, and they generally refuse it. Red mint (*Mentha rubra*) shows a stem upright and zig-zag. The leaves are ovate, sharply serrated, and globrous. Its pedicels are smooth; and the flowers, which are whorled, are of a reddish purple. The sea starwort (*Aster tripolium*), with smooth stem, has linear leaves, lanceolate, and fleshy. The flowers are in corymbs, with yellow disk, and blue or purple rays. The golden rod (*Solidago virgaurea*) might be mistaken for the great rag-wort (*Senecio jacobea*), but the leaves distinguish it. They are long and narrow, though the lower ones are broader and stalked. Its stem leaves are lanceolate; and the spikes of golden-coloured flowers, erect and crowded. Dyer's rocket, or wild mignionette (*Reseda luteola*) is found in great abundance at the foot of Dunmyat. The white variety of the purple fox-glove (*Digitalis purpurea*) grows on the Ochils near Menstrie. Deadly night-shade or dwale (*Atropa belladonna*), the berries of which are highly poisonous, abounds on the Abbey Craig. *Mimulus luteus* is got on the banks of the Forth below Causewayhead, at a great distance from gardens, and perfectly naturalized. Crooked yellow stonecrop (*Sedum reflexum*) may be seen on the roof of a house, in the above-mentioned village, beside the common house leek (*Sempervioum tectorum*). Jagged-leaved crane's bill (*Geranium dissectum*) is very thick in this neighbourhood. In 1827, the hay-crop was considerably damaged by it, having, no doubt, been sown with the seed.

Throughout the King's park, Stirling, there are various pretty plants. Woody nightshade, or bitter-sweet (*Solanum dulcamara*), is a climbing shrub, with heart-shaped leaves, and bright purple flowers in drooping clusters. The stamens are yellow, and two green tubercles appear at the base of each petal. The berries, which are red, are poisonous. Heart's-ease (*Viola tricolor*), so sweet, modest, and unassuming, is an old favourite with the poet and florist. Its stems are angular and spreading; its leaves oblong, and deeply scooped; its stipules leafy; and its petals longer than the calyx. The flowers vary much both in size and colour. This plant shows, in a remarkable manner, what can be done by cultivation; for the wild species, compared with their garden relations, look puny and starved. The meadow saxifrage (*Saxifraga granulata*) has leaves of a kidney shape, and lobed, while the lower ones rest on long petioles. Its root is tuberous, and flower white. The great wild valerian (*Valeriana officinalis*) rises to a height of about 3 feet, and produces a large bunch of pale flesh-coloured flowers. The root is aromatic and antispasmodic. It is said that cats are very fond of the smell.

St. Ninians parish possesses some splendid specimens of the fir tribe. The most extensive plantations are on the lands of Sauchie and Touch, where they amount to nearly a thousand acres. In front of Bannockburn house there are two silver firs, *Pinus picea*, remarkable at once for their size and beauty; and in the same park stands a magnificent chesnut. In the woods of Touch some grand old oak trees are to be seen, together with a fine cedar, supposed to be the largest in Britain. This district of country, including almost every variety of soil and surface, except high hills and sea shore, presents a fertile field for research. The following are a few of the more rare and interesting plants to be found:—

Alisma plantago (Water plantain).
Plantago media (Hoary plantain).
Prunus padus (Bird cherry).
Pyrola medea (Winter green).
Stellaria memorum (Wood stitchwood).
Viola palustris (Marsh violet).

And there is also the thyme-leaved flax seed (*Radiola millegrana*), a most curious little plant, so minute as only to be observed by the searching eye of a botanist. It is scarcely more than an inch in height, and must be sought for on boggy soils and in the wet parts of heaths.

The Larbert district is not considered to be highly favourable to the growth of timber. In Kinnaird park, however, are some oaks of a large girth, and a fine avenue of limes. Near the house of Carronhall stands a Wych elm of singular beauty, which, at 5 feet from the ground, measures above 14 feet in circumference. There are also several Huntingdon willows (*Salix alba* of Linnæus) of nearly 12 feet girth. The timber of this tree is of great value, combining toughness with lightness; and, on the deep soil of the carse, its growth is rapid. Almost all the ordinary wild flowers and herbs are to be found in the woods, waysides, or fields. Both the purple and the white foxglove are common. The freckled and spotted bell of this stately plant is elegantly shaped, and the stamina, two long and two short, are curiously formed and placed so as to touch the pistil. Centaury (*Erythræa centaurium*) is abundant in most of the dry pastures. Its pretty rose-coloured blossoms are not unlike jessamine in shape; but the flower is so sensible of damp that it is only seen expanding during the brightest sunshine. Here, too, is the little eyebright (*Euphrasia officinalis*). It is a delicate and lowly herb, extremely sweet and attractive in appearance. The country people use it for diseases of the eye.

The trees planted or indigenous around Falkirk are oak, Scotch fir, ash, birch, beech, hazel, and larch. All the species thrive well; but hard wood is chiefly grown. The wild plants are more numerous than rare. Only one is worth being specified — the *Osmunda regalis*, or flowering fern, which is found on the banks of the Avon near Polmont. It is very noble in size, being commonly 7 or 8 feet high, and we have seen it here nearly 12. In most cases it is erect, in large masses, so as to form a thick bush; but near the water it is gracefully pendant. Withering, the botanist, calls this noble plant the "flower-crowned prince of British ferns."

CHAPTER XXXV.

ZOOLOGY.

NOW for a little laughter in the fields with the butterfly and wagtail. And to sit under a tree and listen to the brief yet rollicking canticle of the blackbird's tenor, the mellifluous and elaborate treble of the thrush, the round harmonising warble of the chaffinch, and to view, amidst odours of uncloying freshness, the bright scenes of nature, excites feelings of the purest pleasure. Civilization, and the downfall of the Caledonian forest, no doubt cleared the county of many of its wilder class of animals, such as the wolf, the wild boar, and various birds of prey; still a zoological hunt, even now, in certain parts of the shire, is neither tame, nor without interest and profit.

The eagle (*Aquilla*) is seen at times on Ben-lomond. Lately, a very fine specimen was caught there in a trap. The ptarmigan, or white grouse (*Lagopus mutus*), is also found on the mountain. But grouse are common over the whole of the bleak upland moors of Buchanan; while roes and black game seem to multiply with the increasing shelter of wood. Pheasants were introduced by the late Duke of Montrose, and have spread throughout the whole extent of Strath-Endrick. The common squirrel (*Sciurus vulgaris*) so completely formed for an arborial life, and so engaging with its long, beautiful, and spreading tail, is a voluntary resident in the plantations, and finds no scarcity of its favourite food in nuts, acorns, and beech-mast.

In Strathblane parish, game of all the ordinary sorts is very plentiful. A few of the common roes are likewise met with. Here, too, we have seen the polecat, or foumart (*Mustela putorius*), one of the most remarkable European species of the weasel tribe, which preys indiscriminately on the smaller animals. The specimen was about 17 inches in length, exclusive of the tail which measured 6 inches. Its colour was a deep blackish brown, with a tawny cast slightly intermixed. That aquatic quadruped the otter (*Lutra vulgaris*), which feeds almost entirely on fish, is no stranger in the waters of the district. Its general length is about 2 feet, from the nose to the insertion of the tail. With a body elongated and much flattened, and legs short and strong, it swims and dives with great ease, and peculiar elegance. Along with the ring-tailed kite, goshawk, raven, hooded crow, jay, and owl, there is also the buzzard (*Falco buteo*). This bird is supposed to be the most common in Britain of all the hawk tribe. It has a thick heavy body about 22 inches in length; while the full expansion of its wings measure near 50. The bird is its dainty; but, sluggish and inactive, it condescends to feed on mice and even frogs.

Roe-deer breed in great numbers in the glen of Boquhan. They also frequent the glen of Leckie. In the woods are seen foxes, badgers, and weasels, with the usual game on which they prey. The badger (*Meles vulgaris*) is a carnivorous animal—solitary and stupid, that seeks refuge in the most sequestered spots, and shuns sun-light. It has very short legs, and a broad flat body. Besides the common species of small birds in the parish of Gargunnock, there are pheasants, magpies, woodcocks, snipes, wild ducks, herons, and hawks. The heron (*Ardea*), for time immemorial, built its nest on a row of Scotch firs near the mansion of Meiklewood; but, after a modern house was erected, it took its departure. The hawks build their nests on the almost inaccessible cliffs of Ballochleam.

A century ago, the golden eagle bred regularly in Campsie; so did the gentil, or gentile, falcon (*Falco gentilis*). This bird is somewhat larger than a goshawk, and of elegant form. The bill is of a lead colour, the cere and legs yellow, and the head of a light ferruginous shade, with oblong black spots. The back is brown, and the whole of the under parts are whitish, with brown spots and dashes. Badgers are still found here occasionally; while foxes are very numerous. Otters and foumarts are still to be seen. A martin-cat was taken in the Finglen some years ago. The goshawk, buzzard, and kite are common in the district. Eagles, however, are no longer observed; neither is the red-legged crow, nor the hen-harrier. Roe-deer and red-deer are now permanent residents. Squirrels are abundant. The jack-daw (*Corvus monedula*) first made its appearance about 1808. Pheasants were introduced some years later. The misletoe thrush, the beautiful kingfisher and the water-ouzel now breed regularly. The dabchick, the baldcoot, the little golden-crested wren, the red-start, and the golden-eyed diver have also appeared of late. In December, 1838, Mr. Stirling of Craigbarnet shot two cross-bills, the first that had been seen in this quarter. They were very beautiful birds, and are preserved in a fine general collection of ornithological specimens. So far good. But why not have given the interesting little strangers a chance of living and breeding in the district they had so pluckily visited?

With other game in the lower parts of Fintry parish, there is a plentiful supply of pheasants. The roe-deer is not unfrequently to be seen bounding through the woods; while the moors are well stocked with heathfowl. The rocks give shelter to the mountain raven, the hawk, and other smaller birds of prey. Here the fox has also secured a snug retreat. Foumarts, and other vermin of a like nature, are not uncommon; and the harmless and graceful little squirrel has long had a residence in the local woods.

The Ochils abound in rabbits, and game of the ordinary kinds is abundant. Foxes are not numerous. A good many grouse are to be found on the uplands, and a few pheasants in the low grounds and plantations. Squirrels number thousands in the woods of Airthrie. Hawks of various sorts are to be met with, and the blue hunting falcon occasionally makes his nest on Dunmyat. Deer are few, and are only to be seen on the hills. The rarest animal found in Alva parish is the *Falco peregrinus*. For ages, this bird has had its residence on a very high perpendicular rock, called Craigleith, projecting from the brow of the Westhill of Alva. Only one pair, it is affirmed by the villagers, build in the front of this precipice. These hatch annually; and when the progeny are of proper age, the parents compel them to seek another habitation—death alone obliging the old or original pair to resign their ancestral quarters, which fall to their next survivors. In ancient times, when "lords and ladies gay" were fond of the sport of falconry, a bird of this species was deemed valuable. From Craigleith, Queen Mary got falcons after her arrival from France; and gentlemen, in several parts of England, have repeatedly sent for these birds, to tame them, from the nest, for hunting. Eagles are now rarely seen among the Ochils.

Otters are plentiful on the water which flows from the old coal workings of Bannockburn and Auchenbowie; but, when they have reached the excavations, they are safe. Squirrels are also common in St. Ninians parish. Roe are numerous in the woods of Plean, Auchenbowie, and Sauchie. Black grouse and other heath fowl are found in the moorland districts. Ducks frequent the smaller lochs, and the wild goose is sometimes to be seen on Loch Coulter.

Badgers, not many years ago, lodged in Dunmore woods; but they have entirely disappeared through an assault which was made upon them one night, by mischievous persons, with dogs. Hares and rabbits, however, are about as abundant as the leaves of Vallambrosa; and pheasants are likewise in great numbers in the deep plantations.

The close population of the eastern part of the county has left little there to be noted zoologically. Still, otters continue to be got, now and again, on the Carron; and are frequently so tamed that they follow the human footstep with even canine sagacity. On the Callendar estate, there is a large stock of game of every ordinary description; while the fox is by no means uncommon between this point and the western portion of Linlithgowshire.

Little need be said here of the smaller birds, which are common all over the lowlands. Their appearance and habits are fully known by the youngest schoolboy, and that from the pawky robin, the piping lark, or the humble sparrow, to the woodland blackbird and thrush. Of late years, the starling has become very numerous throughout the shire; and has been blamed, not without reason, for playing havoc with the lark. Notwithstanding its capabilities of vocal imitation, both in song and speech, it is not a bird that repays the trouble of such teaching; for, domesticated, it seldom reaches its third year, and the same may be said of about the whole of the soft-feeding species. The rock, or heather, linnet is indeed the only one of our sweet outdoor songsters that takes kindly to the cage for a lengthened life. The bullfinch is another pretty warbler, with its jet black cap and crimson breast. It wants trigness, however, for beauty of form; but some of its notes are very rich and melodious. It is by no means a bird common in the county, although a number are to be found in Torwood glen, and other similarly secluded parts. Of the migratory class, we have only to mention the swift-winged swallow and the shy cuckoo. Feathered stranger was perhaps never more honoured by poet's song than the latter bird of "modest brown." In spite of its trick of leaving the hatching and rearing of its young to native birds—dropping its eggs into a stolen nest—it is ever warmly welcomed as the harbinger of spring.

> " Last night a vision was dispelled
>   Which I can never dream again ;
> A wonder from the earth has gone,
>   A passion from my brain.
> I saw upon a budding ash
>   A cuckoo, and she blithely sung
> To all the valleys round about,
>   While on a branch she swung.
>
> . . .
>
> And twice to-day I heard the cry,
>   The hollow cry of melting love,
> And twice a tear bedimmed my eye—
>   *I saw* the singer in the grove,
> I saw him pipe his eager tone,
>   Like any other common bird ;
> And, as I live, the sovereign cry
>   Was not the one I always heard."

The wanton lapwing was almost overlooked. In the quiet of a summer evening, few sounds are more stillness-striking than the shrill notes of this scheming trumpeter, as, with low and circling flight, it would decoy the intruder from off the field of its guardianship.

As we write these lines in city pent, a blackbird caged on a neighbouring window-sill pipes bravely, as if it would strain its little throat, recalling many a similar, but not sweeter, song, to which we have listened enraptured, in leafliest woodland. In another box cage, too, a merry mavis hops and sings day after day, just as happily and contented as if it were perched in some shrubbery garden, miles removed from the dirt, dust, and disorder of a great city.

CHAPTER XXXVI.

AGRICULTURE.

THE soil of the county is greatly diversified. It may be divided into five kinds—carse, dryfield, hill, moor, and moss. The first extends along the banks of the Forth from the neighbourhood of Bucklyvie to the eastern extremity of the shire, about 28 miles long, and on the average 2 miles broad, making towards 30,000 acres. It is composed of the finest clay, without stones, and interspersed with strata of marine shells. The quality is the finer, the nearer to the present boundary of the parent ocean. The highest elevation is 25 feet above high water, and the depth in some places has been found to be upwards of 20 feet. The etymology of *carse* is conjectural. The word is used by Barbour, who says

"Our thwort the Kerse to the Torwood he geed."

Of the carse of Falkirk, Trivetius, describing an invasion by Edward I., remarks, "*causantibus majoribus loca palustria, propter brumalem intemporiem, immeabilia esse.*" The meaning seems to be, that the English army could not arrive at

Stirling, without passing through some of the carse grounds, and that they were impracticable for cavalry at that season of the year. *Kors*, in the Cambo-British, is marsh. The ancient Swedish, and the Icelandic, use *Kaer* in the same sense, while *Ciers* has also that meaning in the Armoric dialect of the Celtic. The operations of rivers in forming such deposits of soil is very justly questioned, and the action of the ocean agitated beyond the effect of either tempest or tide is alone conceived to be adequate to the production. A tempest, indeed, affects the mighty deep only superficially, and the tide is merely an undulation, or heaving.

The following is an analysis of the carse soil:—

Water,	10 parts.
Silica,	44 ,,
Alumina,	28 ,,
Carbonate of lime,	2½ ,,
Organic matter,	6 ,,
Oxide of iron,	1½ ,,
Soluble salts,	1 ,,
Soluble matter,	2 ,,
Loss,	5 ,,
	100 parts.

The valleys form the richer parts of the dryfield, in which there is some very inferior land. The Lennox hills, stretching from Strathblane to the neighbourhood of Stirling, and occupying nearly a fourth of the county, have a soil chiefly arenaceous, mixed with till, sometimes interspersed with peat earth, and constitute the most valuable pasture tract in Scotland. Ben Lomond may be classed with the hill tract, for, although his base be moor, his sides and shoulders are covered with verdure. Another fourth of the shire consists of moor, or ground more or less inclined to heath. Some parts of it are cultivated, and afford a moderate vegetation of artificial crops. Mr. Nimmo, in 1777, classed as "moor," what, in 1812, Dr. Graham calls "dryfield." We may here discern the progress of cultivation. Perhaps a thirtieth part of the county, in various quarters, may be occupied by peat, some of which is incumbent on a fine clay. At Airth alone there are about 300 acres of moss, on an average 12 feet deep, and covers ground of most excellent quality. Much, no doubt, has been done to reclaim this waste land, by at least two of the late Earls of Dunmore; but it takes not less than £30 to clear each acre, while the rent of the acre when cleared and cultivated is, over all, about £2.

The advance and general diffusion of agricultural knowledge, of late years, has completely changed the character of the county in its soil. Apart from systematic husbandry, the importance of thorough draining and trenching where the land was damp began early to be understood, but it was only when the landlord found it convenient to do the work at his own expense that any progress in this direction was made; for, however willing the tenant might be to have his ground improved by tile draining, it was rare that he could command the funds thus to be sunk. Subsoil ploughing—the invention of Mr. James Smith of Deanston—was also soon found necessary for a good crop, especially in the dryfield. This was done by means of a large plough, in the shape of an old Scotch plough, without a sock, and generally drawn by four horses. Liming and guano, with its chemical compeer, dissolved bones, were next gradually resorted to, that the best possible return might be got out of the land.

The primitive home-made utensils contrast strangely with the improved agricultural implements of the present day. Ploughs in the earlier times were seldom bought, but, as a rule, manufactured on the farm. In 1330 we find their price one shilling. Between 1351 and 1370, however, their value was one shilling and sixpence. The implement, of course, was common carpenter's work, and subject to no demand. Even after the iron plough was in general use, there were several parishes—Slamannan, for one—where the old Scotch plough was still preferred on account of its making a wider furrow. But what see we now in the fields? Steam ploughs and grubbers; potato planters and diggers; turnip lifters, toppers, and tailers; drill harrows; sowing machines; reaping machines;

sheaf binders; and weed eradicators, which weed wheat before the wheat plant begins to ear. Then at the farm-steading, in addition to the portable threshing machine, there is the engine for fodder cutting, which cuts ten trusses of hay for one pennyworth of gas; also, the Scotia incubator, for the wholesale manufacture or hatching of chickens. And if landlords and tenants are to derive any profit from agriculture, all this inventive energy cannot be overrated. At the present moment any country that has a fertile soil which produces more than its inhabitants can consume, is devising means to forward to us its surplus. Wheat may soon be sold in our great centres at an average of 35s. per quarter. Fresh meat in unlimited quantities can be imported from Australia at 3d. per pound. Chickens, reasonably fat, can be bought in Hungary and Transylvania for 3d. each, and could be sent to us in refrigerating waggons. No doubt the scene of a band of the young of both sexes, striving with the sickle as to who should have the honour of carrying off the "maiden" for the crown of the harvest-home, was attractive; but although hoeing and weeding, and even sheafing, may still be done on our smaller farms by manual labour, the days of the corn-field are gone for both sickle and scythe. Some great feats in shearing were, however, performed with the "hook," notwithstanding the fact that the reaping machine sweeps down the grain, in regard to time, in the ratio of ten to one. One old woman was known to make over 400 good-sized sheaves daily; while George Bruce, in the parish of Tough—a wiry man with very long arms—could shear 36 threaves in a day. He drove the "rig" of say 18 feet from side to side, and never lifted his hand till he had a sheaf. He used a long sickle, and drew the corn to him.

Wheat is one of the most commonly cultivated of the cereals. It belongs to the natural order *Graminea* (grasses) of which it is the most prominent member. The genus of plants which yield the various sorts is called by the botanist *Triticum*, from *tritum*, ground or rubbed, because the fruit or seed, in its preparation as a food for man, requires the process of grinding or trituration. No other grain assimilates so well with the human constitution, and so fully represents the two great classes of constituents necessary to sustain the wear and tear of human life, viz., food fuel, and food materials. In earlier times, oats, barley, peas, beans, and rye, entered more largely than at present into the ordinary food of the people; but, when these are used exclusively as substitutes for wheat, they generally derange the bodily health of the consumer. Formerly, wheat was frequently divided into two classes—the winter, *Triticum hibernum*, and the summer, *T. æstivum*. This classification, however, is no longer recognised, as it is now well-known that the cereal, by being constantly sown in the spring, quite changes its habits as to its time of ripening. The produce of wheat sown in the spring acquires the habit of perfecting its growth quicker than the produce of the same wheat sown in the autumn. In soils containing large proportions of sand, or of organic matter, but deficient in clay, we often see the young plant very luxuriant at first, but without the power to build up its stem, for which a certain amount of silica and potash is necessary. Silica and lime are also required for the chaff, with potash, phosphoric acid, magnesia, and ammonia for the seed. In no other description of soil will wheat flourish. These substances are generally found to exist in clays to a greater extent than in other kinds of earth; hence the fertility of the Stirlingshire carse for this important crop. In a wet, late season, on inferior land, its weight may not exceed 60 lbs. per imperial bushel; but on the better class farms its yield is not unfrequently as high as 68 lbs.

Oats form the genus to which the name of *Avena* has been assigned, and the range of soils suitable for their cultivation is very large. Indeed, wherever farming is carried on there is some variety of this cereal grown. The last agricultural statistics of Scotland show that, while the three other grain crops—wheat, barley, and rye, were cultivated to the extent of 449,135 acres, the area occupied by oats alone amounted to no less than

938,613 acres. The potato oat, which takes its name from having originally been found growing in a field of potatoes in Cumberland, in 1788, is probably the most largely sown of all the varieties of the *Avena sativa,* or common oat. With a straw rather short, but clean and stout, it is highly esteemed for mealing, or for feeding purposes. The sandy oat, a harder variety, is generally preferred for late or uncertain districts. The straw is heavy, firm in texture, and rarely seen lodged or broken by bad weather. It was discovered in Aberdeenshire, in 1825.

Barley is generally admitted to the second place in the order of our cereal crops, but our climate and soils being, as a rule, better adapted for oats, the latter take the precedence in the farmer's estimation. In light soils, the chevalier is commonly sown. Where the soil is strong, or in ungenial districts, some of the coarser varieties, however, frequently give a better return. The naked Peruvian, or the black four-rowed barley, yields the largest amount of available food. This cereal is cultivated farther north than any of the other grains. Fields of it are to be seen in the northern extremity, in the Orkney Islands, in Shetland, and even at the Faroe Islands.

The bean belongs to the natural order *Leguminosæ,* of Jussieu, from bearing its fruit in legumes, or pods, which follow a butterfly or papilionaceous flower. It is termed by the botanist *Faba vulgaris*. There is only one species, though long cultivation has produced a well-marked division between those of the garden and those of the field. The tick bean and the Scotch, or horse bean, are the two sorts grown throughout the carses. The ancients entertained some curious notions in regard to this forage crop. The Egyptians, for example, held it a crime to look at beans, judging the very sight unclean. But the bean was not everywhere thus contemned, for Columella notices them in his time as food for peasants, and for them only—

" And herbs they mix with beans for vulgar fare."

There are two different methods of sowing practised—"broadcast" and "drilling." "Dibbling" is now a thing of the past. In Stirlingshire, broadcasting is still common. The process is a simple one. The seed to be sown is carried by the sower in a bag or basket of a convenient form, suspended from the neck in such a position that the sower can have access to it, either with one or both hands, according to the manner in which he intends to distribute the seed. The practice of drilling was introduced by Jethro Tull, to obviate the difficulty of keeping the land sown broadcast free from weeds. Owing to the vast improvement in the adaptation and manufacture of agricultural machines generally, this practice has widely spread of late years. The advantages it offers are—a considerable saving in the quantity of seed (measuring from one-third to one-half), on account of the greater regularity in the proportion of seed sown, and the depth at which it is deposited; also the power it gives to sow the seed in parallel lines at any distance apart that may be desired, so that the surface may be stirred after the heavy rains of winter, and kept free from weeds, either by hand or horse-hoe, during the early growth of the plants.

Of the root and fallow crops, turnips naturally take the precedence, being the keystone of our improved system of farming—the crop by whose success or failure the welfare of the whole rotation is mainly influenced. The common green-top is the oldest variety of the Swedish turnip in cultivation. It has, however, fallen into comparative disrepute, owing to the great attention that has been paid to the purple-top varieties; but where care has been bestowed on its cultivation, it has proved as productive, as hardy, and as high in its feeding qualities as any of the more favoured sorts. Of the common turnip there are some forty-six varieties. The white globe is that most generally grown, and is an excellent description of root for early consumption.

The potato (*Solanum tuberosum*) is, without doubt, a native of South America, having been found growing wild in Chili, Buenos Ayres, and along the coast of the Pacific. Although its first appearance as a field crop in this country was about 1730, its introduction into Britain is supposed to have been in the year 1584. Difficulties which it did not meet with elsewhere, seem to have opposed its reception in Scotland. The zealous but mistaken religious opinions of that period were against the new plant, which was declared a sinful root because no mention of it was made in the Bible. For its general cultivation, the lighter class of loams form the best soil—the produce being of superior quality. But even on peat and bog lands good crops are obtained, especially where there has been the previous application of lime. The sad visitation of the disease, in 1843-5, greatly checked the planting breadth of this tuber. It has, however, again resumed its place on the fallow portion of the farm, not only as an important article of diet, but as a supporting crop of the soil.

While there are no celebrated breeders of live stock in the county, there are several successful exhibitors who have also studied the physiology of nutrition, and advanced with the times in the treatment of farm cattle. They have had materials analysed to ascertain the extent of their suitability as food for stock. Oilcake, and still more corn, appear to injure the constitution of the beast; grass, turnips, and straw, are its only healthy food. There can be no substitute for the natural feeding, except for a limited period, though in times of scarcity, and to give the last dip to fat cattle, the other materials are valuable auxiliaries. Twelve years ago, the dairy stocks of the shire were all but decimated by an outbreak of rinderpest. The plague was of the most virulent type, and veterinary skill was utterly unable to grapple with the mysterious epidemic. All were alike ignorant of how the disease was generated, and how propagated, and all helpless alike in their efforts to arrest its progress. Common slaughter was the only panacea. Daily there were reports of fresh farms and districts being most capriciously seized, and latterly there seemed no hope of the abatement and extermination of the plague until our entire bovine stock had gone. In 1873, it reappeared in one of the richest grazing districts of Yorkshire, and naturallly created some alarm amongst our larger stockholders. The herd, twenty-two in number, which were swept away, came from the coast, and it is not unlikely therefore, that the infection was caught by contact with foreign cattle. On that occasion, however, prompt and stringent measures were adopted for isolating the infected victims. With the local magistracy there was neither hesitancy nor delay. Realizing the seriousness of the outbreak, they acted with praiseworthy vigilance and decision. A cordon of police were at once placed round the unlucky farm, and the few surviving animals of the herd that had not yet succumbed to the malignant pest were swiftly slaughtered and buried in quicklime.

Each district has naturally its own peculiarities of soil. The lands in Alva parish are arable and pasture. The former may be distinguished into four kinds. That which extends from the bottom of the hills consists of a rich hazel mould, intermixed with gravel and small stones. This is succeeded by a stratum of moss over a bed of clay, and extends from 50 to 100 yards in breadth, and in some places it is found 7 feet deep. Next to this is a strong clay, extending a considerable way towards the Devon. Then follows what is called haughing ground, such as is usually found on the banks of rivers; and the inundations of the Devon, which occur twice or thrice a year, leave great quantities of sand behind. The soil at the river's bed appears to be, in many places, more than 20 feet deep. The improvement of the land here, as elsewhere, was long kept back by the farms remaining limited to a few acres; and also by the farmers being bound by their leases to drive coals from the pits on the south bank of the Devon to the shore of Alloa. Lord Alva, however, at length prohibited this absurd and unprofitable practice. Since 1796, the extent of the farms has been enlarged with great advantage to the landlord, and greater respectability to the tenant.

Dairy, pastoral, and mixed husbandry are all pursued in the district of Campsie. Green crop is chiefly raised, particularly potatoes. The oats sown are of the earlier sorts, which, in moist climates, are the most suitable. Lime is to be had prepared at sundry places in the parish, and the soil being generally of a ferruginous quality, it is often found to act with good effect. Peas and beans are rarely sown; flax only in small quantities, if at all. Carrots have sometimes been successfully tried in patches of deep free soil. Only a small breadth of turnips are raised, chiefly for the use of the cattle, as the ground can be more profitably employed in potato cropping. The dairy is a branch of chief importance in the farming throughout the parish, on account of the ready and profitable market found in Glasgow for all its produce. The Ayrshire breed of cows has been carefully cultivated for many years, and few crosses are to be seen in the district.

The arable land of Dunipace parish is of a very inferior quality. Two-thirds of it lie on a substratum of sandstone, the remainder on whin-rock. A considerable quantity of turnips are grown in this district, and still more of potatoes, which are generally of a good quality. Formerly, flax was sown on every farm; but since foreign flax was so plentifully imported, that crop has given way to wheat, which grows here well.

The Agricultural Association of the Eastern District of Stirlingshire was formed in Falkirk about forty years ago. The late Earl of Dunmore was patron, and Mr. Forbes of Callendar, president. Its object was, and still is, to promote scientific and practical improvements in agriculture. Two prosperous auction marts were opened here in 1875. The sales which take place weekly, create considerable stir, the fat stock brought forward for the hammer from the farms of the surrounding districts being large and varied. There is nothing peculiar to the husbandry of this parish. With respect to cropping, experience has proved the six years rotation system to be best adapted for the land, viz., first year, fallow; second, wheat; third, beans; fourth, barley; fifth, clover and ryegrass; and sixth, oats.

The lands of Gargunnock parish consist of various kinds of soil, which are called moor, dryfield and carse. The moor is of a wet, gravelly and clayey soil; yet it affords sound healthy pasture for sheep and black cattle in the summer months. The term dryfield is not descriptive of the soil, but is used merely to distinguish it from the moor and carse lands. Its average depth is 6 or 7 inches. It rests on a subsoil of gravel or till, and under this subsoil are found strata of red and white sandstone. The soil of the carse lands consists of 3 or 4 feet of mixed clay of excellent quality, which lies on a subsoil of yellow or blue clay; but the blue clay prevails. And below this blue clay, a bed of sea shells is deposited about 10 feet from the surface. In some places along the banks where the carse joins the dryfield, the ground has the appearance of having been washed at one time by a river, or by the waves of the sea. Particular attention has been paid in this district to the improvement of the breed of black-faced sheep, and of cattle of the Ayrshire breed.

Throughout the parish of Kilsyth, oats, barley, and green crops are adhered to as most productive and profitable. Wheat was tried, but proved a failure. By far the largest produce, however, is that of the dairy, to which the rest is subsidiary, and consequently the husbandry is what is called the mixed. Indeed, no other would suit the soil and climate. From a memoir presented to the Board of Agriculture by William Wright, M.D., of Edinburgh, it appears that potatoes, after their introduction into Scotland, were first planted in the open field in Stirlingshire. Thomas Prentice, a day-labourer in the parish of Kilsyth, is recorded as having set the example in 1728. Mr. Robert Graham of Tamrawer had brought the practice to some degree of perfection eleven years after; and, for the supply of the public, rented lands near Renfrew, Glasgow, Perth, Dundee, and Edinburgh.

Farming in the Larbert district, where the lands have a retentive sub-soil, was at first much improved by what was called wedge-draining; the section of the cutting being a frustrum of a triangle inverted, whose base was about 10 inches.

A wedge of peat moss was then placed in the top of the drain, so as to leave a space of 8 or 10 inches perpendicular for a water-course. This system, however, was found to have only a temporary effect; and the plan of laying for a water-course a semicylindrical tile, which reposed on a flat tile of a breadth exceeding the diameter of the curved one by about half an inch, proved more effective. A foot of space above the tiles was filled with broken sandstone, or Carron cinders, through which the water percolated. About 1837, a considerable work for making drain tiles was established, by the late Mr. Stirling of Glenbervie, on the beds of clay in the low ground near the Poo. Two or three years after, another field for a similar purpose was opened near the same place by Mr. Bauchop of Bogend. That species of moss, *Hypnum*, commonly called "fog," is very frequent in the local pastures. It abounds on all sandy soils, as well as on moist ground, and is by no means nutritious to cattle.

The soil in the vale of the Avon (Slamannan) yields excellent crops of meadow hay, and when not flooded proves wholesome and fattening for cattle. As the grounds rise in regular ridges towards the south, they produce good crops of oats, some barley, and occasionally a little wheat. The lands towards the western district of the parish, being of a black mossy nature, yield but indifferent crops when the season happens to be wet and cold. Towards the south and south-west there are several hundreds of acres, entirely moss, varying from 3 to 12 feet in depth; and the substratum being chiefly sand, no inducement lies to remove it.

The following tabular statement shows the acreage of each parish, with the number of acres under cultivation, and in pasture, waste, and wood.

	Acres.	Tillage.	Pasture.	Waste.	Wood.	Abstract from Valuation Roll of the County for the year 1880-81.
Airth,	5,477	4,857	270	350	...	£12,149
Alva,	5,458	3,150	2,120	...	188	13,532
Baldernock,	4,322	4,082	...	...	240	6,610
Balfron,	7,820	3,420	...	4,295	105	6,615
Bothkennar,	1,774	...	...	...	...	14,365
Buchanan,	41,598	2,800	..	34,548	4,250	8,336
Campsie,	17,872	6,380	5,492	5,600	400	27,834
Denny,	8,309	5,840	789	1,499	181	22,712
Drymen,	30,850	9,944	1,350	21,700	556	16,376
Dunipace,	5,586	3,800	986	300	500	9,246
Falkirk,	19,551	11,000	4,851	1,900	1,800	44,943
Fintry,	13,772	1,020	972	11,680	100	5,252
Gargunnock,	9,859	1,120	3,638	4,527	574	7,788
Killearn,	15,370	5,370	...	8,860	1,140	10,630
Kilsyth,	13,121	10,901	2,050	...	170	26,582
Kippen,	6,342	1,420	4,360	...	562	7,134
Larbert,	3,963	3,703	...	...	260	19,537
Lecropt,	692	...	...	...	...	2,162
Logie,	3,026	1,026	1,000	...	1,000	22,977
Muiravonside	7,963	...	...	...	...	11,507
New Kilpatrick,	2,747	...	...	...	...	11,859
Polmont,	5,512	4,881	...	531	100	14,886
St. Ninians,	38,012	9,882	2,450	...	11,420	53,243
Slamannan,	7,062	...	...	...	...	19,116
Stirling,	1,212	...	...	...	...	1,545
Strathblane,	9,068	3,680	3,388	...	2,000	9,236
Totals,	286,338					£406,153

CHAPTER XXXVII.

LANDOWNERS.

THERE are several extensive estates in the county, but property is very much divided. Farms in the lower districts vary from 20 to 300 acres. In the hilly and mountainous districts, however, they are considerably larger.

THE CALLENDAR ESTATE (William Forbes, Esq.), which is one of the most extensive and valuable, stretches from the vicinity of Slamannan on the south and east to Greenhill on the west, falling down upon the river Carron at Camelon and Larbert, a length of about 15 miles. In Muiravonside parish, Mr. Forbes owns the farms of Myrehead, which, in the valuation roll of the county for the year 1880-81, is valued at £380; Haining, &c., at £397; Waulkmilton, at £277; East Manuel, at £245; Avondale, at £170; Gilmeadowland, at £150; Manuel Haugh, at £83; and Snabhead, at £67. In Falkirk parish, he owns 40 farms; West Carmuirs, valued at £520; Mumrills, &c., at £520; Randieford, at £250; Woodburn, at £221; Middlesfield, at £200; Carmuirs, at £200;

Loanfoot, at £200; Kilbean, at £192; Craigieburn, at £190; Lochlands of Carmuirs, at £180; West Newlands, at £164; Bogton, at £152; Muirhouses, &c., at £133; and Bantaskine, at £105. His grass parks are valued at £180; woods, copse, and underwood of Callendar, at £400; and mansion house, at £550. Pirleyhill and Standalane colliery is fixed at £1,264; and Loanfoot ironstone, at £846. In Larbert parish, he has Broomage Mains farm, which is valued at £146; in Dunipace parish, property valued at £2,735; and in Denny parish, lands and minerals, at £5,078. The total annual value of Mr. Forbes' possessions in the county is as under:—

Parish of Muiravonside,	- - -	£1,984
,,	Falkirk, - - - -	9,868
,,	Larbert, - - - -	146
,,	Dunipace, - - -	2,735
,,	Denny, - - - -	5,078
		£19,811

Callendar, as we have previously stated, was purchased by William Forbes, Esq., of London, in 1783, for £85,000.

The Right Hon. the Earl of Zetland, of Kerse estate, is another large proprietor in the shire, holding property to the annual value of £10,850. In Falkirk parish, he has 16 farms, and amongst these, West Mains and West Thorn, valued at £290; East Thorn, at £334; Fouldubs, at £263; Walton, at £193; Dalgrain, at £178; Kerse Mains, at £166; Dorrator, at £157; Cauldhame, at £155; Eastend, at £145; Seabegs Place, at £116; Westfield, at £131; and part of Thicket, at £108. His lordship's grass parks at Kerse are valued at £370. In Bothkennar parish he also owns the following farms:—Heuck Island and Crofthead, valued at £290; Town Croft, at £209; Newtonplace, at £149; Carronflats, at £105; and lands of Crofthead, Towncroft, Thicket, and part of Newtonplace, at £266; while £2,076 are set against the Zetland pit colliery. In Airth parish his lands of Halls of Airth are valued at £485; and those in Polmont parish at £1,830.

The Stirlingshire possessions of the Right Hon. the Earl of Dunmore, which lie in the parishes of St. Ninians and Airth are valued at £8,133. His lordship's grass parks in hand are put down at £1,356, and the Dunmore Home farm, at £900.

William Graham, Esq., of Airth Castle, has an annual valuation of £2,601. His farms in the parish are Eastfield, valued at £235; South Greens, at £230; West Westfield, at £229; North Greens, at £230; Airth Mains, at £207; Dougalshole, at £189; and South Westfield, at £182. He also owns the farm of Auchentyre, in Bothkennar parish, which is valued at £116.

The Carron Company, who hold property in nine parishes of the county, are down on the valuation roll for £8,890. In Airth parish, they possess 4 letham farms, valued at £681; in Bothkennar parish, West Mains, valued at £92; in Muiravonside, Crosscroes, valued at £88; Kendrieshill, at £95; and Gateside and Shankend, at £40; in Polmont parish, Bellsrig, valued at £75; Burnside, at £50; Muirpark, at £40; and Wallacerig, with freestone quarry, at £214. In Falkirk parish they have 7 farms, and among these Jaw, valued at £250; Mungalmill, at £122; Middlethorn, at £104; and Mungalhead, at £96. In Larbert parish, the year's valuation of their property is £5,191, £3,870 of which is placed against the iron-works. In Dunipace parish they possess Herbertshire farm, valued at £102; in Denny parish they are down for £515; and in Kilsyth parish, for £657, of which £338 is against ironstone.

The trustees of the late William Dawson, Esq. of Powfoulis, appear for £3,921. In Airth parish they have the farm of Mains of Powfoulis and Saltgreens, valued at £414; and Greendyke, &c., valued at £196; in Bothkennar parish, the farm of Middlerig and Stonehouse, valued at £362; Backrow, at £230; Upper Gairdoch, at £212; and Pinfoldbridge, at £176. The coal and ironstone of South Mains is valued at £1000. In Falkirk parish their farms are Dalderse, valued at £425; Carronside and Langlees, at £219; Coblebrae, at £143; Yonderhaugh, at £102; and Millflats, at £90.

Against the property of Thomas George Dundas, Esq. of Carronhall, there is a total valuation of £3,220. In Bothkennar parish, farm of Kirkton and Closs, at £355; Carronhall farm, at £169; Carronhall Colliery, at £300; and harbour, &c., at Carronshore, £95. Under Larbert parish, the mansion house and policy of Carronhall is valued at £207; and the farm of Kersebrock and Powleys, at £209. For the lands in Dunipace parish the amount is £573.

The lands, &c., possessed by the Right Hon. Lord Thurlow, of Kinnaird, are valued at £1,981. The farm of Halls of Airth and Bellsdyke, at £340; Drum, at £340; Back o' Dykes, at £205; Cuttyfield, at £200; Grass parks, at £163; and coal at Kinnaird, £173.

John Bell Sherriff, Esq. of Carronvale, appears for £1,256—the farm of Kersie Mains being valued at £650; South Kersie, at £356; and Carronvale, at £250.

For Mrs. Ann C. Stirling, of Glenbervie, the amount is £1,256—the valuation of the farm of Shields being £170; of Hamilton farm, £145; of Grass parks, £344; and of her possessions in Dunipace parish, £439.

The sum against the lands, &c., belonging to Joseph C. Bolton, Esq. of Carbrook, M.P., is £2,234—for Wholeflatts, in Polmont parish, £290; for property in Dunipace parish, £523; and in St. Ninians parish, £1,421.

Next to Mr. Forbes, of Callendar, His Grace the Duke of Montrose is the wealthiest proprietor of the county lands. His yearly valuation is as follows :—

Parish of Buchanan,	…	…	£8,259
„ Drymen,	…	…	4,000
„ Fintry,…	…	…	2,852
„ New Kilpatrick,	…		105
„ Strathblane,	…	…	361
„ St. Ninians,	…	…	296
„ Kilsyth,	…	…	688
Total,	…	…	£16,561

His Grace owns the whole of the parish of Buchanan, which is about 29 miles long and 5 miles broad, with the exception of what belongs to the School Board and the minister's manse and glebe, valued in all at £77. He has here 17 farms, with an acreage of 41,598, so that the estate only averages 4s. per acre. The lands and farm of Gartfarron are valued at £352; Cobrach, at £320; Benlomond and Blairvockie, at £1,100; Cashell and Sallochy, at £360; Corriearklet, at £270; Inversnaid, at £250; Gartincaber, at £170; Creityhall, at £165; Auchmar, at £160; Cailness, at £120; Grass parks, at £443; Woods, at £328; Rowardennan shootings, at £300; and Inversnaid shootings, at £250. In Drymen parish his Grace holds 14 farms, valued as above; in Fintry parish, 5; in Strathblane parish, the farm of Quinloch, and Mugdock castle; in New Kilpatrick parish, Drumcloy and part of Milton,

Milngavie; St. Ninians parish, the farm of Kirk-o'-Muir, and part of Todholes; and in Kilsyth parish, Slachristock, and a portion of Binns, Carronbridge.

In the parish of Drymen there are 76 farms—its extreme length being 15 miles, and breadth 10. Here there are numerous proprietors, but of the farms William Cunningham Bontine, Esq. of Gartmore, possesses 19, valued at £2,053.

The whole lands of Fintry, which are about 6 miles long by 5 broad, may be said to be owned between the Duke of Montrose and Sir George Home Speirs, Bart. There are 9 farms in the parish, and of this property Sir George holds a value of £1,465.

In Killearn parish there are 35 farms, and the chief proprietors are—Archibald Orr Ewing, Esq. of Ballikinrain, M.P., £2,395; John Blackburn, Esq. of Killearn, for the trustees of the late Peter Blackburn, Esq., £2,373; Vice-Admiral Sir Wm. Edmonstone, Bart., C.B., of Duntreath, £884; John James Pollock, Esq. of Auchineden, £831; David M'Laren Bryce Buchanan, Esq., Boquhan, £540; Michael Connal, Esq., Glasgow, £245; and Sir G. H. Speirs, Bart. (Glenboig farm), £210.

Strathblane parish is fully 5 miles long by 4 broad. Its farms number 19. The principal landowners are—Sir William Edmonstone, Bart., £1,940; Sir Andrew Buchanan, Bart., Craigend castle, £858; Miss Janet Gloriana Graham,

£715; Allan G. B. Graham, Esq. of Fereneze, £587; John Cameron Graham, Esq. of Ballewan, £450; Walter M'Culloch, Esq. of Ardwell, Gatehouse-of-Fleet, £380; Misses Mary and Agnes Aitken, Lomond Lodge, Killearn (farm of Auchengillan), £230; Major Charles Campbell G. Stirling, of Craigbarnet (lands and farm of Broadyett and part of Hillhead, &c.), £576; Trustees of the late Ellis Wood, Esq. (printfield and land, Blanefield), £350; Ebenezer M'Allister, Esq., £332; Trustees of late Alexander T. Russell, Esq. (farms of Easterton and Bankhead), £240; and Trustees of Moses Provan, Esq., C.A., Glasgow (lands and farm, Townhead of Auchengillan), £108.

Campsie parish, which is 7 miles in length and 6 in breadth, has 45 farms. The chief proprietors are—the Hon. Charles Spencer Bateman Hanbury Kincaid-Lennox, £8,217; Sir Charles Elphinstone Fleming Stirling of Glorat, Bart., £2,080; Lady Agnes J. Gordon, £1,345; Capt. John Warden M'Farlane of Ballincleroch, £1,179; Major Charles Campbell Graham Stirling of Craigbarnet, £1,043; James King, Esq. of Campsie, £1,042; Messrs. Hurlet and Campsie Alum Co., £850; Thomas Reid, Esq. of Carlston, £617; John Reid, Esq. of Hayston, £614; Alexander M'Nab, Esq., £589; J. S. Fleming, Esq. of Balquharrage, £491; James Ferrie, Esq., farmer, £269; Samuel M'Farlane, Esq., £259;

Robert Dunlop, Esq. (Watshod and Balfleurs farm), £206; Mrs. James Laing (lands of Broadleys, Todhills, Sandyfaulds, &c.), £205; James Maitland, Esq., farmer, West Balgrochan, £160; Robert Buchanan, Esq., Blairquhosh (Crosshouse farm), £85; and William Simpson, Esq. (farm of Carlston), £60.

In Baldernock parish there are 14 farms. The principal landowners are—Robert Ker, Esq. of Dougalston, £1,408; John Buchanan Hamilton, Esq. of Leny House, Callander, £911; Hugh Bartholomew, Esq., £650; Trustees of late Sir William Stirling Maxwell, Bart. (farms of Back o' Hill and Redbog), £403; Robert Moyes, Esq. (Easter and Wester Bogside farm), £536; Hon. C. S. Bateman Hanbury Kincaid-Lennox, £337; John Marshall, Sen., Esq. (Laverockhill farm), £230; William Johnston, Esq., Barraston, £200; Robert Ronald, Esq., farmer, £200; Trustees of late John M'Culloch, Esq. (East Blairskaith farm), £200; Mrs. Janet Colquhoun (Upper Blochearn farm, Torrance of Campsie), £180; Robert Watson, Esq. (farm of Bardowie and West Blairskaith muir), £178; George Donald, Esq., farmer, £160; Walter Craig, Jun., Esq., £112; The Old Man's Friend Society, Glasgow (Blairnile farm), £75; Andrew Winning, Esq. (Balmore farm), £72; James Bowie, Esq. (farm of Whitefauld, Torrance of Campsie), £85; James Maitland, Esq. (farm of Balmore), £60.

There are 11 farms in the portion of New Kilpatrick parish that lies in Stirlingshire. The chief proprietors are—the Trustees of Sir George Campbell of Succoth, Bart., £1,683; Robert Ker, Esq. of Dougalston, £1,342; John Craig, Esq., Allander paper mill, £600; Messrs. Allander Printing Co., £600; Archibald Campbell Douglas, Esq. of Mains (farm of Keystone and lands of Craigdow), £577; Representatives of the late Alexander Dunlop, Esq. of Clober, £484; Rev. John Erskine Campbell Colquhoun of Killermont, £450; Mrs. M'Intosh's Trustees (farm of Lower Barloch), £195; and James Weir, Esq. (lands and farm of Barrachan, Milngavie), £110.

Balfron parish has 28 farms. Its length is 11 miles, and breadth 3. The chief landowners are—Henry Ritchie Cooper, Esq. of Ballindalloch, 6 farms, £889; Archibald Orr Ewing, Esq. of Ballikinrain, M.P., 3 farms, £706; Sir George Home Speirs, Bart., 4 farms, £694; James Galbraith, Esq. of Balgray, 2 farms, £675; William C. G. Bontine, Esq., 4 farms, £461; and Major Charles C. G. Stirling of Craigbarnet, 1 farm, £299.

In Gargunnock parish, which is 6 miles long and 4 broad, there are 26 farms. The principal proprietors are—the Tutors of Alastair Erskine Graham Moir of Leckie (minor), £3,077; Capt. Henry John Fletcher Campbell of Boquhan,

£1,783; John Stirling Stirling, Esq. of Gargunnock, £1,426; Patrick Francis Connal Rowan, Esq. (Meiklewood estate), £541; and Trustees of late John Gowans, Esq., Park Terrace, Stirling (East Culmore farm), £222.

In Kippen parish there are 30 farms, over a length of 8 miles and breadth from 2 to 4 miles. The largest holders of property are—W. C. G. Bontine, Esq., £1,929; Michael James Jamison, Esq., £916; Captain Henry John Fletcher Campbell, of Boquhan, R.N., £879; James Stirling, Esq. of Garden, £764; Thomas Littlejohn Galbraith, Esq., sheriff-clerk, Stirling (farms of Blackhouse and Little Kerse), £429; and Moses Buchanan Scoular, Esq. (farm of Middle Kerse), £280.

In the parish of Stirling, which is only 2 miles in length and 1½ in breadth, there are 3 farms. The chief proprietors are—Cowan's Hospital, £545; The Crown (part farm of King's park), £364; Right Hon. Lord Balfour of Burleigh (Burghmeadow), £229; Messrs. James Sinclair & Co., Forthbank, £115; and Rev. George Alexander, D.D., minister first charge (fishings in Forth), £75.

There are 7 farms in Alva parish, all of which are possessed by James Johnstone, Esq. —Strude, £503; Balquharn, £414; Myreton, £365; Burnside, £364; Carsiepow, £250; Boll, £170; Greenhead, £146; and lands of East and West Bank, £74—annual valuation in all, £2,286.

The principal landowners in Logie parish, where there are 12 farms, are the Right Hon. Lord Abercrombie of Airthrie Castle, £1,925; Sir James Edward Alexander of Westerton, £1,102; Bridge of Allan Hydropathic Company (Limited), £450; Trustees of the late James Robertson, Esq. (farm of Cornton, Causewayhead), £283; Bridge of Allan Water Company, £245; General Trustees of the Free Church of Scotland (farm of West Haugh), £200; and Right Hon. Lord Balfour of Burleigh (part lands of Dunmyat and Blairlogie), £142.

The 6 farms of Lecropt parish belong to the Trustees of the late Sir William Stirling Maxwell of Pollok, and are valued at £1,810.

In St. Ninians parish, which has the highest valuation of the county, there are 140 farms. The chief proprietors are John Murray, Esq. of Touchadam and Polmaise, £9,824; Sir James Ramsay Gibson Maitland, Bart., £5,700; Sir Henry James Seton Stewart, Bart. of Touch and Allanton, £2,586; Trustees of the late William Simpson, Esq., £2,286; George Frederick William Callander, Esq., £2,160; Major Herbert Buchanan of Arden, £1,943; Michael Hugh Shaw Stewart, Esq. of Carnock, £1,670; Rev. James M'Gibbon Burn Murdoch, vicar of Riverhead, Seven Oaks, Kent, £1,077; Allan's Hospital, £968; Trustees of late William Wilson, Esq. of Skeoch, £924; Cowan's Hospital, £850; Alexander Wilson, Esq. of Alford, Dunblane, £696; Captain David Stewart, London (farm of Stewarthall and Balfornought), £653; John Dick, Esq., Stirling, £635; Alex. Binning Munro, Esq. of Auchenbowie, £627; Alex. Bennet M'Grigor, Esq., Glasgow, £575; Alexander Henry Murray Menzies, Esq., £350; Trustees of late Edwin Sandys Bain, Esq., £350; John Saunders Muschet, Esq. of Birkhill, £318; Mrs. Anna Bow, or Monteath (farm of Small Burn, Bogside, and Kermock), £315; Robert M'Brayne, Esq., Glasgow (farm of Craigannet and Kirkburn), £300; Mrs. Elizabeth Honyman Gillespie of Torbanehill, £283; Adam Smith, Esq. (farm of Meikle Canglour), £273; Sir Robert Stewart, Q.C., Allahabad, India (Glenhead farm), £255; Society in Scotland for Propagating Christian Knowledge (farm of Whitehouse), £230; Peter Lennox, Esq. of Oakfield, Helensburgh (farm of Muirmill, Glendales, and Briglandsteal), £230; Trustees of late John Christie, Esq., £219; James M'Pherson, Esq., Townfoot of Dundaff (grass lands), £185; Right Hon. Lord Balfour of Burleigh, £180; Mrs. Elizabeth Dobbie (farm of Easter Craigannet, Denny), £145; Robert Buchanan, Esq., £183; Trustees of the late Alexander Munnoch (farm of Wester Cringate), £124; and James Turnbull, Esq., Hallquarter of Canglour, £118.

In Kilsyth parish there are 32 farms. The principal proprietors are Sir William Edmonstone, Bart. of Duntreath, £6,783; Trustees of the late John Wilson, Esq. of Hill Park, £429—including farm of Berryhill, £150; Auchinreroch, £135; and Auchenvalley, £85; Joseph Wilson, Esq., Glasgow, £395; Heirs of the late Andrew Walters, Glenample (lands and farm of Inchterf), £197; John Christie, Esq. of Slafarquhar (lands of Slafarquhar and Bentend), £300; Henry Morrison, Esq., Orchard, £120; John Wilson, Esq. of South Bantaskine, £114; and William Wilson, Esq. of Banknock, £95. The minerals on the Kilsyth estate (Messrs. William Baird & Co.) are valued at £2,823; and Banton coal and iron (Henry Caddell, Esq. of Grange), £879.

Denny parish has 79 farms. The principal landowners, apart from Mr. Forbes of Callendar, are William Wilson, Esq. of Banknock, £960; William Ritchie, Esq. (farm of Knowehead, &c.), £280; Peter Lennox, Esq. (farms of Overton and Easter Langhill), £230; A. M. Monteath, Esq. (farm of Greenburn), £154; Mrs. John Laing of Leys, £154; Thomas Keir, Esq. (lands of Linns), £119; Trustees of Mrs. Campbell (farm of West Thomaston), £115; Executors of the late Robert Millar, Esq. (Bankhead farm), £110; Mrs. Agnes M'Farlane (farm of Broadside), £105; D. W. Paterson, Esq. (farm of Garvauld), £110; Trustees of the late William Wilson, Esq., W.S.,

Edinburgh (farm of Cowdenhill), £95; and John Hay, Esq. (Glenhead farm), £90. The Banknock colliery (J. W. Burns, Esq. of Kilmahew) is valued at £423.

In the parish of Dunipace there are 30 farms, and the chief proprietors, in addition to those already mentioned, are John Harvie Brown, Esq. of Quarter, £1,604; Messrs. William Baird & Co. (Denovan farm), £143; and the Representatives of Alexander Duncan, Esq. (farm of Risk, Denny), £130.

Larbert parish has 18 farms. The property of Sir William C. Bruce, Bart., of Stenhouse, is valued at £1,685, of which £285 is placed against the Tryst ground; that of Henry Cadell, Esq. of Banton, at £336; Larbert House (John Hendrie, Esq.), with Broomage farm and grass parks, £722; and the Stirling District Lunacy Board, £670—£40 of that valuation being against the farm of Gowkhill.

In Airth parish there are 34 farms—Bellsdyke farm (Robert William Gillespie Stainton, Esq.) is valued at £396, and the minerals at £125; Pocknaive farm (Charles Edward Walker Ogilvie, Esq.), at £213; farm of Neuck (the Hon. Lady William Godolphin Osborne Elphinstone, of Bantreath), at £100; and Brackenlees (Mrs. James Foord), at £82.

Bothkennar parish has 16 farms—farm of Westerton (Guardians of Henry Callander, Esq. of

Prestonhall), is valued at £280, and the colliery at £150; lands of Thislet, Howkerse, and Pinfoldbridge (Alex. Nimmo, Esq., Falkirk), at £146, and the coal at £576; farm of North Newton (Trustees of the late Alex. Bell, Esq.), at £137, and the coal at £168; farm of Springfield (Messrs. J. S. & G. G. Mackay), at £120, and colliery at £100; farms of Orchardhead and Hardilands (Charles E. Walker Ogilvie, Esq.), at £193, and minerals at £230; farm of Bellsdyke (R. W. G. Staniton, Esq.), at £134, and colliery at £125; Land of South Mains (Mrs. J. Watt or Beveridge, Culross), £41, and minerals £80.

There are 107 farms in the parish of Falkirk—farms of Redbrae, Lippy, and Glenrig (Mrs. Eliza G. W. Ralston), valued at £276; part of Merchiston and Mungal (Mrs. J. G. Stainton), at £240; Mid and Easter Newlands (Thomas S. Maccal, Esq.), at £190; farm of Newhouse (Trustees of William Marshall, Esq.), at £172; Dyke (James Haldane, Esq., and others), at £155; Jawcraig (Trustees of William Scott, Esq.), at £105; Oakerdyke (Mrs. Margaret Thomson Rankine), at £73; farm of Strathavon (J. C. Douglas, Esq. of Polmunckshead), at £70; lands of South Bantaskine, &c. (John Wilson, Esq.), at £396; Summerford, &c. (Ralph Stark, Esq.), at £151; and colliery pit, Redding (His Grace the Duke of Hamilton), at £350.

Many of the resident proprietors in the parish

of Polmont, though the value of their lands be not great, are possessed of independent fortunes from other sources; and for several generations the same estates have been held, in various instances, by family succession. There are 39 farms in the parish. Abbotsgrange (Charles Stirling Home-Dummond Moray, Esq. of Blair Drummond) is valued at £700; Bowhouse (D. S. Robertson, Esq. of Lawhead), at £510; Polmonthill and Middlerig (His Grace the Duke of Hamilton), at £395; Inchyra Grange (Finlay Anderson, Esq.), at £307; Reddock (G. K. M'Callum, Esq. of Braco), at £242; Saltcoats (James Aitken, Esq.), at £191; Crossgatehead (William Napier, Esq.), at £160; Awells (William Hodge, Esq.), at £150; Powdrake (Miss M. B. Ferguson, Rivalsgreen), at £140; Overton, Polmontside, Loanhead, Candylands, Oxgang, and lands of Polmont house (Major John Kincaid Smith), at £512; Candie (Alexander Robertson, Esq.), at £120; and Powdrakes (Trustees of the late Henry Aitken, Esq. of Darroch), at £107.

Westquarter estate (T. L. Fenton-Livingston, Esq.), is valued at £1,026; Millfield (Thomas Hinton Campbell, Esq.), at £522; Parkhall (Thomas Livingstone Learmonth, Esq.), at £308; Lathallan, including farm of Nicolton (Mrs. Henrietta O'Valiant or Spens), at £209; Whiteside (Trustees of Duncan M'Millan, Esq.), at £162; and Meadowbank (Trustees of the late Matthew Waddell, Esq.), at £324.

In Muiravonside parish there are 54 farms. Andrew Stirling, Esq., whose valuation is £1,034, owns, in addition to the Drumbowie minerals (£500), the farms of Castlehill, West Bowhouse, East Bowhouse, and Muirland, with grass parks, valued in all at £336. William Stirling, Esq. of Tarduf, who possesses the lands of Greenknowes and Lochhead, with the farm of Gillanderland, has a valuation of £312. Henry Cadell, Esq., owns the farm of Melon's place, valued at £101; Woodside, at £65; and grass parks, Quarter lodge, at £18; Thomas Newton, Esq., the farm of Parkhall, Burnside, and Eastfield of Wellshot, at £378; Alexander Dick, Esq., Knowhead and Haugh of Craigend, at £151; George Gray, Esq., Windy-yett and lands of Hareburn, Avonbridge, at £225; Andrew Stevenson, Jun., Esq., White-rig, Manuelrig, etc., at £221; the Trustees of the late James Russell, Esq. of Arnotdale, whose valuation is £1,164, own the farms of Bogo, Blackbraes, Craigmad, Wester Blackrig, etc.; Alexander Peddie Waddell, Esq., W.S., Kaemuir and Hillhead, valued at £148; the Trustees of Alexander White, Esq., Glenhead, Glenend, East and West Hirst, and Hirst Park, at £250; N. W. J. Strode, Esq., the farm of Candie, at £90; Robert Clarkston, Esq., Tor-avon lands, at £100; John Calder, Esq., the

Hill farm, at £70; John Boyd, Esq., the lands of Greencraig, Hillhead, Beedyke, and Harestanes, at £114; Andrew Bryce, Esq., Blackstone farm, at £120; Miss Ann Black, grass lands and farm of Hillend, at £132; and George Bayley, Esq. of Manuel, grass parks and lands valued at £488.

There are 39 farms in Slamannan parish. James Rutherford, Esq., M.D., Woodielee, Lenzie, owns Easter Loanrig, valued at £110; Mrs. Eliza G. Waddell Ralston, Balmitchell, at £120; Alexander Reston, Esq., Easter Whin and Wester Burnhead, at £115; Miss Aitken, Darroch lodge and Newfield dyke, at £120; Mrs. Margaret T. Rankin, Southfield, at £110; Binniehill, at £95; and Thrashiehill and Blackrig, at £160; James Gowans, Esq. of Gowanbank, Edinburgh, East Burnhead, at £106; Andrew Aitken, Esq., and others, Drumclair, at £145; Matthew Cleland, Esq., Crosshill and Whitehill, at £70; Alexander Watt, Esq., Roughrig, Todsbuchts, at £100; and James Paton, Esq., Edinburgh, lands of Avonhill and farm of Craigend, at £164.

Mere acreage means nothing, as showing the monetary value of the districts of such a county as Stirling. Few shires are so much diversified in the productive quality of their lands. All along the thinly-populated line, from Buchanan to Gargunnock, for example, there is a preponderance of bare rocky uplands and barren moss or heath, of which the yearly average value per acre scarcely reaches the sum of ten shillings. In Strathblane, however, there is an acreage of 9,068, with a valuation of £9,236; in Baldernock, 4,322, with £6,610; in the portion of New Kilpatrick, 2,747, with £11,859; and in Campsie, 17,872, with £27,834. Here, the residential estates, too, although not so extensive as several of those farther west, are on the whole of richer quality in their soil, and more generally wooded.

The tract of country along the foot of the Ochils is well known for its rare fertility. The acreage within the shire, from Stirling on to Alva, is 9,176, with a valuation of £48,670, being an average of about five guineas per acre. Airthrie castle and Westerton are naturally rich estates. Their grounds are not only finely-wooded, but the deep verdure of their pastures are in complete harmony with the prolific yieldings of the outlying fields. The average value per acre of Logie parish, in which they lie, is fully £7 10s.

On the south side of the Forth, eastward, the soil is also exceptionally good in quality, in spite of the general presence of minerals. The Sauchie estate has been long noted, both for its fine timber and the luxuriance of its grass. It stretches for about three miles from north to south, with the old and new mansion-houses lying concealed in the woods on the east. All the ordinary wild fruits—rasps, brambles, blaeberries, sloes, and nuts are very abundant over the grounds. Indeed, we have seen the first-mentioned berry so rich and numerous in one of the copses, as to fully justify the local simile of "soldiers' coats outspread." Along the eastern portion of the estate, from the old "Black Row," runs the public road to Loch Coulter and Fintry.

Polmaise, too, with Airth and Dunmore—although a considerable area of moss lies throughout this tract—are not less valuable in fertile fields and extensive plantations. None of the estates, however, are of any great length; but they are highly cultivated, and most tastefully kept.

More than one-third of Bothkennar parish belongs to the old estate of Kerse (Earl of Zetland). Here coal is extensively wrought and continues a leading industry south through the Grangemouth, Redding, Muiravonside, and Slamannan districts. Many of the farms or lands were originally purchased and are, in many instances, now held, for the value of the minerals underground. The residential estates over this eastern portion of the shire are of no account, with the exception of the few small but picturesque policies in the neighbourhood of Polmont. We have already referred to those further west—the most interesting of which, within a distance of ten miles, are West Quarter, Callendar, the two Bantaskines, Larbert, Dunipace, Glenbervie, Torwood, and Carbrook.

In Muiravonside parish, which has an acreage of 7,963, with a valuation of £11,507, Mr. Stirling, for the minerals of Drumbowie, is down on the roll for £500; His Grace the Duke of Hamilton, for coal work, £398; Mr. Strode, for coal and ironstone, £160; the Trustees of Mr. Alex. White, for Craigend brick work, £180; and Mr. Alex. Dick, for free-stone quarry, £168.

Slamannan shows by far more waste ground than any parish in the county, and whatever soil is clear of moss is generally inferior and cold. It is, however, a valuable mineral field. Mr. John Watson's colliery has a valuation of £2,119; Drumclair, £1,031; Mr. Matthew Clelland's minerals, £150; and Southfield (Mrs. M. T. Rankine), £971.

Westquarter estate (T. L. Fenton-Livingston, Esq.), as we have shown, is comparatively small, but its beautiful glen and romantic linns render it very attractive. It possesses, too, the mellower charms of antiquity in various phases, such as are associated with its historical stones, and relics of ancient armoury.

In the adornment of Millfield grounds, the late proprietor, Mr. Miller, took a special delight. Scarcely a stranger, in days bygone, came to the district who was not taken to the sweet little estate for the enjoyment of the principal local treat. At that time the clever engineering of the demesne into romantic features was a novelty, but these are still carefully preserved in all their original picturesqueness.

Callendar estate (Wm. Forbes, Esq.) is one of the largest as well as one of the most interesting properties, historically, in the county. Its woods cover several hundreds of acres, and its fields, for the most part, are fairly fertile. In its ancestral mansion both Queen Mary and Prince Charles Stuart found hospitality; while General Monk had the house for a home while his troops remained in Scotland.

South Bantaskine (John Wilson, Esq.), in its northerly grounds, which rise with some boldness from the banks of the Union Canal, consists of a succession of gentle " hillocks " and hollows stretching about a mile in length from east to west. An inviting plantation surrounds the nobly-situated house. And impressive is this woodland for the genuine lover of nature. Now, as the day-light fades, the sweet melodies of the birds are momentarily hushed. Extreme is the silence. But hark! the stillness is suddenly broken by the blackbird's song. The brilliant burst of music, however, is like the flicker of a dying light. Along the southern boundary of the estate runs a public road called " Standalane," from which is seen one of the grandest landscapes that any portion of the country presents—a valley, indeed, tempting one to think that not in all Italy could a finer vale be found. And besides its rare beauty, its connection with historical incident, has turned it into classical ground. It formed one of Wallace's battlefields in the stirring times of the Wars of Independence, and the spirit of Prince Charles still hovers around it. Not yet has it had any tribute from the poetic muse, but the spell which the great Scottish knight threw over its fields will remain, so long as patriotism is a ruling feature of the national character. A considerable part of the country to the south and west of Standalane is very bleak, and the barren character of the district is shown by the scantiness of its human habitations. Those that are to be seen are either farm-houses or labourers' cots; but, when Bonnybridge, Dennyloanhead, and Castlecary appear in the valley, the landscape loses much of its dreary appearance. Patches of cultivated ground and stretches of undulating pasture-land, with occasional pieces of woodland scenery, covering some rounded knoll, is the pleasing prospect which meets the eye. Still, all through this moorland strath, from Glenfuir westwards, the antiquarian with a taste in this direction may find great scope for the exercise of his science. There are, for instance, the Roman wall and its fort-vestiges.

North Bantaskine (James Wilson, Esq.,) is fully entitled to a place of some consideration among the notable estates of Stirlingshire. The grounds contain some of the finest specimens of the yew, larch, plane, and chestnut in the county, together with a fine fragment of the Roman wall. The lawn in front of the mansion is in beautiful condition, and the garden and green-houses are also in a very perfect state. Mr. Wilson, who only became proprietor of the place about two years ago, has not only enlarged, but greatly improved the residence.

About a mile east of the Larbert Tryst-ground lies Kinnaird house (Lord Thurlow)—

> " A rural mansion on the level lawn
> Uplifts its ancient gables, whose slant shade
> Is drawn, as with a line, from roof to porch,
> Whilst all the rest is sunshine."

Here Robert Bruce, the preacher, and James, the Abyssinian traveller, spent their latter years, and both died within the grey old building. There are still veterans in the parish who have a vivid remembrance of the traveller's *physique*—sturdy champion as he was of his name—and tell with zest many amusing stories of his home-life: of Bruce, when he rode out one day, having been pitched from horseback into the heart of a plot of whins at the Goose-muir; of the profound pity, too, that existed all over the country-side for the steed he rode, whose back was strikingly "howed" from the man's extraordinary weight; and of "daft Jamie Wilson's" services on the occasion of the great funeral—marching in front of the burial procession with drawn sword and open Testament. The lands of Kinnaird, which consist chiefly of farms, are rented at from £4 to £5 an acre. Coal, however, of good quality, both for domestic and foundry use, is also extensively wrought over the estate; and beyond the immediate surroundings of the shaft-bottoms the pits are comparatively dry. Their air-currents are likewise so thorough as to render the remotest excavations—

> "Those caves whaur vent'rous men
> Hae houkit mony a fathom ben."

fresh and cool, even though several of the passages are not more than 2 feet square.

Any reference to the estates of the shire would be imperfect without allusion to that of Stenhouse, the property of Sir William C. Bruce, Bart. The mansion, in part, is one of the oldest in the county, and within the grounds stood that puzzling piece of antiquity, Arthur's O'on. An avenue, breaking off from the main one between the two lodges, and lined on either side with trees of great size, leads to the baronet's residence, which, however, has been let for some years to a Glasgow brewer. The property, with its other fields, or farms, has the widely-known old Tryst-ground—a common of about 80 acres. Stenhousemuir was also feued off the estate. The village does not present any special features of interest to the stranger, but it has a sturdy and independent look for all that, and numerous handsome villas are growing up around. Its position is certain to insure its success, as well because of the fine open character of the neighbourhood, as because of the rapid and frequent railway communication it enjoys to and from Glasgow.

Larbert estate is one of the smaller sort. Snugly embosomed among trees, it has, however, many features of beauty. Pasture lands, wood, and a lovely sheet of water, much prized by the local curlers, all combine to form a pretty property. Originally, it was possessed by Sir Gilbert Stirling—a perfect type of old *noblesse*—from whom it passed into the Chalmers family, and was latterly purchased by John Hendrie, Esq. Opposite the south-eastern extremity of the grounds lies the parish grave-yard, where repose alike the ashes of the men of yesterday and of those who fought the battle of life hundreds of years ago. Many of the tomb-stones which lie scattered about are very old, and exhibit the sculpture marks of a rude and unlettered age—"arms, angels, epitaphs, and bones"—such as are not uncommonly seen in country burying-grounds.

> " You ask me where I would be laid,
>   In what beloved spot
> I would repose my life-tired head—
>   It matters not.

> "You ask me if this heart would like
>   Some one to trace my name
> On the memorial-stone of grief—
>   'Tis all the same.
>
> "But stay! methinks I'd like to sleep
>   By Carron's gentle flow—
> I'd like to have an humble stone—
>   Well! be it so."

Dunipace estate, which belongs to John Harvie Brown, Esq., is rich in historical interest. It is situated in a vale of great natural beauty, falling back northwards from the banks of the Carron; while the two mounds referred to in an earlier chapter stand out boldly in the foreground of the mansion. Close by their base is an "auld kirkyard," into which not a jarring sound enters to break the dead silence of the sleepers, nor a breath of wind gets admission to wave the long rank grass that hides many a neglected grave. A dyke, 5 feet high, conceals while it surrounds the burial-ground; and out of the walls grows the sweet-eyed feather-few—an herb, from its stimulant virtues, popular with the botanist. At the east corner an aged elm outspreads its massive branches; while a plane opposite, like some hoary saint with uplifted arms, seems ever imploring a blessing on the hallowed wild. Within the enclosure are also the barberry, the henbane, the bracken, and a variety of common shrubs. About forty years ago a chapel stood close to the churchyard, in which Dr. Knox, who was at that time minister of the united parishes of Larbert and Dunipace, occasionally preached. An old friend of the writer's, who was present at several of the meetings, says, further, that so numerous were the bats throughout the building the young folks used to catch them during divine service and bring them out of church in their handkerchiefs and pockets.

The property of Dunipace formerly belonged to the Primroses, but was forfeited through a service done the Highlanders on the occasion of the second battle of Falkirk. Here Edward I., in 1301, signed a warrant to his plenipotentiaries for a truce with the Scots, and Sir William Wallace was also familiar with the finely wooded strath. But two thirds of the arable lands in the parish lying partly on a substratum of sandstone, and partly on whin-rock, is rendered of a very inferior quality. Jean Livingston, at whose instigation, her husband, John Kincaid, of Wariston, Edinburgh, was cruelly murdered in 1600, was, by birth, connected with Dunipace. She was young and he was old. The ill-fated marriage form, the subject of an old Scottish ballad :—

> " It was at dinner as they sat,
>   And when they drank the wine,
>   How joyful were laird and lady
>   Of bonnie Waristoun !

> "But he has spoken a word in jest;
> Her answer was not guid;
> And he has thrown a plate at her,
> That made her mouth gush bluid."

Murderer and accomplice having been caught while still bearing unequivocal marks of guilt, were immediately tried by the magistrates of Edinburgh, and sentenced to be strangled and burned at a stake. The lady's father, the laird of Dunipace, who was a favourite of James VI., used all his influence to procure a pardon for his unfortunate daughter; but all that could be obtained from the king was an order that she should pass away by decapitation, and at such an early hour as to make the execution as little of a spectacle as possible.

We had almost omitted to mention the Stirlingshire poet, William Cameron, author of "Dinna cross the burn, Willie," who was born in this neighbourhood, December 3, 1801. Like David Gray, the Merkland bard, whose life was "but a piece of childhood thrown away," he was, in earlier life intended for the ministry, but ultimately became, through the death of his father, one of the schoolmasters of Armadale. His first song, "Jessie o' the Dell," had its origin in Miss Jessie Harvey of the *Mill*. Then followed into equal popularity, throughout drawing-rooms, nurseries, concert halls, workshops, and farm steadings, such beautiful melodies as "Meet me on the Gowan

Lea," " Bothwell Castle," " Morag's Fairy Glen," " Far may ye roam," " My Willie and me," &c.

Carbrook estate, the property of J. C. Bolton, Esq., M.P., lies on the very edge of all Torwood's historical traditions and incidents. Nature may be seen in wilder aspects, but the scene of quiet beauty which meets the eye both within the grounds and in their surroundings cannot fail to linger in the visitor's memory. Nothing could be finer than the golden tints imparted to the contiguous heights and plantations as the wave of ebbing day recedes towards the west. The Glen is situated a few yards distant from the famous old thorn on the estate. Its dell, as may readily be imagined, is thickly covered with brushwood and brackens, but it has also a musical burn in its rocky centre, which in spate seasons bounds with real cascadian passion over the Sheep's Linn that lies a short way down. The streamlet has a tenantry of trout, too, and by the angler, with the freedom of its waters, many a decent lot of " beauties " must be basketed. Not a few local Waltonians *take* the liberty occasionally of an hour's cast, and the finny folk (all praise to their considerate courtesy!) take as frankly to the bait of the trespasser as to that of the proprietor.

Buchanan house, on the east side of Loch Lomond, near the right bank of Endrick water, a mile west of Drymen village, is the seat of the Duke of Montrose. It succeeded a previous mansion which was accidentally burned in 1850, and has extensively-wooded grounds. Strathendrick, opening fully to the view at the adjacent shores, extends away to the east like a vast landscape garden, with George Buchanan's monument standing like a sun-dial in its centre, and the Lennox hills engirdling most of it like a grand defensive barrier. Under the name of Sweet Ennerdale it is celebrated in the old song of the "Gallant Grahams."

Finnich Glen, which lies about two miles distant, is a romantic gorge through sandstone rock, with mural sides nearly 100 feet high, but not more than 10 feet wide; and has, in one part, a large tubular mass of rock called the Devil's Pulpit.

Gartness house was a favourite residence of Napier, the inventor of logarithms; and at the Pot of Gartness is a cauldron-shaped cavity, with a picturesque cataract, in the course of the Endrick. Killearn house, Carbeth house, Boquhan Place, and Ballikinrain, all interesting mansions, are in the vicinity of Killearn village; while a short distance south are Dualt Glen and Carnock Glen—two romantic wooded ravines, with traversing streamlets and waterfalls. Duntreath castle, adjacent to Blane water, was long noted for its dungeons, stocks, and other appurtenances of strong feudal domination. Balglass castle, on the left bank of the Endrick, claims a high antiquity, and is said to have given refuge to Sir William Wallace.

Flanders moss, which extended formerly about 14 miles from the vicinity of Gartmore to that of Stirling, is an extensive, but flat and uninteresting territory, rising no higher at the very watershed between the river systems of the Clyde and Forth than 240 feet above sea level. It was formed partly by the decay of the Caledonian forest, and underwent modern reclamation to the aggregate of nearly 10,000 acres, chiefly by means of channel cuttings to the Forth. The improvement operations resulted in excellent meadow and arable land, and yielded several interesting Roman relics, now preserved in the antiquarian museum of Edinburgh.

Leckie house, near the base of the Lennox hills, is an elegant mansion in the old baronial style, and has charming grounds, commanding brilliant views of the upper basin of the Forth, and of the frontier Grampians. Touch house is the seat of Sir Henry J. S. Stewart, Bart., and stands in a picturesque ravine, traversed by a brook with a fine waterfall. Craigforth mansion takes its name from a bold, bosky crag of similar formation to Stirling Hill and Abbey Craig. If the disembodied spirits of the old marauders of the Highlands could revisit the scenes of their power and their feuds, and see the change that time has wrought on this meet nursing ground for a brave and energetic race, it is difficult to imagine with what kind of feelings they would be seized. Would they not endeavour, all sinewless though they are, to beat back the invader—civilisation ? Would there not be an aerial wail of all the Macgregors, " We're landless, landless, Gregalach ?"

The annual value of the real property of the shire, as assessed in 1812, was £189,626; in 1815, £218,761; in 1842-3, £272,634; and in 1880-1, £406,153.

CHAPTER XXXVIII.

IRON INDUSTRIES.

EARLY in January, 1760, the first furnace was blown at Carron. Dr. Roebuck, who was the founder of these works, which, with the exception perhaps of Coalbrookdale, are the oldest of any importance in the country, was also manager until 1773; when, getting overwhelmed in difficulties, from the flooding of his mines, he was obliged to sell out; and, in that same year, the company received a charter of incorporation by which its capital was fixed at £150,000. Roebuck's father was a manufacturer of cutlery in Sheffield. The son studied medicine at the University of Edinburgh, and afterwards graduated at Leyden. Returning to England, he ultimately turned his attention to the chemical and metallurgical arts, and, along with Mr. Samuel Garbett, became a manufacturer of sulphuric acid in the village of Prestonpans. Here he got acquainted with Mr. William Cadell of Cockenzie, who was anxious to engage in the production of iron, and a company for that purpose was forthwith organised, consisting of Roebuck, his brothers Thomas and Ebenezer, Samuel Garbett, William Cadell, sen.; William Cadell, jun.; and John Cadell. The leading articles by which the works, even at the outset, got a world-wide fame, were the cannons, mortars, and chain-shot manufactured for the arsenals of Europe. Ordnance, mortars, and carronades were sent out to Russia, Denmark, and Sardinia; while the latter country received, in addition to a quantity of extra large mortars, a shipment of guns ten feet in the bore. The British Government, however, were by far the most extensive purchasers—the whole battering train of the Duke of Wellington having gone from Carron. The last order for guns came from France. Not since 1852 has there been a single carronade moulded; and this war-casting, which had its name from the works, has in fact become obsolete. It was cast solid in an upright position, and afterwards bored to the required calibre.

It was undoubtedly an unequalled superiority of material and workmanship that gave this establishment unrivalled fame, both at home and abroad, and induced many distinguished men to pay it a visit. In 1821, Prince Nicholas, afterwards Emperor Nicholas, went over the foundry, and was followed by Prince Leopold and Prince Maximilian of Austria. The latest royal visitor was the Prince of Wales, who, in July, 1859, inspected all the chief departments of Carron; and, as an illustration of the moulder's work, the casting of a common three-legged pot was shown him, the patterns for which consist of nine pieces —two for the body, three for the feet, and two for each of the ears. But, one Sunday afternoon, another prince—the prince of Scottish bards— knocked at the Carron gate. Need we further mention his name? Burns, the Ayrshire ploughman—the poet whom all Scotland delights to honour. No admittance, however, could that day be granted the "Great Unknown." So with diamond, and a stroke of keenest satire, he scratched the following verses on a window-pane of the neighbouring inn :—

> " We cam' na here to view your warks,
>   In hopes to be mair wise;
> But only, lest we gang to hell,
>   It may be nae surprise.
>
> But when we tirl'd at your door,
>   Your porter dought na hear us;
> Sae may, should we to hell's yetts come,
>   Your billy Satan sair us."

It is generally allowed that the lines were first seen by Mr. Benson, a traveller to Carron Company, who immediately copied them into his order book, and afterwards penned the following reply—Burns having applied for admission *incognito*.

> "If you came here to see our works,
>   You should have been more civil,
> Than give us a fictitious name,
>   In hopes to cheat the devil.
>
> Six days a-week to you and all,
>   We think it very well;
> The other, if you go to church,
>   May keep you out of hell."

An unlimited command of mineral resources, together with the readiest channels of export, have always been highly advantageous spokes in the Carron wheel. Now, as in days bygone, the company have rich and extensive workings, both in coal and ironstone, the "hands" of which, from their numbers, form several well-populated villages. Upwards of a century ago, they opened a pit in the parish of Kilsyth, where the ironstone strata have been found from four to fourteen inches in thickness. The coal in the neighbourhood of the works, which dips, for the most part, to the south-east, has been wrought for ages. It is of various qualities. Some of it, being brittle, falls to be chiefly used for the furnaces and forges; while other sorts burn clear, giving a good heat and cake, so that the very dross is valuable. At one time, the company held an enormous quantity of pig-iron, which was made and stored under Mr. Joseph Dawson's managership. A workman concerned, alluding to one of the immense piles, received the following characteristic reply from plain "old Joe,"—"Gang on, man, ye're a lang way frae the roof yet," referring to the sky. In 1872, however, when the revenue demanded the best appearance possible, this "sunk capital" was thoroughly cleared out, and realised in cash.

By water, as by rail, the company are at no loss either for the bringing in of raw material, or the throwing out of manufactured goods. A railway, which was laid down some twenty years ago, stretches from the interior of the works to Burnhouse, where it meets the Polmont branch of the North British line, connecting with that of the Caledonian on the west; and where a large basin also adjoins the Forth and Clyde Canal. On this railway one or two powerful locomotives are kept ploddingly at work, while others do gigantic service in coal traffic between the outlying pits and furnaces. What changes come about with time! It is scarcely sixty years since the rails leading from Carron to the Bainsford basin were laid, and even that enterprise in its day was considered no mean undertaking. The first line, stretching from Kinnaird colliery into the interior of the works, was constructed in 1766. The rails in that instance were of wood, covered with a sort of hoop-iron. In the course of the following year, however, rails wholly of iron were got from Coalbrookdale. Six magnificent screw-vessels, that sail from Grangemouth, are likewise owned by the company, and carry the produce of the foundry to London, for the extensive warehouse there; but large quantities of freight, are, at the same time, taken from local and metropolitan traders. For the conveyance of goods to the west and east, sixteen lighters, or other small craft, ply on the canal.

Throughout the works, some splendid machinery plays its part in the smelting and manufacturing processes. There are, for example, the patent hammers, in the forging departments, devoted to axle-making; and the stationary engine, of enormous power, employed in the production of blast. The steam-cylinder of the latter machine is 6 feet in diameter, the piston having a stroke of 10 feet. The blast cylinder is 104 inches in diameter, and 10 feet deep. But a gigantic piece of similar mechanism, which was erected by James Watt for pumping work, is also to be seen, in the old "engine-house," wonderfully complete, barring the furrows of oxidation, taking into account that its services have been dispensed with for the last 30 years. This engine, which was constructed on the atmospheric principle, was fitted with 4 pumps, which raised to a height of 36 feet 40 tons of water per minute. Its cylinder was 6 feet in diameter by 8 feet in depth, and the beam about 30 feet long. The steam was supplied by 3 cast-iron boilers, two of which were globular in form. Two of the original water wheels, 5 feet in diameter, and overshot, are still going. One drives a turning lathe, &c.; and the other Smeaton's blowing engine, which was erected in 1766. This engine embraces 4 air cylinders, about 3 feet in diameter, and is so arranged as to give a continuous blast.

But the furnaces are undoubtedly the head-quarters of danger. In 1788 there were only eight of these in blast in Scotland, of which four were at Carron, two at Wilsontown, one at Bonaw, and one at Goatfield—the two latter being fired with charcoal. The largest of the kind, however, is that at Ferryhill, in Durham, whose height is $103\frac{1}{2}$ feet, with cubic contents of 33,300 feet. A few years ago, the Carron Company erected three new blast furnaces upon the plan which has so generally commended itself to the experience of the Cleveland ironmasters, who may be regarded as the most skilful, scientific, and enterprising members of their craft in the world. This step was taken on account of the then high prices of pig-iron, which were realizing to some of the larger manufacturers a clear profit weekly of over £10,000.

Notwithstanding the great, and in many instances powerful, competition now connected with the casting departments of the iron trade, Carron is still *the* iron-works of Britain. And such general public confidence in its various domestic and industrial products, which include grates, cooking ranges, stoves, boilers, kettles, pots, stew-pans, sugar-pans, rain-pipes, &c., is due, no doubt, to the shrewd and devoted conduct of those men who, for the last 120 years, have held successively the onerous position of head of the works. Mr. William Cadell was one of the earlier managers. He was eventually succeeded by Mr. Charles Gascoigne. Getting embarrassed financially, the latter, while in office here, accepted an offer from the Empress of Russia, who wished to have works constructed in her dominions for the casting of guns, shells, and shot, and, taking with him a number of skilful hands, foundries were accordingly erected at Petrozabodsky, and elsewhere in the country. For Gascoigne this proved a step on the way to position and fortune. In course of time he was created a knight of the order of St. Wladimir, had the rank of general in the Russian service, and died worth £30,000. Next in order came Mr. Joseph Stainton, a native of Cumberland, who had been for several years chief clerk in the counting-house of the works. This was a man of great decision of character, and, as is engraved on his monument in Larbert churchyard, "by economy, diligence, and scientific skill, he relieved the company from embarrassment, and placed it in unrivalled prosperity." He died in harness in 1825, at the age of seventy, and was followed in the management by his nephew, Mr. Joseph Dawson, also a native of Cumberland. "Joe," as he was familiarly called, was likewise much respected by the workmen, and controlled the destinies of Carron for about a quarter of a century—his career terminating in January, 1850, when he had reached his seventy-second year. A brother, Mr. William Dawson, then got hold of the managerial reins, but who did little, from his retiring, "jog-trot" spirit, in whipping the concern into anything like enterprise and progress. Afflicted latterly with partial blindness and other physical infirmities, he resigned his managership, and went to the grave at the ripe age of eighty years. Mr. Thomas Dawson, another brother, was now entrusted with the same responsible duties. Scarcely, however, had he been installed in office, when he took seriously ill and died suddenly. This led, in December, 1873, to the appointment of Mr. Andrew Gordon, than whom none have shown more of energetic and practical oversight.

Although Carron for many years turned a listless ear to the demand for improvement, she no longer rests on her oars in sluggish inertia. Under the late able management, the works have been carried on with a vigour and enterprise which will compare favourably with the most spirited of their modern competitors. Extensive alterations and improvements are at present being executed. The public road on the north side has been diverted outwards with a considerable sweep, and the future boundary of the works at this part will consist of a substantial wall with the chief entrance and offices intervening. Indeed, these are now so far forward that a short time will suffice for their completion. Internal reconstructions are also being rapidly pushed on. The additional space, which the diversion of the road above referred to gives the company, is being allocated for workshops, to take the place of those dilapidated and smoke-begrimed buildings which, throughout the rise and progress of Carron, have been scattered over the works without either plan or method. These modernising operations will throw the centre of the vast industrial establishment entirely open, and, apart from the desirable appearance of order, will afford increased facilities both for productive power and the despatch of goods manufactured. The alterations at present contemplated will, according to estimate, cost about £100,000. Above the main entrance to the works there is now a tower with vane and clock. Underneath are the Carron "arms"—cannons crossed, with the motto, *Esto Perpetua*. Still, the old east gate, with the counting-offices on the south, fronted by a narrow enclosure containing a few stunted and blackened trees, and the "stable-row," humble and retiring on the north, will not soon pass from local memory.

The farm connected with the iron-works is called the Roughlands, and its lands, extending to 400 acres, lie, for the most part, in the immediate neighbourhood. From the well-stocked steading and the Mulloch field, everything necessary in the form of feeding and fodder is got for the foundry horses; but these have been comparatively few since the locomotives were introduced.

The Carron Company are also amongst the oldest merchants of Glasgow. In 1765, they projected Duke Street, for the purpose of obtaining a direct route from Cumbernauld to the city; and, in 1816, acquired ground in Buchanan Street, upon which they erected a warehouse and manager's residence.

An amusing circumstance is attached to the preliminary arrangements for the Carron works. There happened to be one more than the landowner to be bargained with in the feuing of the 14 acres as a site; viz., the farmer, whose lease of the grounds extended over some couple of years. A very reasonable sum was asked for the right of immediate possession; but the demand, from its mistaken exorbitance, could not be entertained. Thus, unable to come to an amicable understanding, the representative of the negotiating firm gave the tenant time to reconsider his terms. In the interim, the farmer had a call from a friend, shrewder, commercially, than himself, who observed that the Englishman had probably mistaken pounds Scots for pounds sterling. And so it turned out; but, just as an explanatory letter was on the eve of being despatched, forward came the company's acceptance, thereby agreeing to pay exactly twelve times the money asked.

From the south is got the most striking impression of Carron, with its ringing industry and flaming furnaces. The latter are a most trustworthy barometer to the surrounding villagers. Should they, in the gloom of night, cast a glowing belt over the atmosphere, the following day is certain to be showery. Opposite the western portion of the works are several heavy hills of ironstone, and as much old metal in patterns as would be a handsome capital for many a smaller foundry; while on the north side of the river, immediately opposite the furnaces, there is an enormous mass of rubbish, called the cinder-hill, and which keeps continually smouldering, like some miniature Vesuvius. Of this mountain of old scraps and ashes—the accumulation of many years—it could scarcely be credited that its every particle, so to speak, had been carted out of the works.

Until lately, the great body of the Carron men were natives of the district, whose forefathers had been in the same service; and, as stock goods were invariably made when a temporary dulness affected the demand for certain articles, few of the employés ever thought of leaving the place. But old men and old customs have passed away. Those now at the head of affairs, in following out the spirit of the age, care nothing for old servants. What is sought for and got is the man who, all through, is cheapest for the masters. The present average rate of wages earned by moulders is 24s. a-week; by pattern-makers, 21s.; by wrights and blacksmiths, 20s.; and by labourers, 15s. Connected with the works there is a friendly society, which holds an interest, by shares, in the company, and provides pecuniary assistance for its members in days of ill-health or accident. This "club" was founded about sixty years ago, and has a membership of over 700. There are, however, other two principal benefit societies, with a number of minor ones. A cooperative store has also been in existence here for upwards of fifty years, and no similar association could be more harmoniously and successfully conducted. From its start, indeed, it has been exceptionally well kept together, notwithstanding the rival societies in almost every adjacent village. About twelve years ago, the company erected a large and commodious schoolroom for the education of the local children; while, on 2nd October last (1880), the memorial stone of a U. P. church was laid by the Rev. John Yellowlees, minister of the congregation, who was, on the occasion, presented with a silver trowel, bearing a suitable inscription. In a cavity in the wall of the west gable, a glass bottle was deposited, containing the leading newspapers and specimens of the current coins of the realm, over which the stone was placed. The building is of Gothic design, and will, when completed, accommodate about 500 people. Its entire cost is estimated at £1,700, and there is every prospect of the church being opened free of debt. The architect for the work is Mr. James Boucher, Glasgow.

The Falkirk Iron Works, now the second largest in Scotland, were started some sixty years ago by a number of enterprising workmen from Carron, and only fell into the hands of the present proprietors in 1848. From the outset, their progress has been steady, but especially during the last thirty years the development of the foundry in its various branches has been remarkable. The buildings now cover 8 acres of ground, and the employés, numbering 900 (men and boys), turn out over 300 tons of castings per week. Here an extensive trade is done in the ornamental or artistic class of goods; but, during the Crimean war, 16,000 tons of shot and shell were manufactured by the Messrs. Kennaird; while their orders for guns of all sizes, for mercantile ships, are considerable. The firm, with Mr. George Binnie as manager, have also executed several foreign contracts of importance. Amongst these were castings for some of the principal iron bridges in India, Italy, and Spain. But fountains for the Calcutta Water Company, and tubular telegraph posts for South America have likewise been supplied. The weightiest portions of work recently made, however, were the columns for the Solway viaduct. These were cast in 10 and 20 feet lengths, to be bolted together as the complete column. No establishment in Britain can cope with the Falkirk Foundry in its elegant and varied stock of patterns for such goods as the following :—register stoves, hat and umbrella stands, garden-seats, verandahs, iron stairs, statuary groups, mirror-frames, inkstands, etc. A small figure of a stag, browsing, was shown, by the Messrs. Kennaird, at the Exhibition of 1862, along with a variety of other castings, as illustrating the capabilities of the sand-moulding process. In order to have the stag cast in one piece, the mould had to be made in upwards of a hundred parts, each part being simply a clod of moist sand, held together by compression. Sugarpans for the West Indies; grates, pots, and pans for the million, are only a further sample of the great variety of iron goods manufactured here. Few foundries, in fact, have risen so rapidly into fame and importance; and it may safely be affirmed that none show greater promise of being able to "hold their own" in the vast competitive field of iron manufactures.

A short distance west the canal bank are the works of the Burnbank, the Gowanbank, the Grahamston, the Parkhouse, and the Camelon iron companies; while at Lock 16 we have the

Union Foundry, with the Port-Downie and the Forth and Clyde iron works. In addition to these eight establishments, there are three of recent date to the eastward of the Falkirk iron works. These are the Abbot's, the Gael, and the Etna foundries—the last mentioned being a branch of the Etna works in Glasgow. There are likewise two new foundries situated close to the branch of the North British Railway at Grahamston, the one being called the Callendar, and the other the Vulcan iron works. Here, is also the extensive engineering establishment of the Messrs. Blackadder. The reason of so many foundries having been thus recently started to the north of Falkirk is not far to seek. Middlesbro' "pigs," which are now chiefly used in the manufacture of castings, are brought by steamer to Grangemouth, and thence conveyed per Forth and Clyde Canal to Glasgow (Port-Dundas); while the manufactured goods are also forwarded along the latter route to Grangemouth for shipment to London. Hence the great and double saving in carriage to the Falkirk ironfounders—the distance to Glasgow from Grangemouth being nearly seven times the distance to Grahamston. The following table will show the rise and progress of iron-working throughout the foundry district of the county :—

IRON INDUSTRIES.

	Started.	Hands Employed in 1880.
Carron Iron Works,	1760	2,500.
Falkirk Iron Works,	1819	900.
Union Foundry,	1854	100.
Abbot's Foundry,	1856	120.
Burnbank Foundry,	1860	140.
Carron Bank Foundry (Denny),	1860	30..
Bonnybridge Columbian Stove Works,	1860	250.
Bonnybridge Foundry,	1860	400.
Gowanbank Iron Works,	1864	300.
Grahamston Iron Works,	1868	350.
Denny Iron Works,	1870	90.
Larbert Foundry,	1870	150.
Camelon Iron Co.,	1872	180.
Parkhouse Iron Co.,	1875	100.
Gael Foundry,	1875	40.
Port Downie Iron Works,	1875	100.
Forth and Clyde Iron Works,	1876	80.
Springfield Iron Works,	1876	20.
Etna Foundry,	1877	120.
Callendar Iron Co.,	1877	80.
Bonnybridge Malleable Iron Works,	1877	8.
Total Iron Workers,		6,058.

Nail making was introduced into Camelon, about eighty-five years ago, by Mr. Caddell of Carronpark, who brought workmen from England for the purpose, and thus the trade was taught those belonging to the district. In 1830, there were about 500 nail-makers here; but, in 1833, the cholera cut off so many of this class that Mr. Fairbairn, who had also become a manufacturer, found it necessary to advance £40 against interments, which was repaid from the earnings of survivors. At that period, a man working from 5 to $5\frac{1}{2}$ days a week, and each day consisting of 10 hours, earned from 9s. to 14s. a week, and with a boy under him 14s. to 16s. Latterly, double that money was got; but the machine-made nails from America and London have ruined the hand-made trade. At present there are only about 50 nail-makers in Camelon, of whom Mr. James Jones employs 15, and Messrs. Fairbairn & Co. 8. In St. Ninians, thirty years ago, there were 200, who made from 1,000 to 1,200 nails in the day; but their working hours were long, and their wages small. 8s. or 9s. per week was the most that could be earned. Here, too, for the reason stated with respect to Camelon, the nail trade is of no account. Only some 30 men are so employed.

CHAPTER XXXIX.

MINING.

COAL, while one of the most valuable of our minerals, is also one of the most abundant, The output in Stirlingshire during 1879 was 967,855 tons—the collieries of the western district producing 257,539 tons, and those of the eastern 710,316. Of ironstone there was likewise raised in the western district 105,947 tons, and in the eastern 2,819; making a total of 108,766 tons. The amount of fire-clay raised, for the same period, was 8,219 tons; and of oil shale, 1,135. Throughout the county, there are at present 34 pits open, the principal of which are in the districts of Bannockburn, Auchenbowie, Denny, Lennoxtown, Kinnaird, Falkirk, Redding, and Slamannan; while the number of men engaged over-all is stated to be about 1,800. As regards the coal-fields of the world, although our own land does not contain the largest amount of fossil fuel, its output is greater than that of any other country. The extent of the coal-fields in Great Britain is said to be 4,251 square miles;

while the annual weight raised is now usually estimated as equal to 35,000,000 of tons. The home consumption is stated to be 23,000,000 of tons per annum; and if coal costs the consumer an average price of 7s. per ton, then 23,000,000 tons will be worth in all over £8,000,000 sterling. The total number of persons engaged in the work of British collieries has been computed at from 160,000 to 180,000; and that the total capital thus employed is no less than £10,000,000.

The following short calculation will give the results of all that can be conjectured as to the amount of vegetation in coal:—Wood affords in general about 20 per cent., and coal about 80 per cent. of charcoal. Apart, therefore, from the oxygen and hydrogen, it must have required 4 tons of wood to yield the charcoal which we find in 1 ton of coal. Let us then suppose a forest composed of trees 80 feet high, that the trunk of each tree contains 80 cubic feet, and the branches 40, making 120; the weight of such a tree, at 700 specific gravity, will be $2\frac{1}{4}$ tons; and allowing 130 trees to an acre, we have 300 tons on that space. Further supposing the portion that falls annually, leaves and wood, to be equal to one-thirtieth, we have 10 tons of wood annually from an acre, which yields 2 tons of charcoal; and this charcoal, with the addition of bitumen, forms $2\frac{1}{2}$ tons of coal. Now a cubic yard of coal weighs almost exactly a ton; and a bed of coal, 1 acre in extent and 3 feet thick, will contain 4,840 tons. It follows, therefore, that 1 acre of coal is equal to the produce of 1,940 acres (*i.e.*, 4,840 divided by $2\frac{1}{2}$) of forest; or, if the wood all grew on the spot where its remains exist, the coal bed 3 feet thick, and 1 acre in extent, must be the growth of 1,940 years.

It need not be said that the pit as a workroom is peculiarly dangerous. The collier, in fact, must be seen "holing," for the more than common difficulties and perils of his trade to be fully understood. Flat on his side, or down on his "hunkers," or knees, long and laboriously he pikes, working out the block of coal from the wall or seam.

When Bruce, the traveller, returned from Abyssinia to Kinnaird, he was greatly dissatisfied with the way in which his collieries had been wrought. After some stormy disputes with the lessees, he agreed to submit the matter to a committee of experienced coal engineers, who accordingly met at Kinnaird, inspected the mines, and made every endeavour to form an impartial judgment. Conversing one day with those gentlemen, he challenged something which one of them said respecting the condition of the mines; whereupon the engineer said, " If you are not afraid, Mr. Bruce, go down and satisfy yourself on the point by personal investigation." The word "afraid" startled Bruce. "Afraid!" said he in his own peculiarly commanding way; "Sir, do you think I should be afraid to go down into my own mines?" At once he engaged to descend with them, the following day, into the "Carse Pit;" and they as eagerly took him at his word, having secretly determined to punish him for the unreasonable way in which he had disputed many of their statements. "He speaks of Nubian sands," quoth one to another that evening; "we'll show him something worse to-morrow, if I am not mistaken." Next day, accordingly, Bruce appeared at the mouth of the pit; and, after donning a suitable suit, went down with his *corps* of engineers. The strata were not very thick at the best, and many of the *wastes* were considerably crushed and fallen in. Walking underground was, consequently, anything but pleasant; nevertheless, as the engineers had arranged, in they went, up one *waste* and down another, leading the adventurer such a dance as traveller never danced before. All the while the engineers pretended to demonstrate to Bruce the conclusions at which they had arrived. Sometimes the party would be stooping in rectangular form; sometimes wading up to the ankles in wet coal mud; and at other times reduced to crawling on their hands and knees for a quarter of a mile. At one part, the engineers passed through an aperture barely wide enough for themselves, who were men of moderate size, and cruelly narrow for Bruce. He tried the passage, but stuck in it; and had to be extricated by the head and shoulders. Again reaching the bottom of the shaft, the figure which he presented is not to be described. Still, up to the last, he maintained his usual composure, and only remarked that he certainly was surprised at the dirtiness of the *wastes*.

The Snab pit at Kinneil, with a depth of 1200 feet, is one of the deepest shafts in Scotland. In that Bo'ness district, both coal and ironstone abound; there being some seven or eight principal seams of the former, one of which carries a thickness of 12 feet, and two seams of the latter which is black-band in character. One of the most remarkable collieries in the country was wrought here under water. The strata of coal being found to extend far out beneath the firth, the colliers had the courage to work half-way across the channel. A building, or moat as it was called, half-a-mile from the shore, and taking the form of a round quay, afforded an entrance into the sea-pit; but, ultimately, an unusually high tide came which drowned the whole of the miners.

Pits are apt to become all the more fiery the deeper they are wrought; and, where the area excavated is extensive, special statutory attention should be given to upcast and downcast shafts. Never in the annals of our mining industry has there been havoc to equal the appalling destruction of human life of which the last few years have been witness. Colliers, considering the critical character of their calling, are careless beyond all credence. They may be reasoned with, fined, and even dismissed, for rashly flying in the face of rules specially framed with the object of protecting life and property, but all to no purpose. A manager of one of the largest of the Scotch collieries once caught a miner filling his flask from a barrel of gunpowder, while an oil-lamp with open flame hung from his bonnet. What, however, from the enlightened provisions of modern science, and stricter regard to the most ordinary chemical precautions, pit labour is ever getting less and less perilous to health and life. The Davy lamp, no doubt, is in some measure to be thanked for the now comparative rarity of explosions, such catastrophes generally having occurred from the workman's light coming into contact with inflammable air, or, in other words, hydrogen gas. And a word with respect to the collier's general health. From his toil, so peculiarly chest-trying, it is easy to see why he so rarely shows the "auld grey frostit head." With an average life of only twenty-seven years, he is little short of a phenomenon at fifty; and when found at that "patriarchal age," is generally a crouching invalid, emaciated and breathless. And the diseases to which he is specially liable are those affecting the respiratory organs. "Housemaid's knee"—an acute inflammation over the knee-pan—is a very painful and common sore throughout his class; but the great hydra of the pit is asthma, with the constant tendency to bronchitis in the winter season, and this ailment not unfrequently ends in enlargement of the liver and dropsy. "Black-spit" is another health-undermining, although not mortal disease comparatively, reaching to such intensity at times that a fluid like tar runs out of the throat. Yet this *melanosis*, strange to say, seems preventive of other affections of the lungs. Consumption, for example, is never heard of amongst colliers; and its absence from the Hebridean poor has also been observed—people who are continually inhaling a carbonaceous atmosphere from the peat-reek of their huts. The tissue of the miner's lungs appears most tenacious of the charcoal deposits. Some years ago, on the occasion of a female body being dissected in the neighbourhood of Falkirk, the surgeon who performed the *post-mortem* operation could tell at once, from the blackness of the lungs, that the woman in early life had been engaged underground, although thirty years had elapsed from the day on which she left the pit. And we have the same baneful dust ruining the health of the moulders in our foundries. The late Dr. Graham, latterly master of the Mint, on analyzing the lungs of a workman who had wrought at Carron for about forty years, found even as much as a fourth of them pure charcoal.

When the oil lamp was abolished from the mine, asthma and black spit were thought to have received their death-blow. And the tallow now in use has certainly done away, to a great extent, with the lamp-black deposits that have hitherto proved so detrimental to collier vitality. It is, in fact, rare now to find any of the younger pitmen afflicted with asthma, except where the disease may be fairly considered hereditary; and further improvements in pit-lighting are at present being contemplated.

A great deal of nonsense has, of late, been written about the dusky heroes of the mine. Everywhere they have been represented as a brutal, illiterate, and godless class; and it cannot be denied that their conduct, so far from being the genuine embodiment of every virtue, is still in a great measure rude, and perhaps not quite up to the ordinary standard. Yet not so sweepingly can they be written down either barbarians or vagabonds. The great bulk of the men employed in our new collieries undoubtedly lead a most riotous life. Nor is it surprising that we should there find so much of the baser dross of humanity. To these young coal workings, all the unsettled Irish of the country flocked; and whatever wealth of wild goodness may be common to the hot-headed Hibernian, at his door assuredly lies, for the most part, the notorious blackguardism of our mining hamlets. That lower and degraded class too, are without exception itinerants. Never certain of steady employment, they keep themselves in readiness to take up their bed at any hour and walk. It would be well, therefore, if by some arrangement the miner could be made to feel sure of permanent work and a settled home. No doubt there are peculiar difficulties in the way. Colliers, of all the "sons of toil," are specially apt to get dissatisfied and restless. Many of the steadiest hands have to be frequently shifted in their workings; and even sent at times into a different pit. By-and-by their power of muscle fails them—their thews and sinews get weakened and worn, and the poor fellows go about, as it were, seeking their lost strength.

As we have already hinted, the general enlightenment and self-respect of the workmen connected with our older collieries are undisputable; while a growing intelligence throughout their ranks is ever raising them in the scale of moral being. From Garscadden, for example, sang David Wingate—himself "a weary bon'd miner," and a poet born. To read his songs, "The Deil in the Pit," "The Burn in the Glen," and "My Little Wife," is as refreshing as a norland breeze.

On some occasions, the pit must be wrought night and day; and this is managed by one set of men working the day-shift, and another set the night-shift. The night-shift is always regarded somewhat of a hardship by the men, but by a change of the sets it is fairly distributed amongst them all. The wages, which are paid according to piecework, vary considerably in different districts, and are liable to fluctuation. In some cases the quantity of coal a man may put out in a day is limited by mutual consent, or in accordance with a rule of the Union; in others, the working hours are limited, each man being allowed to put out as much as he can in the stated time; and again, there are collieries at which there is no limitation either as to time or quantity. A century ago, the wages of miners, all serfs, was from 7s. to 8s. 4d. a-week. In those days candles were used in the pit, which were supplied by the masters without charge. The average wage is at present 3s. 6d. a-day. In 1851, the average was 2s. 6d.; and in 1854, it was 5s. A gradual decline then took place; and in 1858 the average was 3s.; below which sum it has not fallen, the figures for the six succeeding years being respectively 3s. 6d., 4s., 4s. 6d., 5s. 6d., and 4s. 9d. From these sums about 3d. a-day falls to be deducted for light, sharpening tools, &c. In 1871 and 1872, the wages rose to 10s. a day; and a man, with two boys, could then make as much as 20s. This was a rare and luxurious period for the colliers; but the times were too good to last. With the close of '72 came a reverse; and wages gradually declined until they reached the present average rate above stated. The relations between the Stirlingshire miners and their employers have been little disturbed by disputes as to work or wages. In the west of Scotland the case has been different — strikes being of frequent occurrence.

CHAPTER XL.

GENERAL INDUSTRIES.

CALICO-PRINTING, although not a common industry in Stirlingshire, is carried on extensively in the western district of the county. The largest establishment of the kind is that of Messrs. R. Dalglish, Falconer & Co., known as Lennox-mill, Campsie. The "field" was first opened as a print-work about 1786. In 1790 it contained 20 printing tables, and 6 flat presses. At that period, however, a great many women were employed to pencil on colour—a method which is now entirely abandoned. In 1807, the present firm became tenants of Lennox-mill, which had, by that time, been considerably enlarged, as it contained 50 tables, and 8 presses. In 1810, the first surface-printing machine was erected, which was an improvement on block-printing; and soon afterwards a cylinder-printing machine, which was an improvement on the copper-plate printing presses, similar to what the "surface" was on the "block." In both cases, what was formerly on a flat surface, was put on a cylinder of wood or copper. This, continually revolving, furnished itself with colour, which it, at the same time, transferred to the cloth.

At present, almost every description of printing is performed at Lennox-mill, and nearly every fabric of cloth printed, from the finest muslin worn by ladies, to the coarsest calico worn by the Pariahs of India. As most of the goods are for the Indian market, the colours are somewhat "loud" and the designs peculiar. The dress-pieces made for people of the Hindoo religion have a broad border of peacocks round the skirt, the upper part bearing a spotted or diaper pattern. The ground-work of all is Turkey-red, but the birds and other designs are produced in blue, yellow, and green. The Mahometans consider it sinful to try to imitate nature too closely; and though peacocks figure in the designs prepared for ladies of that faith, they are drawn in the rudest fashion, and worked out in mosaic. None of the designs of these Indian garments would find admirers in this country; and as the artists are bound down by certain conventional rules, they have no scope for the creation of original patterns. In cloth for turbans there is the same limitation in variety. The dress pieces are short, being only from $1\frac{1}{2}$ to 8 yards in length; and owing to that and other technical causes, it would be unprofitable to print them on a cylinder machine, so they are done by the block method.

What is printed on the cloth is not the complete colour, but a substance to discharge the red and absorb another colour. This substance is applied in the form of paste, which has no resemblance to the ultimate colour.

Lennox-mill now contains 7 printing cylinders, and 200 tables. The water-power is equal to about 20 horses, and the steam-engine is 30 horse-power. The heating and dyeing are all done by steam, for which purpose about 250 horse-power of steam is employed. The coal consumed daily is about 30 tons. The engraving of the copper rollers is all performed on the premises, and requires very nice machinery. The stock of copper rollers is heavy, amounting in number to 1,500, weighing about 155,000 lbs. At present the works give employment to 545 hands—men, women, boys, and girls. About 250,000 pieces are produced annually, consisting of garments for home and export trade.

The art of calico-painting was introduced into Europe from India, about 1676; but a considerable time elapsed before the trade gained general attention. In 1774, however, the law which prohibited the printing of English-made calicoes was repealed, and, by the aid of a series of wonderful inventions and improvements, the industry flourished and increased, though the Excise duty of 6d. on every square yard of calico printed, stained, painted, or dyed, was not removed until 1831. The invention in 1785, of cylinder-printing by Mr.

Bell, of Glasgow, worked a revolution in the trade; and the tedious process of painting designs by hand was immediately superseded by the use of blocks. There are five general styles in calico-printing, namely :—(1.) The fast-colour or chintz style, in which the mordants are applied to the white cloth, and the colours of the designs are afterwards developed in the dye-bath. The term "mordant" is applied to certain substances with which the cloth to be dyed must be impregnated, otherwise the colouring matters would not adhere to the cloth, but would be removed by washing. Thus the red colour given to cotton by madder would not be fixed unless the cloth were previously steeped in a solution of salt of alumina. (2.) Where the whole surface receives a uniform tint from one colouring matter, and figures of other colours are afterwards brought up by chemical discharges and reactions. (3.) Where the white surface is impressed with figures in a resist paste, and is aftewards subjected to a general dye. (4.) Steam-colours, in which a mixture of the mordants and dye-extracts is applied to the cloth, and the chemical combination is effected by the agency of steam. (5.) Spirit-colours, consisting of mixtures of dye-extracts with nitro-muriate of tin. The latter are brilliant but fugitive. The machine printers at Lennox-mill earn from 30s. to 50s. a-week; small-block printers, 25s. to 30s.; large-block printers, 30s. to 40s.; and boys 4s. to

7s. In addition to Messrs. Dalglish, Falconer, & Co.'s establishment, there are extensive calico print works at Blanefield, which lies about 5 miles west of Campsie. There was also a cotton-mill in Killearn parish; but the building was destroyed by fire in 1806, and has not been rebuilt. A printfield in the same district was likewise abandoned the following year.

Yarn spinning and woollen manufactures are confined for the most part to Alva, Stirling, and Bannockburn. Up till 1829, blankets and serges were the only goods produced in the first-mentioned village, when the manufacture of shawls was introduced. There are nine spinning-mills in the place, employed on yarns for making shawls, tartan dress goods, tweeds, &c. The mills contain 37 sets of carding-engines, driven by steam and water power. The number of persons engaged is about 220; and the amount of raw material put through in the course of a year is valued at £123,000. Some of the yarn is used in the locality, but the greater part of it goes to agents in Glasgow. The weaving of shawls, handkerchiefs, plaids, and shirtings is the staple trade of the village, and gives employment to about 700 journeymen and 100 apprentices in the busy season, besides from 500 to 600 women who do the winding, twisting, and finishing. A number of young boys are also employed as drawers and twisters. Since shawls and tartans ceased to be fashionable articles of female attire, and since the closing of the ports of the United States to our manufactured goods, trade has been limited to a few months of the year; and that circumstance presses hard on those employed in the weaving business, who generally seek work during the winter months in Galashiels, Selkirk, and Hawick. The value of the manufactured goods runs from about £200,000 to £250,000 annually. The chief market is Glasgow, but a considerable quantity also goes to Manchester, London, and some of the principal Irish towns.

In point of antiquity, the Tillicoultry woollen trade ranks among the first, if it was not the first, in Scotland. Mention is made of its woollen goods in the chartularies of Cambuskenneth so early as the reign of Mary Queen of Scots. At that period, and for about two centuries afterwards, the village was famous for weaving a coarse woollen cloth called "serge," which is described as a species of shalloon, having a worsted warp and woollen weft. It sold at about 1s. a yard, and was long known throughout the country as "Tillicoultry serge"—indeed, that name appears ultimately to have been applied to all serges made in the district. Towards the end of the eighteenth century the current of manufacturing enterprise in Tillicoultry seems to have become stagnant, and the making of serges was transferred to Alva; though it would appear from the old "statistical account" that a market for Alva goods was not easily obtained, it being a common saying that "a serge web from Alva would not sell in the market while one from Tillicoultry remained unsold." Notwithstanding such preference, Alva ultimately carried the trade in that class of goods. In 1792-5 the woollen trade of Tillicoultry appears to have been at its lowest ebb. There were then but 21 weavers in the parish, and the stamp-master (who kept no note of the goods) supposed that 7,000 ells of serge, and an equal quantity of plaiding, would cover the produce that passed through his hands annually from Tillicoultry. The manufacture of muslins was introduced about that time, but apparently met with small success. In 1789, or 1800, John Christie, "an ingenious and energetic native of the village," erected the first woollen factory in Tillicoultry. At a later period he introduced carding machines with improvements of his own. In 1817 the present firm of Messrs. R. Archibald & Sons began business, and soon other woollen factories were erected. The trade at the time was almost solely confined to the production of blankets and plaidings. It is worthy of note that the first "self-acting mulejenny" and "slubbing billy" made in the kingdom were purchased from the inventor and maker, Mr. Smith of Deanston, by Messrs. R. Archibald & Sons, in 1839. The machines are still in the possession of the firm, and in operation.

In these days, when strikes and intimidation are common, it may be interesting to relate an incident which happened in Tillicoultry in the transition period of its manufactures. When spinning machinery was first introduced to do the work which the wives of the village had formerly done with their "muckle wheels," Mr. William Archibald, who possessed the mill now occupied by Messrs. William Gibson & Co., endeavoured to introduce water as a driving power, and for that purpose erected a dam on the Mill Glen burn to divert the water to his mill. The wives considered that such a scheme was neither more nor less than "a new way of playing off an old-fashioned trick—taking the bread out of their mouths by taking the work out of their hands;" and a council of matrons was convened. What transpired at the meeting is not reported; but the result was that they mustered in a body, and armed with spades, hoes, pick-axes, pokers, and tongs, proceeded, "without let or hindrance," to the mill-dam, which they speedily demolished.

About 1824 the manufacture of tartans was introduced into Tillicoultry, and such were the enterprise, energy, and taste brought to bear upon it, and the success by which it was attended, that general prosperity prevailed, and that to such an extent as to add in twenty years over 3,000 to the population. The tartan trade has undergone a considerable change since then;

"clan" patterns, which for many years were paramount, being now almost discarded for "fancy" patterns. Messrs. Paton, of Tillicoultry, have long held a high place in the market for these goods, and their manufactures in tartan have decorated the person of her Majesty the Queen, and serve as hangings in the Royal Palace at Balmoral. The woollen productions of Messrs. Paton are of a varied description, and consist of shawls, tartans for dress, and cloakings of various kinds. The firm employ from 900 to 1000 operatives, and pay annually in wages about £20,000. They have 16 sets of carding-engines in operation, each of which puts through wool to the value of about £2,600—the goods when finished representing about three times that amount. Both water and steam are used to drive the machinery—the former of 25, and the latter of 75 nominal horse-power.

Messrs. R. Archibald & Sons carry on an extensive business in shirtings, shawl goods, tartans, and thin tweeds; and Messrs. J. & R. Archibald, Devondale, have long been famous for the excellence of their Scotch tweeds.

In the parish there are twelve woollen factories, containing 46 sets of carding machines, and employing upwards of 2,000 persons. Besides these there are nine establishments where handloom weaving is carried on, containing in all about 180 looms, and employing nearly an equal number of weavers, whose chief productions are shawls and napkins. In connection with the factories there are 340 hand-looms and about 230 power-looms. Australian and Cape wools are those principally used in Tillicoultry; neither that grown on the Ochils nor on the Cheviots being suitable for the class of goods manufactured.

In Stirling two woollen manufactories are in operation. The most extensive is Forthvale mill, belonging to Messrs. John Todd & Sons. The chief branch of the woollen trade for which these works are used is spinning yarns for the manufacture of tweeds, shawls, and fancy stuffs. There are 6 sets of carding machines and 6,284 spindles employed in the spinning department. The machinery is propelled by an engine of 50 horse-power. The quantity of wool (all foreign) used annually is 376,000 lbs., and the value of the annual production is £30,000. There are 65 persons employed.

The Parkvale and Hayford mills, situated near the village of Cambusbarron, about 2 miles from Stirling, belong to Messrs. Robert Smith & Son, and comprise dyeing, spinning, and weaving by power. The goods manufactured are a superior quality of winceys and other materials for ladies' dresses. Wincey has been brought to the greatest perfection by Messrs. Smith. The warps are composed of cotton yarn, which is chiefly spun in

Lancashire; the wefts are of wool, the produce of the spinning department of the works. In the weaving factory, there are 530 power-looms, and in the spinning department 13 sets of carding-engines. The whole machinery is driven by 6 steam-engines of 300 horse-power in the aggregate. The wools manufactured are English, German, and colonial, and the quantity used annually is 610,000 lbs. The goods made amount in value to from £170,000 to £200,000 per annum, according to the price of raw material. There are in all 950 persons employed. The wages paid annually amount to £19,000.

At Bannockburn there are two extensive works —one owned by Messrs. William Wilson & Sons, the other by Messrs. J. & W. Wilson. That of William Wilson & Sons, embraces spinning, dyeing, and the weaving of carpets, tweeds, and tartans. 14 carding-machines are employed. The quantity of wool used annually, including 50,000 lbs. purchased from other spinners, is 680,000 lbs. The value of the annual production is £80,000; and the number of persons employed is from 500 to 600. Messrs. J. & W. Wilson manufacture carpets only. The wool used annually is 500,000 lbs., and the value of their annual production is about £25,000. They employ 180 hands, including weavers, dyers, and wool-sorters. There are, besides, two small manufactories, in which about 50 persons are employed in weaving tartans and kiltings. The value of their annual production is £45,000.

Manufactories for chemical products are numerous throughout the county. The works of the Hurlet and Campsie Co. were originally the property of Messrs. Mackintosh & Co.—the Mr. Mackintosh who invented the celebrated waterproof cloth, which bears his name. They were started in the year 1806, for the manufacture of alum, copperas, prussiate of potash, prussian blue, &c. The alum and copperas are derived from a schist or aluminous shale, which is found in the coal strata of the Campsie district, and is embedded between the coal and the limestone at a thickness of between 18 inches and 2 feet, the limestone being above and the coal below. The constituent principles of the schistus are various. After the coal has been wrought out, the schist, being exposed to the action of the air, undergoes decomposition. The sulphur it contains is, by the absorption of oxygen, converted into sulphates of the metallic bases with which it is combined, and by its exfoliation readily separates itself from the limestone, and falls down into the space formerly occupied by the coal. When in a state of complete decomposition, the schist assumes a beautiful efflorescent appearance, like that of flock silk, and is very soluble in water. This schistus, as drawn from the coal wastes, is lixiviated at the works in large stone cisterns, and the liquid being afterwards evaporated till it attains the requisite specific gravity, it receives the portion of sulphate or muriate of potash necessary to its formation into the state of crystallizable salt. This is the alum of commerce. In this process, the copperas, existing in the ore, is separated. The prussiate of potash manufactory, which was the first, and for many years the only work of the kind in Great Britain, is upon an extensive scale, and well arranged. This salt is the ferro-cyanate of potassium of chemists. It is used by calico-printers in blue dyeing, also by wool-dyers, and likewise in the manufacture of prussian blue. The exquisite beauty of this salt contrasts strangely with the filthiness of the animal matter out of which it is made. The prussian blue manufactory, which is in connection with the above, produces an article of the finest quality. This product is the result of mutual decomposition of prussiate of potash and sulphate of iron. The present proprietors, with their branch establishment at Port Downie, Falkirk, employ over 300 hands.

At Stirling, Denny, and Falkirk there are several pyroligneous acid works, in which the distillation from wood is used in making iron-liquor for printfields, and also vinegar. The oldest of the firms engaged in this manufacture are Messrs. William M'Laren & Sons and Mr. James M'Alley, Grahamston. The Lime Wharf Chemical Works were started in 1845 by Mr.

James Ross, who has now retired from the business, but the manufactory is still being carried on vigorously and successfully by the present co-partnery.

The spelter works at Lower Greenhill were originally started by Mr. William R. Hutton, who employed between 60 and 70 men. There are 8 double furnaces connected with the manufactory, each of which required 4 men a shift, and were wrought night and day. The charge put into each furnace is 20 cwt. of calamine mixed with ground coal for a flux, which is then heated up—the zinc coming off as a distillate. The produce from the charge is about 7 cwt. This industry was quite a new one to Scotland, the great bulk of the zinc required being previously brought from Germany. There are now, however, a few works of the same kind at Swansea, in England. The calamine, before being put into the furnace, at one time required to be calcined, but Mr. Hutton discovered a process by which this could be done without, and which effected a saving of about 5 per cent. of zinc, apart from the value of coal and labour necessary in the calcining. The working of ore was stopped here some years ago owing to the great difficulty of obtaining the same, and the low prices ruling for spelter. There is, however, one furnace still working, but this produces the spelter from the refuse of the galvanizers, which is an oxide of zinc, and usually contains from 30 to 60 per cent. This refuse formerly had to be carted away as rubbish. It will now produce to an average sized galvanizing work about £300 per annum—the price obtainable for it being from 30s. to £6 per ton. The ore used in the manufacture of calamine and zinc blende is principally found in Spain and Italy, and the mines being eagerly bought up by the continental manufacturers, it can only be got by the British smelter at what to him is ruinous prices. The zinc blende has been occasionally found in England, but in no great quantity. There is, however, a considerable amount of blind blende turned out from the Great Laxey mines in the Isle of Man.

Paper-making is one of the principal industries of the Denny district. Herbertshire mill is the oldest establishment of its kind in the parish, and is the property of William Forbes, Esq. of Callendar. Messrs. Alexander Duncan & Sons carry on at this mill the manufacture of writing and printing papers. They employ about 100 hands—men and women. No material has yet been discovered to supersede the use of linen and cotton rags in making the finer qualities of paper. Many attempts have been made to find other kinds of fibre that would be equally suitable, and the list of substances which have been subjected to a trial is an exceedingly curious one. Up till the year 1857, upwards of 200 patents had been taken out in Britain for the protection of inventions of this kind, and they relate to about fifty varieties of fibre. The list includes asbestos, bean-stalks, clover, dung, gutta percha, heather, moss, nettles, peat, sawdust, seaweed, thistles, and tobacco-stalks. In the year 1772, a book was published at Regensburg, in which there were eighty-one specimens of paper, made from as many different substances. The demand for paper has always threatened to exceed the supply of rags, and hence the desire to find a substitute or auxiliary. The application of machinery to the manufacture of paper is of recent date. Both in preparing the pulp and in making the paper, the appliances used by the early paper-makers were of the simplest kind. The rags, after being thoroughly washed and bleached, were, while still wet, laid in heaps and covered over with sacking. In that way they were allowed to ferment for about a week, when they were taken out and cut into smaller portions by means of a sharp hook. They were next placed in large mortars made of oak, and there pounded with iron-shod rods, kept in motion by either wind or water power. So slow was this process of pulping, that eighty pairs of stamps produced only 1 cwt. of pulp a-day. Even then the work was so imperfectly done, that the stuff had to be pressed into boxes, and allowed to "mellow" for several weeks. After that, it had to be subjected to a series of beatings in the mortars, before it was ready for use. The pulp was next placed in a "vat," along with a certain quantity of water. The fibrous matter was held in suspension by the liquor being constantly stirred by a revolving frame or series of wooden arms. The first important mechanical contrivance introduced into the trade was the pulping-engine invented in Holland about the middle of last century. The tedious method of fermenting the rags and bruising them in a mortar was superseded by this machine, which, in its present improved form, reduces the rags to pulp in a few hours, and is capable of comminuting 5 or 6 tons a-week. The following is an account of the process of paper-making at Herbertshire mill :—As soon as the rags are cut by women across a scythe-blade fixed into a table covered with wire-cloth, for the purpose of getting rid of the dust and sand, they are passed into the boiling-house, where they are boiled for twelve hours; afterwards, they are washed, and broke into a pulp by an iron cistern, called a paper-engine, capable of boiling 1 cwt. of rags, which are beat by a roller with 36 steel bars, which turn on a plate in the bottom of the cistern. 5 of these engines, of 20 steel bars, are kept going night and day, requiring upwards of 40 horse-power to drive them and the other requisite machinery. After the rags are broke in, and bleached for twenty-four hours, they are beat into pulp, or stuff, ready for passing on to the paper-machine, perhaps one of the most complete pieces of machinery ever invented in this country; as, in one room, 60 feet in length by 25 feet wide, one may see the material, much resembling churned milk, passing, by means of a fine web of wire-cloth, 15 feet long, into a series of rollers used in pressing out the water, and forming the paper into a firm body. It then passes into a set of cylinders heated by steam, from which it is reeled into rolls in a perfectly finished state, quite dry and pressed, ready for use. Six of the rolls are then put on to the cutting machine, which cuts them into the sizes required. This machine is capable of cutting 144 sheets per minute of post or writing paper. On an average, 26 cwt. of rags are cut per day, and 21 cwt. of them beat into pulp. The waterwheel for driving the paper-engine is 24 feet diameter, and fully 12 feet wide. It is wholly of iron, and weighs 33 tons. Another small wheel is used for driving the paper-machine, 22 feet diameter, and 18 inches wide. Nearly £150 a-month is paid in wages, the following being the rates:—mill-workers (men and lads), 17s. to 19s. a-week; women, from 7s. to 10s.

A number of extensive quarries have been opened in Stirlingshire since the advent of railways. These have competed with the local quarries in supplying stone to both Edinburgh and Glasgow. The most important are those of Dunmore, Polmaise, and Plean in the neighbourhood of Bannockburn, where the coal measure sandstone terminates. The stone obtained from these quarries is durable, and a number of the houses recently built on the south side of Edinburgh have been constructed of stone from Stirlingshire. In 1867 Mr. James Gowans of Rockville, Edinburgh, who is the most enterprising and extensive lessee of quarries in Scotland, sent from the Plean Quarry a large quantity of stone to be used in the erection of a new warehouse in Paternoster Row, London, for Messrs. Nelson & Sons, publishers. It would be interesting to note the effect of the London atmosphere on the stone of Messrs. Nelson's warehouse, which is composed entirely of silica, as compared with the limestone generally used in London. Had the new Houses of Parliament been built of Scotch stone, there is every reason to believe that the nation would have been spared the regret caused by the premature decay of that costly edifice. And good building stone is abundant all through the west of Scotland. To the north of the Ochil range the rock for a long distance belongs to the old red sandstone. The Scottish Central Railway passes over that formation during its entire route from Stirling to Perth. The stone all through the district referred to is suitable for building purposes. It is durable if used with the strata lying horizontally, but if laid with the strata in a perpendicular position it wears away rapidly. Cases of decay arising from ignorance or neglect of this peculiarity may be seen in the houses of Perth. About 150 men are employed in the freestone quarries of the county. They receive from 20s. to 25s. a week, which is an increase of 25 per cent. on the wages paid thirty years ago. Steam-power is used in the quarries to work cranes, pumps, and inclined planes. Horses are also employed.

Lennoxtown (Campsie) is the favourite district for limestone. There are here three firms presently engaged in the lime trade. Mr. Matthew H. Muirhead of the Balglass works, Mr. Daniel Wilson of the Glorat works, and Mr. John Kirk of the Balgrochan works, who employ in all about 160 hands. This limestone is of the very finest quality, being almost a pure carbonate of lime, as will be seen by the following analysis of a portion of the stone:—

Carbonate of lime,	93.00
Protoxide of iron, ...	2.99
Magnesia, ...	1.30
Insoluble earthy matter,...	2.21
Iron pyrites,	0.50
	100.00

The limestone lies about 2 feet above the coal, and is about 3 feet 10 inches in thickness. Another stratum is found at 9 inches under the coal. It is provincially called the white limestone, and is of very excellent quality. From the quantity of siliceous matter it contains, it possesses peculiar properties of binding where exposed to the weather, as also of setting, in buildings under water. Indeed, it is a stipulation in the schedules of all important contracts that the lime must be that of Lennoxtown. The following are its constituents in 100 parts :—

Carbonate of lime,	83.20
Protoxide of iron, ...	2.17
Insoluble earthy matter,... ...	11.87
Iron pyrites, ...	0.13
Carbonate of magnesia, moisture, &c.,	2.63
	100.00

Stirling is the seat of coach-building. Mr. George Thomson, whose establishment has for many years been foremost in the trade, is known far beyond the bounds of the county, even in the metropolis south of the Tweed, and his handwork is admired wherever it is seen. For waggonettes, landaus, broughams, &c., he carried off the prize medal at Perth in 1850 and 1871; at London, in 1851; at Dublin, in 1854 and 1865; at Edinburgh, in 1869; at Glasgow, in 1870 and 1872; at Dumfries, in 1870; at Kelso, in 1872; and at Stirling in 1873. Strength, lightness, and elegance, combined with suitable accommodation and easy springs, are the objects to which the coachmaker has to pay chief attention, so that the material used must be carefully selected and judiciously combined. In the construction of a carriage six distinct trades are directly concerned, and contributions from as many more are required. Take a brougham, for instance, and trace it through the various stages of construction. As in building a house or a ship, the first thing to be done is to prepare a design—a full-sized chalk drawing of the proposed vehicle on a black-board. The different kinds of carriages derive their names from some peculiar arrangement of the more important parts, but carriages of the same designation may differ widely in details. Persons ordering carriages are allowed an opportunity of inspecting the design, and suggesting alterations thereon, and the result is that it is rare to find two carriages exactly alike. After the chalk drawing has been approved of, operations are commenced. The body-makers take measurements of the upper or principal parts of the drawing, and forthwith begin to make that part, to which their attention is exclusively confined. Equally distinct are the occupations of the carriage-makers, the wheel-wrights, and the smiths. The carriage-makers construct the framework on which the body of the carriage rests, and the pole or shafts. The wheel-wrights are solely occupied in making the wheels. The amount of smith work required for a carriage is considerable, and some of the pieces are exceedingly complicated in shape. The woods chiefly employed in coach-making are ash, mahogany, and oak, and these must be thoroughly "seasoned." Ash strengthened with iron is used in the framework of the "body." The nave, or centre, of the wheel is made of elm, the spokes of oak, and the felloes or rim of ash. Last of all, the painters and trimmers execute their part of the work. In the best class of broughams, however, a piece of currying work has to be done before painting can be proceeded with. The roof and upper part of the back and sides are covered with a hide of leather, which is so manipulated, that, without a seam, it covers the parts mentioned, imparting strength and rendering the carriage waterproof. In all, twenty-five coats of paint and varnish are required. Most carriages are decorated on the wheels, shafts, and other parts, by fine lines of a light colour. These are executed before the varnishing is done, and so are the armorial bearings or monograms, which few carriages are without now-a-days. The heraldic painting is done by a superior tradesman, and some specimens of this kind of work are remarkable for clearness of outline and vividness of colour. When the painting is completed, the carriage is put together and passed to the trimmers, of whom there are two classes—one doing the upholstery work for the interior, and the other the "black-work," or leather fittings. The metallic beading, door-handles, and other decorations of the kind, are obtained from manufacturers who devote special attention to their production. Mr. Thomson, in addition to an extensive home trade, exports a large number of carriages annually. Mr. William Kinross, of Stirling coach works, also does a considerable business throughout the county; while Messrs. J. & A. Fea, Messrs. James Robertson & Son, and Mr. Thomas Hastie, carry on the same industry, on a small scale, at Falkirk. The following are the current rate of wages, earned by piecework and otherwise, in the shops of the two leading firms:—Bodymakers, 20s. to 35s. a-week; carriage-makers, 20s. to 25s.; smiths, 17s. to 30s.; wheelwrights, 21s. to 25s.; painters, 19s. to 26s.; and trimmers, 20s. to 24s.

A distillery was erected in the village of Fintry, by Messrs. Cowan & Co., in 1816, who sent out 70,000 gallons of spirits annually, produced from malt. The kinds of grain used are maize, rye, buckwheat, oats, and barley. For "grain whisky" the latter is converted into malt, which is used in certain proportions, with the other grains in a raw state. There are distilleries also in the Blane Valley (Glenguin), at Gargunnock (Glenfoyle), at Cambus, Bankier, Bonnymuir, Rosebank, and Camelon,—the latter of which was established, some thirty-eight years ago, by the father of the present proprietor, Mr. R. W. Rankine. In the year 1799 there were 87 licensed distillers in Scotland, who paid duty on spirits retained for home consumption to the amount of £1,620,388. That was the first year of the change in the mode of levying duty. Previously so much was paid according to the capacity of the still, but now a 4s. 10¼d. duty was laid on every gallon of spirits made for home consumption. The change was not approved of by the distillers, about a third of whom gave up business in the following year, and the duty decreased to £775,700. The lowering of the duty to 3s. 10½d. in 1802 revived the trade, and the returns for 1803 showed 88 distillers paying £2,022,409. In 1804 progress was checked by another advance in the duty, and the number of distillers dwindled down, until, in 1813, there were only 24. The duty reached 9s. 4½d. a gallon in 1815, but the produce was considerably under a million pounds. It is probable, however, that the quantity of whisky actually made in the county was greater than at any previous time, the high duty tending to foster illicit distillation and smuggling. The lowering of the duty to 2s. 4¾d. in 1823 had the effect of giving an impetus to the trade. The number of licensed distillers greatly increased, and the revenue rose steadily. There were 243 distilleries in 1833, who paid duty to the amount of £5,988,556, the rate then being 3s. 4d. a gallon. Passing over many changes that have taken place in the interval, it may be sufficient to state here that the license duty at present payable by distillers is £10 10s., with 10s. of spirit-duty for every gallon of whisky sent out for home consumption.

The brewery of the county is situated in Falkirk, and belongs to Messrs. James Aitken & Co. The business, which has been conducted for four generations by the same family, has, from first to last, been very successful on account of the superior quality of the "brew;" and year by year "Aitken's Ale" continues to gain wider ground as a favourite beverage. The process of malting embraces four operations—namely, steeping, couching, flooring, and kiln-drying—the object of all being to force the barley to germinate, and then to check the germination at a certain point. Across the end of each of the malting floors is a steep for containing the barley. The grain is run into the steep from the store-loft, and when the steep is partly filled, water is allowed to flow in. After the grain has been steeped for about sixty hours, the superfluous water is run off, and the barley is thrown out of the steep. At this stage it is measured by the excise officers, and charged with malt duty. It is then "couched," that is, allowed to lie in a heap on the floor for twenty-six hours or so, during which time its temperature rises about ten degrees, and it gives off some of the superfluous water. This "sweating," as it is termed, is the result of the partial germination of the barley. On examining the grain at this stage, it is seen that rootlets have begun to appear, and traces of a stem may be detected beneath the husk. Now is the time for "flooring." The barley is spread in an even layer on the floor, to a depth of 6 or 8 inches, and as it dries it is frequently turned. The operation extends over several days, at the end of which the barley is placed in a kiln and dried thoroughly. The action of the kiln in drying is not confined to expelling the moisture from the germinated grain, but serves to convert into sugar a portion of the starch which remained unchanged. Malt is generally distinguished by its colour—as pale, amber, brown, or black malt—arising from the different degrees of heat and the management in drying. The pale and amber coloured varieties are used for brewing the lighter kinds of beer; a darker variety is used for sweet ale; and the darkest for porter. A remarkable change takes place in the grain during its conversion into malt, as will appear from the following analysis:—

	Barley.	Malt.
Hordein (a form of starch),	55	12
Starch,	32	56
Sugar,	5	15
Gluten,	3	1
Gum,	4	15
Resin,	1	1
	100	100

These figures show that the amount of the convertible starch and sugar has been nearly doubled at the expense of the hordein, a portion of which has also passed into the condition of mucilage, or a soluble gum, while the gluten is reduced to one-third of its original quantity. In converting barley into malt a loss of material occurs. Thus, 100 lbs. of barley yield only 80 lbs. of malt; but, on the other hand, there is an increase in bulk, 100 measures of barley yielding 101 to 109 measures of malt. This change in weight and bulk may be tested by casting some grains of barley and malt into water, when it will be seen that, while the barley sinks at once, the malt keeps afloat. The extract of malt is called "wort," and when the tuns are filled, yeast is added to it, in order to start fermentation. In a short time carbonic gas is evolved, and the liquid becomes covered with froth. The gas is so abundant that it becomes dangerous to breathe over the tuns. Even after the vats have been emptied, the gas hangs about, and workmen entering them without ascertaining whether the fatal gas has disappeared, have fallen victims to their negligence. Great skill is required in determining the temperature to which the wort should be reduced before adding the yeast. In summer it is usual to cool it some 20 degrees below the temperature of the tun-room, while in winter it is worked at several degrees above the temperature of the room. The pale amber colour and mild balsamic flavour which characterise Scotch beer are owing in some degree to the low temperature at which it is fermented. The process of fermentation is completed in from three to eight days, and then the yeast is skimmed off and the beer "cleared" by being subjected to a filtering and settling process, which removes all traces of fermentation. That completes the manufacturing operations, and all varieties of beer, ale, and porter are made by processes similar to those above described. The liquor may differ in strength according to the quantity of water used, or in colour from the malt being more or less charred in drying. That beer making has passed through many stages is a matter of history. Our Anglo-Saxon ancestors drank a sweet beer or mead made either from malted grain or from honey, partially alcoholised or fermented; and it was not until the introduction of hops at the beginning of the sixteenth century that any change in national preference for bitter over sweet beer occurred. For some time, indeed, the taste for mead remained, and the old conservatives of the days of Henry VIII. were those who resented the introduction of the newfangled notion from Germany that hops and malt made the best brew. Such as had overcome the repugnance to the bitter flavour, which was first given by means of cloves, wormwood, camomile flowers, &c., to preserve the beverage for prolonged periods, were obstinate in their opposition to the foreign invader, and it required one of Henry's sharp laws to make the employment of hops compulsory and universal.

Shipbuilding is confined, for the most part, to Grangemouth. There Messrs. Dobson & Charles build vessels both of iron and wood, varying from 300 to 1000 tons. The first steamboat built in the port was launched in 1839, being a towing vessel for Memel. To favour this branch of industry, an excellent graving dock was constructed by the late Lord Dundas in 1811, which was capable of taking in two vessels of 300 tons each, and had a depth of water at spring tides of 14 feet. Boatbuilding, chiefly for the canal trade, is also carried on prosperously at Port-Downie, by Mr. Gilbert Wilkie, whose business was established about twenty years ago, under the firm of Messrs. Mackay & Wilkie. Sails and ropes are manufactured both at Grangemouth and Bainsford. Timber yards and saw mills are very numerous in this district, the most extensive being situated in the "Port," Grahamston, Bonnybridge, and Larbert.

In St. Ninians there are two leather manufactories, and in Falkirk four, in the majority of which currying as well as tanning is performed. The latter is the more important process. The object of the tanner is to destroy in the hides and skins the liability to putrefaction common to animal matter, and to render them impervious to the action of agents which would decompose them under ordinary circumstances. This is done by steeping the skins in an astringent liquid prepared from bark. The active principle eliminated from the bark is called *tannin* or tannic acid, which forms a chemical combination with the skins. The bark of the oak is the most valuable to the tanner, and is most extensively used; and for a long time no other substance was employed in tanning. The demand for oak bark having come to exceed the supply, various substitutes were tried, among these being heath, myrtle leaves, wild laurel leaves, birch bark, and oak sawdust. Varied results attended the experiments, but oak bark has never lost its supremacy. The hides arrive at the tannery in one of three states—they are either fresh from the slaughter-house, salted, or dried. The fresh hides give least trouble, but the salted and dried ones require special manipulation to make them soft. The hair in all cases is removed by steeping the hides in a solution of lime and water. As the hides, after steeping a certain time, are withdrawn from the pits, they are laid on a sloping bench, with a convex top, and subjected to scraping with a large two-handled knife. That operation completed, they are conveyed to the tan-yards, in which are a series of square tanks of various sizes, divided by walls; while each is also furnished with a waste-pipe, by which it may be emptied. The hides prepared for sole leather are washed and dried after being taken from the tan-pits, and are then ready for use. Those that have to be dressed are removed from the tan-yards to the currying shops, where the leather is scoured, and, by a series of operations, brought into a condition for use. The currier's occupation, though not one of the most pleasant-looking, is one of the most healthy of trades. The work, however, is very laborious. The average wages may be stated at 26s. a week; tanners earn 20s., and tannery labourers 16s.

Dynamite is manufactured at Redding, near Falkirk, by the British Dynamite Company (Limited), who have a still larger establishment at Stevenston, near Saltcoats. At these works sulphuric acid is made in the usual way from sulphur or pyrites. By the action of the acid on nitrate of soda, nitric acid is got and bisulphate of soda, which is a bye-product. These are the only chemical re-agents required. A mixture of two parts of sulphuric acid and one of strong nitric acid is made, and to this glycerine is added with careful regulation of temperature. After standing, the mixture is poured into cold water, when the nitro-glycerine sinks to the bottom as a heavy oily fluid. It is washed to get rid of the sulphuric acid, which is afterwards recovered, and then it is converted into dynamite by mixture with some inert substance. That which was originally employed by Nobel was *Kieselguhr*, a very friable siliceous matter from Oberlohe, in Hanover; an intimate mixture of about 25 parts of this was made with about 75 of nitro-glycerine in a porcelain vessel. This is the material used both at the Stevenston and Redding works. Instead of it charcoal powder, fine sand, sawdust, finely ground burned clay, &c., have also been employed. The last stages of the manufacture consist in making the dynamite into cartridges, in which form it is packed and ready for sale. This substance is a most valuable agent in mining and quarrying. It is not affected by damp, and it requires far less labour in boring blast holes than gunpowder, besides being about eight times more powerful.

Candlemaking, before the invention and introduction of gas, was no mean industry. Excepting the finer sorts, such as wax and spermacetic candles, no great business, however, is now done in this branch of trade. Mr. John Rintoul, of Falkirk, is the oldest representative of candle manufacture in the shire, and his chief work in these more illuminated times is tallow for the mines. But common candles are still made, which are either dipped or moulded. As the quality of the article depends on the material employed in the manufacture, the first part of the tallow-chandler's process is the sorting of the tallow. Mutton suet, with a proportion of ox tallow, is selected for mould candles, because it gives them gloss and consistence. Coarse tallow is reserved for the dipped candles. After being sorted it is cut into small pieces preparatory to being melted; and to prevent putrefaction this is done immediately after the fat is taken from the carcase. When fused a considerable time, the membranous matters collect at the surface, constituting the *cracklings* used sometimes for feeding dogs, after the fat has been squeezed out of it by a press. The liquid tallow is strained through a sieve into another copper, where it is treated with water at a boiling temperature in order to wash it. After a while, when the foul water has settled to the bottom, the purified tallow is lifted out by means of tinned iron buckets, into tubes of moderate size, where it concretes, and is ready for use. It is a remarkable circumstance that the wicks for the best dipped candles are still cotton rovings imported from Turkey, notwithstanding the vast extension and perfection of cotton-spinning in this country. Four or more of these Turkey skeins, according to the intended thickness of the wick, are wound off at once into bottoms or clues, and afterwards cut by a simple machine into lengths corresponding to those of the candles to be made. With modern machinery about 8,000 dipped candles can be manufactured per day by a single workman. But the more outlandish districts of the country can only produce a demand for the means of supply. And that demand is comparatively a *bagatelle*. Lime-light, however, may, by-and-by, do the same for gas as gas has done for candle. City streets and railway stations have begun it.

CHAPTER XLI.

SPORTS AND GAMES.

MUCH has been said for and against gymnastic exercises. One folly committed arises from the conclusion, that if exercise is good for the health, the more violent and exhausting it is the more good is done. But, judiciously conducted, the practice of gymnastics is essential for shaping and moulding frames of manly grace and vigour. They fortify the general health, strengthen the nerves, and induce an address, a hardihood, and a presence of mind in danger, difficult of attainment without them. Their mental and moral influence is consequently great. They tend to equalise the spirits, invigorate the intellect, and calm the temper. Physical culture, in short, means the effectual training of the body in the offensive and defensive warfare of the battle of life.

At a time when national safety depended on the superiority of individual muscular exertion, rather than of refined strategies and polemical machinery,—when a battle resembled rather a scramble of wild beasts, in which the strongest took the best share of the booty, than an united, organised, and scientific system,—institutions tending to the development of the bodily powers began to be recognised among the Greeks as advantageous, if not necessary to their military success. But the champions of old, so renowned for strength of sinews, with their massy clubs and sevenfold shields, would at present make but a poor figure in a battle, or at a siege, against muskets and artillery; and, even in ancient times, Cicero remarks that though Ajax was much more robust than Nestor, yet the Grecian general says nothing of the former, but avows that if he had ten such as Nestor in his army he should soon demolish Troy. Setting aside the morality of the question, it is by no means certain that we should be at all the better off were we systematically to weed out all our weaker branches. Many of our most useful men—statesmen, merchants, manufacturers, poets, scientific workers, artists, and handicraftsmen—have been persons of weak or medium physique. Nay, even our own greatest soldiers are not always the strongest and stoutest of men. The Napier family, race of born warriors as they are, have always been noticeable for their ill health; and Moltke has a frame which he would hardly pass in one of his own corporals. It is thus that gymnastic excellence, considered by itself, is asserted to be of little use; that the occasions are few on which society requires us to leap over a five-barred gate, or to climb a pole, or to hang with our head downwards. Though this be true, it is apparent to every one that health is generally found in conjunction with strength, and that strength is without doubt increased by muscular exertion. The connection between life and health is too patent to be insisted on. For some other purpose, then, is the leaping-pole necessary than that of avoiding the necessity and delay of clambering over or unlocking gates; it is necessary—we speak generally—for our strength, and the prolongation of our health and existence. Life and health walk hand in hand; health is nothing but integrity of life; disease is nothing but an offence and abbreviation of it. Gymnastic exercise will not, under all circumstances, be successful, but, *cæteris paribus*, it will be in creating fine men. By which expression is not to be understood plump or fat men, for that fatness is the result rather of ease than of labour may be gathered from a visit to the cattle show. We have, however, at last discovered that Providence has made lambs to skip and kittens to play; and it has come to be pretty generally understood that boys and girls are not so unlike other small young creatures which make little foolish runs and rushes and bounds and summersaults, expressive of the simple truth that they find existence a joy.

But, first, as to the sports of the shire. During the later life of Mr. Ramsay of Barnton and Sauchie, some thirty years ago, horse-racing occurred annually on the course at Stirling. The animals that ran, were, as a rule, the finest and foremost in the country; but with the death of the leading spirit of the meetings their career also closed. This, however, was by no means a matter of general regret. The turf was then, as it still is, on the decline. And little wonder. Its speculations increase the cares of life—do not suspend them. A set of unprincipled miscreants, with their deep-laid stratagems as depredators, have sealed its doom. No doubt it is interesting and exciting to see displayed, in perfection, the full powers of the race-horse; but there was a wide moral difference between the Olympia games of Greece and the modern Newmarket. At the ancient sports, honour was the reward of the winner, and no man lost either his character or his money.

The tournament, evidently derived from the Ludus Trojæ, is now the subject of antiquarian research. James I. had used his influence to suppress the sanguinary tournament; but James II. revived it. In 1449, two noble Burgundians named Lalaine, one of them, Jacques, as celebrated a knight as Europe could boast, and the squire Meriadte, had challenged two of the Douglases and Halket, to fight with lance, battle-axe, sword, and dagger. Clad in complete mail, and having been solemnly knighted by his Majesty, they engaged in the valley of Stirling. Soon throwing away the lance, they had recourse to the axe, when one of the Douglases was felled outright, and the king, seeing the combat unequal, threw his baton down—the signal of cessation. James Douglas and De Lalaine had approached so close, that of all their weapons none remained save a dagger in the hand of the Scottish knight. De Lalaine seized him so firmly by the wrist of the hand which held the weapon, that Douglas could not use it. The other arm he held below the arm-pit, so that they turned each other round the lists for a considerable time. Simon de Lalaine and Halket were strong, but unskilled in warding the axe, and had soon crushed their visors, weapons, and armour. Meriadet's antagonist, a Douglas, had attacked him with the lance. The butt end of Meriadet's axe knocked it out of his hand, and, ere he could undo his own axe, he was felled to the ground. Regaining his feet, and renewing the assault, he was once more laid prostrate, never to rise.

Wrestling, long a favourite athletic exercise, for the discontinuance of which in the gymnasia we see no reason other than the mutability of fashion, is generally falling into contempt. Hawking has disappeared. Shooting, while still common where game abounds, has lost the wild sportsman-like character of earlier days; though, all credit to the pluck of our young aristocracy, when with the early autumn they take to the heather and stubble as young ducks to water, and with cutting winds full in their face, under driving rain and sleet, stalk the deer on the bleak highland hills. Fox-hunting, no doubt, stands its ground; but fears are entertained even for the king of sports. It is difficult to determine when the first regularly appointed pack of fox-hounds appeared among us. Dan Chaucer gives us the thing in *embryo:*—

> "Aha, the fox! and after him they ran;
> And eke with staves many another man.
> Ran Coll, our dogge, and Talbot, and Garlond,
> And Malkin with her distaff in her hond."

At the next stage, neighbouring farmers, probably, kept one or two hounds each, and on stated days met for the purpose of destroying the sneaking vermin that had been doing damage in their poultry yards. By-and-bye, a few couples of strong hounds seem to have been kept by small country squires, who, on occasions, joined packs. Such were called trencher hounds, implying that they ran loose about the house, and were not confined in kennel. For several years, the Stirling and Linlithgowshire fox-hounds have met regularly for sport, and many a lively day has been enjoyed "through bush through briar."

Ladies, too, were wont to unsex themselves for the run. With scarlet riding-dress, masculine head-gear, flushed countenance, and dishevelled locks, the huntress came bounding to the covert side. Undismayed by showers of mud from horses' hoofs, by hedge and fence, gate and stile, she scoured the country, screeching forth a tally-ho! at reynard's departure, and a whoo-hoo-hoop! at his death.

The games, past and present, of the county are endless in their variety. Bullet-throwing on the public highway has happily been discontinued through the action of the police; pitching the quoit is confined to agricolous persons after their day's toil; and the ball is too generally, and without cause, despised. The latter would hardly, perhaps, at the present day be considered worthy of a place amongst gymnastic exercises; but that it is an exercise of the greatest advantage there can be little doubt, and more dignity may be imparted to it by mentioning it under other names, as football or cricket, which, says Johnson, is a sport in which the contenders drive a ball with sticks in opposition to each other. This definition would, in fact, apply equally well or better to hockey; but, on reflection, we may discover, without the aid of the lexicographer, that cricket, our national pastime, of which we are so justly proud, is essentially and primarily a game at ball. For a sport, however, which can be enjoyed at any time of the year, in any weather, and without any of the trouble that is incidental to so many of the other kindred pastimes, commend us first of all the game of rounders. There are few, perhaps, who cannot recall the luxury of an occasional relaxation in that way, after the fatigue and *ennui* of a long and tedious outing at cricket. We can picture, as if it were but yesterday, the jollity that reigned supreme in the cricket-field when rounders were proclaimed as the sport next on the programme; and it seemed like a waif from the great ocean of the past, when, last summer, we had a chance of renewing our old intimacy with the game, at the invitation of a *posse* of mirth-loving schoolboys, as we passed across the airy tryst-ground at Larbert. The bowling-green is another popular place of resort for recreation. And it has this advantage that it suits the old as the middle-aged. It has been imagined that gymnastic exercise is exclusively profitable to the young. It is not so; it is of advantage, of great advantage, likewise to the old. With our seniors, the increasing weight of the body, and the loss of the so-called "animal spirits," induces the desire of repose, and they need an increase of exercise beyond that which inclination enjoins on them. Thus they are brought within the province of the gymnastic code. Though the pastime mentioned has not the magical effect of beauty—

"A withered hermit, fourscore winters worn,
   Might shake off fifty, looking in her eye"—

some perceptible advantage may yet be obtained by any old man who will be childish enough to play even at ball. Military ardour, combined with a love of their country, has formed our youths into various rifle companies, in which the exercises prescribed are advantageous for the same reason, viz., general muscular development, though perhaps to a lesser extent than with those of the golf, cricket, or foot-ball fields. And this fusing together of civil and military life is a matter of which to be proud. We have it on reliable anthority that many of these Volunteers manœuvre with as much apparent facility, and perform not only battalion but divisional movements with as great precision and accuracy, as if soldiering were the business of their lives. Few even of its bitterest enemies longer dare to call our "cheap defence of nations" a mere myth; or have the boldness to deny its *prestige* as a moral and physical power in the land.

A Denny archers' club was instituted in 1828, which competed annually for the captaincy, at a distance of 100 yards, the captain being preses for the year; for two poisoned arrows from the island of Mombase, at the distance of 160 yards; for a silver medal, at 50 yards; for three prizes of arrows, at 30 yards; and for a silver arrow, at the same distance—the successful competitors being vice-presidents. The medal and arrows remained in the possession of the successful competitors; while the others were shot for annually. Many picturesque proverbial expressions belong to the bow. "An archer is known by his aim, not by his arrows." "Draw not thy bow before thy arrow be fixed." "He hath twice or thrice cut Cupid's bow," says Don Pedro in the comedy of *Much Ado about Nothing*; "and the little hangman dare not shoot him." "A word spoken is an arrow let fly." The maiden who kept a lover in reserve, lest her admirer should prove faithless, was said to have two strings to her bow—an expression which arose from the military archers having used a double string in the field, to prevent delay in refitting the bow in case of accident. "Even the holy man of God will be better with his bow and arrow about him." Homer says—

"the string let fly
Sounds shrill and sharp like the swift swallow's cry;"

but though the *Iliad* has frequent allusions to this sport, the most finished picture of Grecian archery occurs in the *Odyssey*. Gibbon, the Roman historian, exclaims, "Methinks I see the attitudes of the archer—I hear the twang of his bow." Many of our early poets indulge in this favourite species of illustration; yet none have so happily applied the technicalities of his craft as Shakespeare, himself a practised bowman from his midnight visitations to Sir Thomas Lucy's deer park. Even at the present day, we "kill two birds with one shaft;" and "get the shaft hand of our adversaries." When familiar with the foibles of friend or foe, we have "found the measure of his shaft." The triumph of making an enemy's machinations recoil upon himself is "to outshoot a man in his own bow." Our ancestors of every rank and profession practised archery, regarding it as an important branch of manly education. Of Henry VIII, Paulus Jovius says, "no man in his dominions drew the great English bow more vigorously than Henry himself; no man shot further, or with a more unerring aim." And the present Queen has given a proof of real British feeling by the appointment of a master of archery among her household officers. But while the example of the noble and the wealthy had, no doubt, considerable influence on the spread of modern archery, its own intrinsic excellencies were its chief recommendations. Requiring no excessive corporeal exertion, and associated, as a rule, with refined and polished society, the bow, of all amusements, appears specially adapted for dissipating the *ennui* of the fair. The piano and embroidery frame are both good enough in their way, but

> "In the good greenwode,
> Among the lilie flower,"

health and vivacity can be got, which the pure breath of nature can alone bestow.

In 1835, a curling club was also started in Denny. Mr. John Carnie, of Curling Hall, Largs, received here the rudiments of his skill as a curler. John was the second son of Mr. Neil Carnie—a principal partner in the firm of Messrs. Thomas Sheils & Co., of Herbertshire printfield. On the Carron and the reservoirs of the establishment, John first shone in the game, and acquired that knowledge which enabled him to write a standard work on curling, and to invent a rink which, on any morning, when there was a little frost, might, by a slight suffusion of water over its surface, present in four hours (the thermometer at 28°) the finest and firmest ice a curler could desire. But now every parish throughout the county has its senior and junior clubs. And one or two of the late winters have afforded rare opportunities for the enjoyment of the " roaring game." Though men talk sadly of the good old years when they could count confidently on so many weeks of black frost, with dams and "dubs" bound in iron, few, we presume, will now dare to repeat the slander that old winter has well-nigh got all his wonted energy and grip drained out of him. He is, we see, when he cares to show his piercing " ivories," still the powerful potentate of the past. Not for some forty years have we had winter storms so protracted and intense. The snow fell generally to a depth of several feet; and many were its deep drifts in nook and by-way.

Such seasonable weather brought forcibly to mind the great snow storm of '23, the flakes of which, as we have been told, began to fall on a Sabbath afternoon in February of that year, when the principal thoroughfares had all to be "cast," and even for weeks after the thaw set in, our seniors speak of having walked to kirk and market between great walls of congelated snow. Another heavy storm fell three years later; and a third in October of '36, when the cereal stooks stood buried in the warm winding-sheet in which mountain, moor, and field were so prematurely wrapped. And when the winter so braces itself up, and thus grandly displays its sparkling ensigns, there is much to interest and even charm the eye. The usual harsh industrial din comes muffled to the ear. Horse-hoofs strike no sound from the crusted causeway, and street vehicles softly spin along. Then, what in art can match the frostal tracery of rime pencilled on the humblest window pane; the eave-array of icicles; and the myriad plumes and pearls of tree and hedge? Beautiful, too, beyond all rivalry, the ice-drapery of the rocks, where the water-springs, trickling down their ragged face, give form to the pendant pillar. And as we pass farm-yards which the snow has turned into vignettes for winter idylls, we thank God for the fall and the warmth it gives the fields, on whose fertility we so much depend for sustenance.

Of all recreations for the unbending of mental strain, curling is, no doubt, the chief. Jovial and jolly are all of the frantic groups that form the pitted players. What a wild flourishing of "cowes!" What airy, eager "soopings," as the missioned stone runs along the rink from tee to tee! The ice may be "bauch," hence the occasional necessity of warmly welcoming up the shot. Let us here give a few of the characteristic phrases of the curliana brotherhood. Social equality is the order of the day:—"O man, Laird, that's a bonnie curl! That's grand wark! Come on, my laddie; I like ye; come on—a perfect pat-lid. I say, Earl, hand up that cowe. Leave her tae hersel'. She's a stane that kens the tee. There she gangs, roarin' in, straucht as a craw's flicht. Weel played, Laird! You for a curler!" Or hear skip No. 2 as the Doctor lifts his stone:—"Noo, Doctor, I want ye tae pit a lang guard on that. Dae ye see my cowe? Weel, jist play till't cautiously, my man. Dinna attempt the tee; the port's stret. There she comes rowin' and spinnin'. O Geordie, soop her! soop her! She's a howg! she's a howg! Dag on't, Doctor, ye've spoilt a'. But let her come hame. There she curls—a bonnie laid-down stane. Leuk at that, Cauldhame. Touch't if ye can. That's what I ca' weedin' them oot tae some purpose. A bonnie curl, Doctor. Come owre and gie's a grup o' your hand. It was a feather i' the kep o' oor club that nicht we brithered ye." And so right merrily goes the match, contested ever with the kindliest feeling, and closed—no matter who wins, for one side or other must—with the friendliest congratulations. But, as we have indicated, it is also keenly contested. Not only "honour" depends on the result, but the dinner of beef and greens that has to be defrayed by the losers.

Skating is another exciting amusement on the ice. Peculiarly enlivening, even for the mere spectator, is the sight of disporting crowds shooting hither and thither in the most graceful groups and gyrations. And the skating part now generally played by the ladies, renders such exhibitions all the more picturesque. Need we say that many of the fair skate with exquisite ease and skill—skim, in fact, over the glassy surface like swallows on the wing, and seem quite as familiar with the *modus operandi* as any of the sterner sex. Here and there, it is true, a mere learner is to be seen snatching, as she toils and staggers along, at the empty and intangible air; but such ludicrous appearances are as common with Tom and Harry as with Berta and Nell. The best lady skaters in the world are probably to be found in the great cities of Lower Canada, Montreal, Quebec, or Ottawa, where balls, carnivals, and other ice parties are matters of regular occurrence, and the skating rink is a national institution. Two of the finest figure pictures in groups that were ever done in photography were those of the "Fancy Ball" and the "Carnival" given at Montreal, on the Victoria Rink in honour of Prince Arthur, H.R.H. Duke of Connaught. They were executed by command of Her Majesty, every figure in them, some hundreds in number, being portraits taken separately, and afterwards grouped by the celebrated photographer, Notman. All the figures in both pictures are on skates, the range of costumes adopted being very wide — Turkish sultanas, gipsies, Indians, fairies, and historical characters alike careering along in dizzy waltzes or stately quadrilles.

The only fishing club in the shire is connected with the county town. This year's competition took place on Loch Leven, at which there was a strong muster, 33 members being out in 17 boats. The united takes of the club amounted to 353 trout, weighing about 274 pounds. The heaviest single fish caught was 2 lb. 2 oz. Inland sport is every day becoming more restricted, owing to causes too obvious to require specification, and sportsmen will be driven, in spite of choice or preference, to the open coasts and sheltered bays to find that enjoyment in fishing or shooting which is to them the salt of life.

To our more youthful readers we would say, on parting—cultivate early, familiar intercourse with the book of nature, and the landmarks of history. Perhaps no study could be found more beneficial for health, and, at the same time, so fraught with mental benefit and pleasure, as the so-called "hobby" of the topographer. And in this world there is need for acquiring sources of enjoyment apart from society and its various spheres of recreation. Let these lines be deeply engraven on the tablet of every juvenile mind :—

> " Life is a thorny beaten track,
> Where man works out his busy day,
> And passes joys upon the way,
> For which he fain would travel back."

CHAPTER XLII.

SOCIAL FEATURES.

"SCOTLAND is drinking itself to death." So we are told from time to time by our neighbours south of the Tweed. And the question naturally comes—How far is the alarming assertion true? We need not, ostrich-like, cover our eyes to avoid the sight of danger. There can be no doubt that matters are bad both in town and country as regards excessive indulgence in stimulants. Unhappily, we live in a land where thirsty men are to be found by the million—human beings overwhelmed by a perpetuity of thirst; and lamentable scenes are the consequence. A score of highly-coloured pictures appeal every day to the heart of the philanthropist. In our police cells, batches of men and women are weekly to be seen prostrate through overdoses of alcohol. On the public streets men reel and tumble, and carry poverty and ill-nature to their wretched homes. No disparaging comparisons; but pride ourselves as we may on our social progress, we have not, after all, got a long way in advance of those days upon which we are so wont to cast a slur. No opportunity is lost of congratulating ourselves on our improvement of behaviour as contrasted with the bacchanalian habits of the last, or penultimate generation. And, unquestionably, *gentlemen* do not get drunk now-a-days in the gross fashion that was common even amongst our grandfathers. At least they do not drink, as a rule, so as to lose their heads or legs. Not so long ago, three bottlemen were common in society; but such human casks have gone the way of the dodo and pterodactyl. Even the formality of taking wine with each other at table, especially the practice of drinking healths, is fast becoming obsolete. Still, while admitting that the scandal of open drunkenness has gone from the upper and middle classes, it must not be forgot that a man may be intoxicated without being helplessly drunk. Inebriation means slow poisoning, and the amount of this suicidal conduct which is constantly going on is terrible to think of. Nothing can be more hurtful to both body and mind than the general habit during the day of "nipping"—the most mischievous phenomena of our social life—whether the liquor taken be bar sherry, petroleum whisky, or doctored gin. Osiris, the great god of Egypt, was the first distiller of whisky on record; and in the Greek epigram of Julian, we find this so-called "barley-wine" described as "false Bacchus, fierce and hot; child born of Vulcan's fire, to burn up human brains." But whence all this morbid craving for narcotics? Comes it from the extraordinary facility with which we exhaust life? Is it to keep up the nervous energy required to go through business, with its pressing cares and worrying anxieties, that alcohol is resorted to? Excess of activity is generally followed by a state of depression in which the subject of it looks at everything past and present in a gloomy light, and which produces in some systems a desire for liquor as a Lethe of the soul. But it is evident, for one thing, that we are deficient in the knowledge of physical laws, and the means of preserving health. If we push brain activity to an extreme, we enfeeble our body; and if we push bodily activity to an extreme, we make our brains inert. And it is this antagonism between body and brain that not unfrequently creates the craving for alcoholic drinks.

Stirlingshire, however, is by no means as black as it has been painted in the sweeping assertion from the south. Statistics could be given from the rolls of co-operative building societies, and savings banks to prove the fact. Indeed, the great bulk of the population bear the highest respectability of character; and many, in the larger industrial districts, sit as landlords under their "own vine and fig-tree." In Falkirk, too, the earliest of the temperance societies was formed—a movement that has done good work, from its institution till now, in checking the havoc which strong drink has made, and is making, with the manhood, independence, and vigour of the people.

Nor has Falkirk ever been wanting in "wags" and "wits." We have heard various jests emanate from the punning brotherhood. Here is one: —Mr. H., "Very cauld the nicht, Mr. G." Mr. G., "Many are called, but few are chosen." Mr. H., "If they are not chosen they wont be lang cauld." On another occasion, Mr. H., having lent a professor of the terpsichorean art about £20, was rebuked by his own brother, who had casually seen the I O U, for his too ready and liberal spirit in thus accommodating all and sundry in his circle of friends. "How can you ever expect, Sandy," said John, "to see such a sum in your hands again from an itinerant dancing-master?" "Leave that to me," was the reply; "if necessary, I can take *steps* to recover it." One morning Mr. H. observed a professional brother, who was one of Pharaoh's lean kine, pushing along the High Street eating a spelding. The salutation was—" Good morning, Mr. A.; glad to see you; never saw you look so like your meat."

In the spring of the present year the homes of many of the moulding class were temporarily darkened by a series of strikes. Prices of goods had fallen, and the masters, to make both ends meet, notified a reduction in the rate of wages. This the men objected to, and "struck;" but latterly and wisely they gave in, and returned to work at the reduced scale. Pity it is that everywhere we see capital pitted against labour, and labour against capital. The very backbone of the great industrial system would seem to have somehow got out of joint. Let us boast no more for the present of our unrivalled success in the paths of the Baconian philosophy. One of the most unhappy signs of the times is unquestionably the lamentable enmity and discord that has of late years sprung up between the workman and capitalist; and if the general trade and commerce of Britain is not to be utterly paralysed, a more harmonious spirit must be introduced into the intercourse of employers and men. In France, some years ago, 28 miners of Auzin were imprisoned as felons, for simple combination with a view to raise the wages of their class; but in this country strikes are no longer put down by the influence of terror. Here the days of feudal servitude, with their penal code and red-hot brand, have been left behind. British labour is completely free to determine its price; and it is the workman's bounden duty to sell his vigour of limb or mechanical skill in the best market. But assuredly they are not the pioneers of our industrial progress—sworn enemies, forsooth, to all order and prosperity—who, in the guise of benefactors of the race, strut stumpingly in public, and, with irritating discussions on the subject of wages, stir up strife and widen the breach for peace and goodwill between the employer and the employed.

Fifty years ago, the ignorance of the collier community was notorious. Isolation, together with universal inter-marriages, had no doubt a good deal to do with their intellectual weakness. Several capital stories are told of several of the class. The Rev. Dr. Knox of Larbert, calling upon a family at Kinnaird, asked Dick, the head of the house, by way of pastoral interrogation, " how many persons there were in the Godhead." Dick was puzzled; and so followed the minister's sharp rebuke. "Noo comes my turn," says the collier, "if ye will aloo me, Doctor, tae pit a bit question tae yersel'. How mony links wud ye say were in our pit chain?" Dick's eyes flashed with delight, for the Doctor was thoroughly outwitted. "I cannot answer that, my good man," replied the pastor; "and, perhaps, nobody but yourself could." "Go, billy!" exclaimed Dick, "every yin, I see, tae their ain trade; you tae yours, Dr. Knox, and me tae mine." On another occasion, the Rev. John Bonar stepped in upon a collier family in the same village, and, amongst other inquiries, asked the mistress whether the gudeman ever took the books? "Books! what's that?" said the simple-minded woman. "Well, well!" observed the clergyman, "but you are in a dreadful state of darkness here!" "Ye maunny say that, minister, for it's no yet a week gane sin' oor Tam put in a bonnie bit window there, whaur we had naething but a bole afore." "You misunderstand me altogether, my good woman," observed Mr. Bonar, in explanation; "I mean, does your husband ever engage in family worship, by singing and praying?" "No, no, sir; I'll tell nae lee. Our Tam's no a singer, but he's the best whistler in a' the raw." It is different now, however, with the community of whom we speak. They have always borne the character of a temperate and hard-working class; and, at the present day, are, in point of intelligence, at least equal to any of the ordinary working men. The children, too, have had a great advantage over their parents in regard to education. No pit village has been without its school for many years; and for the support of the teacher the coalmaster reserves a fee of two-pence per week from each man, and that quite irrespective of the number of his family. To make matters still plainer—he who has no progeny to educate, has nevertheless the fourpence a fortnight to pay, towards the salary of the schoolmaster, with his neighbour who may have given a dozen "hostages to fortune." Girls are held somewhat at a discount. When a daughter, for example, comes home to the family, she is practically spoken of as a "hutch of dross;" whereas, when the little stranger appears in the sex of a son, he has the higher valuation of a "hutch of coals."

The feeing-fair, either in Stirling or Falkirk, is the great half-yearly holiday of the farms. Many of both sexes visit the market purposely for an engagement; but the majority, having been previously hired, go merely on pleasure bent. A registry has been frequently spoken of for this class of servants, and such an institution, where something of the character of the applicant could be known, would certainly be more satisfactory for the employer. At present, the farmer, as a rule, engages his ploughman and dairymaid, if they happen to be single, from mere physical appearance and a casual question with reference to their former master. But the feeing-day, as we have said, is devoted chiefly to "daffin." Let us attempt to recall the spirit-stirring spectacle. A merry crowd, indeed! in which there is the very extreme of gaiety and *abandon*. Everywhere, along the public street, the swarming, streaming mass shout and jostle in riotous merriment. The girls—coarse and coaxing—appear in the strongest colours of gala attire; and, as they seldom get the opportunity of turning out in their best gear, they come to town on a fair-day (to use their own figurative language) "dressed to death." Jolly beyond description are one and all of the jubilant throng. A fiddle, above all things, they cannot stand. Its music takes their heels, just as intoxicants take their heads. But when the weather is wet, the "droukit" and drunken scene is truly pitiful. Then it is that the taverns are also crowded with a roaring rabble; and from out these lower dens the country lads, "fouish and frisky," swagger and reel, ready for any *role* of rollicking rudeness. "Sandie" could not be a whit more amorous though he were wooing "Nancie" under the milk-white thorn.

> "And in a fit of frolic mirth,
> He strives to span her waist;
> Alas! she is so broad of girth,
> She cannot be embraced."

But it must be remembered that manners in the country are different, in degree, from those of the town. Were certain city belles—modest Flora, for example, who puts the legs of her piano into pretty frilled trousers—present to see how their rustic cousins fare at harvest-homes, how their feelings of propriety would be shocked.

And what of the dancing? such an impassioned scene gives the lie to the French impeachment, that we take our amusements dolefully. We have frequently been spectators of the rustic festival; and our country cousins are *par excellence* the dancers. They are a noisy but joyous race, who seem to feel gladness more than any other class. No doubt their terpsichorean frolic is somewhat vulgar and boisterous. We could scarcely speak of the festal hall—"Rankine's Folly," or the Corn Exchange—as a temple

> "Where love possessed the atmosphere,
> And filled the breast with purer breath;"

but even a rude joviality of temper is surely neither sign nor proof of an utter disregard of morality. They are indeed greatly at sea who would have the cheery and happy lot placed on the same platform with the drunken Helots of old, who were a laughing-stock for Spartan boys. Why should the "Haymakers," for example, be to the rustic lads and lasses, on a feeing-day, another "Danse Macabre?" And if there is nothing wrong, but something rather commendable, in a Volunteer or foundry ball, why should our isolated ploughmen and their sweethearts be denied similar festive recreation? Many a time we have seen "the doves censured while the crows were spared."

Recently a Cockney critic gave a clever, but somewhat distorted and exaggerated picture of a Scotch feeing fair. He describes the lads and lasses as dressed out "in their best"—the former with well-groomed heads and brilliant neckties, and the latter with "staring gowns," "flaunting ribbons," and towering chignons of "frizzled wool and horse-hair." He sees, moreover, only the crowds and the dissipation, and discovers in the scene an easy and unerring clue to all the national scandal which figures in the Registrar's returns. Surely this sweeping conclusion errs in so far as it seems to ascribe too much good behaviour to all the rest of the year. The *Saturday* reviewer takes no account, for example, of the temptations which prevail at other seasons, such as the "coming through the rye," the wooing "when the kye come hame," or the gallant conveys "amang the rigs o' barley." We may rely upon it that the great majority of the ploughmen and dairymaids who attend the feeing market, and share in its exuberant hilarities over much hearty renewal of acquaintance, know very well how to take care of themselves. Not in vain have these agricultural serving men and maidens attended parish schools and churches, and been present at the "Saturday nights" of venerable and pious cottars. The writer in the *Saturday*, aiming, not without success, at a highly spiced literary performance, clearly makes too much of it. He has endeavoured to produce, in prose, a kind of companion picture to Burns's "Holy Fair," and unduly slandering our honest rustic population, has laid on the coarser colours with much too unsparing a brush.

But while we refuse to rank the hind community with the ruffians of the "Inferno," and to regard the hiring-fair ball-rooms as nurseries of lust, let it not be supposed that we are blind to the dissipation, vulgarity, and vice, which are ever conspicuously mixed up with such motley gatherings. These are phases of revelry—common to all promiscuous assemblages of pleasure-seekers, where a certain number invariably hold high carnival with the glass—that we would not for a moment think of extenuating ; and it would be well were recreation everywhere made subservient to the higher ends of mental and moral improvement.

British agriculture, ever becoming more and more scientific, will yet have greater need of labourers of skill and intelligence ; and there is an important fact that must be forcibly urged upon the ploughmen guild. They must be led to understand, that it is by the cultivation of their mind and morals chiefly, by a more general diffusion of brains throughout their ranks, that they can either elevate their character or increase their power.

"They sleep, they eat, they toil : what then ?
Why, wake to toil and sleep again."

We frankly grant the peculiar difficulties of such an educational task. It would be no joke, the attempt to keep the hind awake over a book, or an exercise, demanding close mental application. His daily work, stiff and stiffening, has the tendency to make him dull and drowsy at night. Whenever he sits down by the blazing fire, in the winter evenings, sleep potently overcomes him, unless his eyes are kept open by story-telling, or by the singing of his own rude roll of ballads. Yet the effort to instruct the class would not by any means be as futile as the pouring of water into a bottomless bucket. There are many improvable intellects among the fustian-clad lads of our farm-steadings, as there are also not a few of their number sober, industrious, and provident—who nobly rise above the influences of their bothy sphere, and look, with a manly heart, beyond the miserable rewards of their present unenviable servitude.

The general festive seasons, especially with the young, are still Hogmanay, New Year's Day, and Han'sel Monday. Persons with a thirst for philological secrets will naturally inquire what the first name signifies. Its meaning, however, is very doubtful. Various interpretations of the word, have, from time to time, been suggested; but while some of these are ingenious enough, no doubt, they strike one suspiciously as being forced—clever, but not convincing. "*Homme est né,*" "The man-child is born;" or, "*Au gui menez,*" "Come to the mistletoe," as the Druids are said to have gone in gay and joyous procession; or "*Aux gueux menez,*" "Come to the beggars," referring to the charity which has ever been a creditable and characteristic feature of the season. Be the ancient reading what it may, children, in the villages at least of the county, enjoy on the occasion a return of "hogmanays;" while parties of boys go about from house to house disguised in old shirts and paper visors. They act a rustic kind of drama, in which the adventures of two rival knights and the feats of a doctor are conspicuous; finishing up by repeating a rhyme, addressed to the "gudewife," for their "hogmanay."

Even in this free country, there is a marvellous clinging to some old customs which have nothing to recommend them but that they are old. First-footing, on New Year's morning, is still to a certain extent practised and encouraged. With whisky or other drink as a gift, visits are made to friends' houses at midnight to wish them "a happy new year." Nor have certain of the old superstitions connected with the season yet passed away. The first-foot is a visitor of great consequence. To come empty-handed is tantamount to meaning ill to the family. A person with plain soles is considered not lucky. A hearty merry fellow is deemed the best first-foot. And should anything out of the ordinary course occur throughout the day, it is remembered and regarded as the cause or forewarning of anything extraordinary happening during the year.

With Han'sel Monday, until some twenty years ago, came a week's holidays for the employés in the principal public works, when family visits were made to friends at a distance, and other social pleasures enjoyed. But now the Monday itself is alone observed as a holiday. Cock-fighting at this time was one of the chief amusements of the lower orders—a barbarous pastime which in the present day is rarely heard of, either in the nailmaking or colliery districts. "Raffle-shooting" for buns and other seasonable articles, was another great institution; but it also has become obsolete. All, in fact, that now remains of this once chief holiday in Stirlingshire is the orange exchanges amongst the younger people, similar to their custom at Hogmanay.

Previous to the year 1832 the poor and parochial funds were managed by the kirk-session. The heritors met twice a year with the session to docquet accounts, and to receive their report of the state of the poor; but the whole of the active management devolved upon the session. Nor did they discharge their duties in a perfunctory manner. Besides exercising a minute and daily care over all the paupers on the roll, on the first Monday of every month, they, and the minister, met, when all the poor who could attend were expected to make their appearance, and personally to receive their monthly allowance. Those who could not appear from ill health, were waited upon by some member of the session, and their condition reported. Thus was the case of every individual brought monthly under the view of the whole session. Sometimes there was in consequence an increase, sometimes there was a diminution of their allowance, according to circumstances. The effects of this system of watchfulness was abundantly apparent. None were admitted on the roll who were not proper objects of charity. None were continued upon it who did not require relief. No case was overlooked. The poor were well attended to and contented, and the funds by which they were supported, exclusive of the church collections, amounted to a mere trifle. There was then, and even for some years after, much of the good old feeling among the people, of reluctance to receive parochial aid. It was no uncommon occurrence, a quarter of a century ago, for the parishioners to raise, by subscription, a sum of money in aid of some individual or family, who had been thrown into destitute circumstances by affliction or bereavement, rather than they should be subjected to the humiliation of becoming parish paupers. Here is a case in point. A poor, industrious family, in the parish of Drymen, had their eldest son (a promising young student), brought home to them in fever; —and he died. The father and mother were seized, and the former also died. Means got exhausted, and there were eight young children to provide for. The poor widowed mother, from her sick bed, entreated of the minister who offered her relief, that whatever he bestowed should not be from the parish funds. Such a spirit of honest pride, however, is fast departing, if it is not now all but gone. The reception of parochial relief, judging at least from the numbers of the applicants, appears to be no longer felt a degradation.

INDEX.

ABBEY Craig, i. 371; ii. 182
Abercromby, Lord, ii. 107
Abercromby, Sir Ralph, ii. 45
Agricola, Julius, i. 2, 10, 22
Agricultural Association (Eastern District), ii. 254
Agrimony, ii. 223
Ainecourt, Sir Gilzame de, i. 185
Aitken, James, & Co., ii. 347
Aitken, Thomas, i. 342
Airth, i. 330; ii. 279
Airth Castle, i. 100
Airth Church (Ancient), i. 101
Airth Minerals, ii. 184
Airthrey Castle, i. 220; ii. 278
Airthrey Mineral Spring, ii. 37
Ajax, ii. 358
Alexander III., i. 144
Alexander, Sir James Edward, ii. 107
Alpine Plants, ii. 215
Alum, Manufacture of, ii. 333
Alva, ii. 1
Anglo-Saxons, ii. 350
Angus, Mary, Countess of, i. 316
Archers' Club, Denny, ii. 365
Archibald, J. & R., Devondale, ii. 330
Archibald, R., & Sons, Tillicoultry, ii. 328
Ardinning Loch, ii. 207
Argentine, Sir Giles, i. 194
Armoury, Stirling Castle, i. 71
Arnothill, i. 270
Arnotdale, i. 272

Arthur's O'on, i. 46
Ashdow Chasm, ii. 194
Athelward, ii. 190
Auchindavy Fort, i. 31
Auchinlilly-linn, ii. 188
Auld Wives' Lifts, i. 56
Avon River, ii. 185
Avondow River, ii. 196

BAILLIE, Alexander, i. 97
Baillie, General, i. 221, 224
Baird, John, i. 252
Baldernock, ii. 3, 182
Balfron, ii. 3
Balglass Castle, ii. 290
Baliol, John, i. 145
Ballagan, Spout of, ii. 32, 186
Bankier Fort, i. 6
Banknock, i. 386
Bannockburn, i. 378
Bantaskine, North, i. 272; ii. 282
Bantaskine, South, i. 273; ii. 281
Barhill, i. 32
Barley, ii. 248
Baston, Andrew, i. 198
Bean, ii. 248
Beaton, Archibald James, i. 367
Belfrage, Dr. Henry, ii. 48
Bell, James, ii. 49
Bellendean, Sir Lewis, i. 263
Bell-flower, Giant, ii. 223
Bemulie Fort, i. 29
Bencleugh, ii. 217
Ben Lomond, ii. 213

Bertram, Rev. —, i. 396
Bird Cherry, ii. 229
Birds of Prey, ii. 233, 234
Blackadder, Lieut.-Col. John, ii. 48
Blackburn, John, ii. 108
Blackburn, Peter, ii. 108
Black Lochs, ii. 207
Black-mail, i. 316
Black-mail Contracts, ii. 153
Blane River, ii. 185
Boat, Iron, the First, i. 293
Boat, Steam, the First, i. 295
Body-snatching, i. 343
Bolton, Joseph C., ii. 43, 109, 263
Bonheur, Rosa, i. 386
Bonny River, ii. 192
Bonnybridge, i. 386
Bonnymuir, i. 251
Bontine, W. C., ii. 265
Boquhan River, ii. 186
Bored Stone, i. 181
Bothkennar, i. 327; ii. 4, 279
Boulder-clay Flood, ii. 172
Boun, Sir Henry de, i. 192
Bowling Clubs, ii. 364
Brewery, Falkirk, ii. 347
Brianjay, Frere, i. 167
Bridge of Allan, i. 374
Bridgeness, i. 42
Bridge, Roman, i. 16
Bright, Hon. John, i. 258
Broich River, ii. 206
Bruce, Alexander, of Alva, ii. 3
Bruce, James, of Kinnaird, i. 324, 341; ii. 56, 283, 313
Bruce, Robert, of Kinnaird, i. 323, 339; ii. 50
Bruce, King Robert, i. 51
Bruce, Sir Michael, i. 46
Bruce, Sir William C., ii. 109
Bruces of Stenhouse, ii. 104
Bruce Castle, i. 100
Bruce's Cave, ii. 216
Buchanan, Peel of, i. 59
Buchanan, Parish of, ii. 5, 181

Buchanan Estate, ii. 289
Buchanan, Sir Andrew, ii. 110
Buchanan, George, i. 299
Buchanan, of Machar, ii. 145
Buchanan, Family of, ii. 92
Bullet-throwing, ii. 363
Burgess Ticket, Copy of, ii. 23
Burghs, Origin of, i. 261
Burgh, Royal, ii. 21
Burns, Robert, ii. 295

CADELL, W. A., of Banton, ii. 74
Cadell, William, of Cockenzie, ii. 293
Cairnfaal, i. 7
Calamine, ii. 336
Caledonians, i. 43
Calico Printing, ii. 322
Calico Painting, ii. 324
Callendar, James, First Earl of, ii. 25
Callendar, i. 39, 392; ii. 281
Cambuskenneth Abbey, i. 108
Camelon, i. 8, 400
Cameron, William, ii. 288
Campbell - Bannerman, Henry, i. 371
Campbell, Robert, of Inversnait, ii. 138
Campfield, i. 232
Campion Bladder, ii. 224
Campsie, i. 317; Fells, ii. 182, 211
Canal, Union, ii. 33
Candlemaking, ii. 354
Canglar, Little, i. 210
Carbeth Loch, ii. 207
Carbrook, ii. 289
Carfarran, Peel of, i. 58
Cargill, Rev. Donald, i. 382
Carnie, John, of Curling Hall, ii. 368
Carnival, Montreal, ii. 372
Carnock, River, ii. 194; Glen, 290

Carpet Weaving, ii. 332
Carriden, i. 42
Carron Bog, ii. 188
Carron Company, ii. 261
Carron Reservoirs, ii. 205
Carron River, ii. 186
Carse, i. 370; ii. 241
Castlecary Castle, i. 96
Castlecary Fort, i. 3, 34
Castlecary Glen, i. 97
Cauldron Linn, ii. 193
Celandine, ii. 224
Centaury, ii. 230
Chapelhill, i. 25, 36
Chapel, Royal, of Castle, i. 68, 138
Charles, James, Baptism of, i. 90
Chemical Manufactories, ii. 333
Cholera, ii. 309
Christie, John, of Tillicoultry, ii. 328
Cicero, ii. 358
Circular Fort, i. 54
Clanronald's Bard, i. 225
Claudius Appius i. 13
Coach-building, ii. 342
Coal-fields, i. 325, 381; ii. 311
Coal, Output of, ii. 311
Coal-workers, ii. 312
Coal Stratification, ii. 171
Coal, the Vegetation in, ii. 312
Cochrane, Lady of, Kilmarnock, ii. 161
Cockburn, Malcolm, Provost, i. 267
Colliers, Character of, ii. 318, 380
Colliers, Diseases of, ii. 317
Collier Serfdom, i. 325
Colzium Castle, i. 322
Connaught, Duke of, ii. 372
Cooper, Henry R., of Ballindalloch, ii. 110
Copper, ii. 32

Copperas, Manufacture of, ii. 333
Coulter Loch, ii. 207
Craigallion Loch, ii. 207
Craigforth House, ii. 291
Craigmaddie Loch, ii. 207
Craigmaddie Moor, i. 56
Craigmuc, ii. 31
Craigrostan, ii. 137
Crane's-bill, Shining, ii. 224
Crane's-bill, Jagged-leaved, ii. 228
Cricket, ii. 363
Cromwell, Oliver, i. 398
Crosses, Stone, i. 330
Cross-hills, ii. 235
Crowberry, ii. 224
Croyhill i. 34
Cumin, John, i. 161
Cunningham, Alexander, i. 356
Cunningham of Boquhan, ii. 140
Curling, ii. 368, 370

DALGLISH, Falconer and Co., ii. 322
David I., i. 102, 107
Dawson, Joseph, ii. 296, 300
Dawson, William, ii. 301
Dawson, William, Trustees of the late, ii. 262
Dawson, Thomas, ii. 301
Dea Matris, i. 35
Denny, i. 384; ii. 5, 183
Devon River, ii. 192
Distilleries, ii. 345
Dobson and Charles, ii. 351
Dock, Graving, Grangemouth, ii. 351
Doig, Dr. David, ii. 63
Dominican Convent, i. 132
Donald V., i. 63
Douglas, James, ii. 362
Douglas, Sir James, i. 196
Dragon, Snap, Great, ii. 222

Draining, ii. 244, 257
Drinking Customs, ii. 374
Drymen, ii. 6
Dualt Glen, ii. 290
Dualt River, ii. 193
Duchray River, ii. 194
Duke Street, Glasgow, ii. 303
Dumbarton Fort, i. 25
Dunbar, the Poet, ii. 199
Dunbroch Loch, ii. 207
Duncan, Alexr., & Sons, ii. 336
Duncanson, Thomas, Reader, ii. 17
Dundas, Thomas G., ii. 111, 263
Dundee, Viscountess of, i. 321
Dunipace, i. 49 ; ii. 6, 286
Dunipace, Laird of, ii. 280
Dunmore i., 331 ; ii. 279
Dunmore, Earl of, ii. 261
Dunmore, Family of, ii. 101, 111
Duntocher, i. 26
Duntreath, i. 103 ; ii. 290
Duntreath, Family of, ii. 86, 117
Dwale, ii. 227
Dynamite, Manufacture of, ii. 353

EAGLE, ii. 232, 234
Earl's Seat, i. 316
Earthquake, ii. 207
Ebroch River, ii. 200
Edmond, Colonel, of Stirling, ii. 65
Edmondstone, Sir Archibald, ii. 74, 201
Edmondstone, Sir William, i. 371 ; ii. 43
Edward I., i. 51, 86, 133, 148, 159, 173
Edward II., i. 196
Election, Parliamentary, ii. 43
Ellaig, Loch, ii. 207

Elphinstone, Charles, i. 330.
Elphinstone Family, ii. 121
Empetrum nigrum, ii. 224
Endrick River, ii. 194
Erskine, Admiral, of Cardross, i. 371
Erskines of Alva, ii. 96
Erskine, Rev. Ebenezer, i. 230; ii. 18, 67
Erskine, John, ii. 66
Erskine, Sir Robert, i. 86
Erth, Fergus de, i. 100
Esker, i. 391
Eyebright, ii. 230

FALCONS, ii. 236
Falkirk, i. 38, 260 ; ii. 8
Feeing Fair, ii. 381
Ferns, i. 336, 390 ; ii. 224, 231
Finnich Glen, ii. 290
Finnich-Tennant Cairn, i. 59
Fintry, ii. 9, 181
Fire-clay Output, ii. 311
Fishing Club, ii. 372
Flanders Moss, ii. 291
Flax Seed, Thyme-leaved, ii. 229
Flying Experiment, i. 83
Foot-ball, ii. 363
Forbes, Lord, i. 216
Forbes, William, of Callendar, ii. 125, 259
Forbes, Wm., of London, i. 395
Forth and Clyde Canal, i. 289
Forth River, ii. 195
Forthvale Mill, Stirling, i. 331
Foumart, ii. 233
Foundries—
  Abbot's, ii. 308, 309
  Bonnybridge, ii. 309
  Burnbank, ii. 307, 309
  Carronbank, ii. 309
  Gael, ii. 308, 309
  Etna, ii. 308, 309
  Larbert, ii. 309
  Union, ii. 308, 309

Foxglove, ii. 227, 230
Fox-hunting, ii. 362
Franciscan Convent, i. 134
Freebooters, i. 315
Fumitory, Rampant, ii. 226
Furnaces, ii. 299, 304
Furze, Dwarf, ii. 226

GARBERT, Samuel, ii. 293
Gargunnock, Peel of, i. 59, 152
Gargunnock, ii. 10
Garrel River, ii. 200
Gartness House, ii. 290
Gascoigne, Charles, ii. 300
Gentiana campestris, ii. 224
Giant's Castle, Rownafean, ii. 204
Gibson, William, & Co., ii. 329
Gilfillan, James, of Killearn, ii. 166
Glazert River, ii. 201
Glenbervie Estate, i. 383
Glenfuir, i. 38
Gordon, Andrew, ii. 301
Gowans, James, of Edinburgh, ii. 340
Graham's Castle, i. 94
Graham's Dyke, i. 36
Græme, Sir John de, i. 169
Graham, Dr., ii. 317
Graham, of Killearn, Chamberlain, ii. 138
Graham-Stirling, Major Charles C., ii. 133
Graham, Robert, i. 278; ii. 256
Graham, William, of Airth, ii. 261
Grange Burn, ii. 192
Grangemouth, ii. 4
Grasses, ii. 220, 226
Gray, David, ii. 288
Greenhorn's Well, Falkirk, i. 281
Guthrie, Rev. Henry, ii. 67
Guthrie, Rev. James, ii. 67

Gymnastics, ii. 357
Gymnodinia conopsea, ii. 224

HADRIAN, i. 21
Haining Castle, i. 102
Hanbury-Kincaid-Lennox, Hon., ii. 125
Hansel Monday, ii. 388
Hardie, Andrew, i. 252
Harvie, Jesse, of the Mill, ii. 288
Harvie, Sir George, ii. 68
Hawking, ii. 361
Hawley, Lieut.-General, i. 231, 241
Heart's-ease, ii. 228
Heath, Fine-leaved, ii. 220
Henry, Dr., ii. 71
Henry VIII, ii. 350, 367
Henry, Prince, Baptism of, i. 71
Henry, Dr. Robert, ii. 68
Herbertshire Castle, i. 95
Herbertshire Paper Mill, ii. 336
Hereford, Earl of, i. 196
Hermitage, The, ii. 189
Heron, The, ii. 234
Hillend Relics, i. 58
Hogmanay, ii. 386
Holyrood Abbey, i. 142
Hope, Sir Thomas, ii. 71
Horse Racing, ii. 360
Hospitals—
　Allan's, i. 356
　Cowan's, i. 355
　Spittal's, i. 355
Hume, Alexander, ii. 73
Hurlet & Campsie Alum Co., ii. 333
Hurly Hawkie Mound, i. 84
Hutton, W. R., of Lower Greenhill, ii. 335.

IMBECILE Institution, i. 352

Implements, Agricultural, ii. 244
India, Pariahs of, ii. 323
Inveravon, i. 40
Iron Industries, Table of, ii. 309
Ironstone Output, ii. 311
Ironworks—
  Callendar, ii. 309
  Camelon, ii. 307, 309
  Carron, ii. 293, 309
  Denny, ii. 309
  Falkirk, ii. 306, 309
  Forth and Clyde, ii. 308, 309
  Gowanbank, ii. 307, 309
  Grahamston, ii. 307, 309
  Malleable, Bonnybridge, ii. 309
  Parkhouse, ii. 307, 309
  Port Downie, ii. 308, 309
  Springfield, ii. 309
  Vulcan, ii. 308
Islands, Floating, ii. 203

JAMES I., ii. 360
James II., i. 66 ; ii. 360
James III., i. 67, 129, 204, 211
James IV., i. 140 ; ii. 199
James V., i. 68, 90
James VI., i. 69 ; ii. 288
Jeffrey, Dr. James, ii. 73
Jug, Stirling, i. 362
Juniper, ii. 224
Justices, Peace, of the, ii. 25

KAY, JEAN, ii. 145, 148
Kay, James, of Edinbelly, ii. 145
Kelvin River, ii. 201
Kelvin Valley Railway, i. 320
Kenneth III., i. 65
Kerse House, i. 287
Kier, Thomas, of Linns, i. 267
Kildean Bridge, i. 153

Killearn, ii. 10, 181
Kilmarnock, Earl of, i. 230, 395
Kilmarnock, Countess of, i. 232
Kilns, i. 272
Kilpatrick, Old, i. 26
Kilpatrick, New, i. 28
Kilsyth, i. 320, ii. 10, 183
Kincaids of Kincaid, ii. 98
Kincaid, John, of Wariston, ii. 287
King's Park, i. 81
Kinnaird, ii. 283
Kinneil, i. 41, Snab Pit, ii. 315
Kinross, William, of Stirling, ii. 345
Kippen, ii. 11
Kirkintilloch, Peel of, i. 29
Knights Templars, i. 142, 382
Knot, The, Stirling, i. 82

LADY'S Loup, ii. 190
Lalaine, Jacques, ii. 360
Lalaine, Simon de, ii. 361
Landowners—
  Airth Parish, ii. 261, 262, 273
  Alva Parish, ii. 269
  Baldernock Parish, ii. 267
  Balfron Parish, ii. 268
  Bothkennar Parish, ii. 261, 262, 263, 273
  Buchanan Parish, ii. 264
  Campsie Parish, ii. 266
  Denny Parish, ii. 260, 272
  Drymen Parish, ii. 264, 265
  Dunipace Parish, ii. 260, 262, 263, 273
  Falkirk Parish, ii. 260, 262, 274
  Fintry Parish, ii. 264, 265
  Gargunnock Parish, ii. 268
  Killearn Parish, ii. 265
  Kilsyth Parish, ii. 264, 272
  Kippen Parish, ii. 269

INDEX.

Larbert Parish, ii. 260, 263, 273
Lecropt Parish, ii. 270
Logie Parish, ii. 270
Muiravonside Parish, ii. 260, 262, 276
Polmont Parish, ii. 262, 263, 275
St. Ninians Parish, ii. 261, 263, 264, 270
Slamannan Parish, ii. 277
Stirling Parish, ii. 269
Strathblane Parish, ii. 264, 265
Lands—
  Alva Parish, ii. 253
  Campsie Parish, ii. 253
  Dunipace Parish, ii. 254
  Falkirk Parish, ii. 255
  Gargunnock Parish, ii. 255
  Kilsyth Parish, ii. 256
  Larbert Parish, ii. 256
  Slamannan Parish, ii. 257
Larbert Estate, i. 344; ii. 285
Larbert, ii. 11, 183
Laurieston, i. 39
Laxey Mines, ii. 336
Leakie's, the, of Forth, ii. 199
Leather, Manufacture of, ii. 351
Leckie House, ii. 291
Leitchtown, ii. 31
Lennox Castle, i. 317
Lennox-mill, ii. 3
Lennoxtown, i. 318; ii. 5
Lennoxhills, ii. 182
Lennox, Captain John, ii. 97
Leopold, Prince, ii. 294
Letham Moss, i. 329
Levenax Castle, ii. 185
Levenax, Earl of, i. 217
Life and Health, ii. 359
Light-Water Burn, ii. 192
Lily of the Valley, ii. 225
Limestone, Lennoxtown, ii. 341
Ling, Common, ii. 220
Livingston, Thomas F., ii. 125

Livingstone, Sir George, i. 388
Livingston, Jean, ii. 287
Livingston, Sir Thomas, i. 67
Livingston, Family of, ii. 104
Livingston, Sir William, i. 393
Lobelia, Water, ii. 222
Lochleggan, ii. 206
Loch Lomond, ii. 202
Logie, i, 55; ii. 12
Loup of Fintry, ii. 195
Lowis, John M., of Plean, ii. 126
Lunatic Asylum, i. 353
Lupus Virius, i. 44
Lyle, Thomas, i. 330

MAGGIE Wood's Loan, i. 232
Mahometans, ii. 323
Malcolm III., i. 278
Mallow, Marsh, ii. 227
Malt, Analysis of, ii. 348
Mansfield, Earl of, ii. 70
Manuel Nunnery, i. 130
Marauders, Highland, ii. 291
Marcellus Ulpius, i. 43
Marion's Well, Falkirk, i. 282
Marischal, Sir Robert K., i. 88
Mar's Work, i. 92
Mary, Queen, i. 397
Maximilian, Prince, ii. 294
Mayfield, Falkirk, i. 271
Meikle Binn, ii. 212
Menstrie House, i. 220
Meriadte, Squire, ii. 360
Middlesbro' "Pigs," ii. 308
Middleton, Dr. David, i. 275
Mignionette, Wild, ii. 227
Millfield, Polmont, i. 391; ii. 280
Milton Bog, i. 187
Milton Village, i. 319
Mimulus Luteus, ii. 227
Minerals, ii. 31
Minister's Well, Falkirk, i. 282
Mint, Red, ii. 227

Moltke, ii. 358
Monkland Canal, i. 290
Monteith, Vale of, ii. 29
Montrose, Duke of, ii. 127, 264
Montrose, Marquis of, ii. 128
Moore, Dr. John, ii. 75
Moravia, Andrew de, ii. 129
Moray, Sir Andrew, i. 156
Mortcloth and Safe Societies, i. 344
Moschatell tuberous, ii. 225
Mugdock Castle, i. 104
Mugdock Loch, ii. 207
Mugdock Reservoir, ii. 208
Muiravonside, ii. 12, 280
Muirhead, Patrick, i. 280
Mumrills, i. 40
Mungal Bog, i. 168
Munro, Sir Robert, i. 237
Murray-Menzies, Alexr. H., ii. 130
Murray, of Touchadam and Polmaise, ii. 129
M'Crombie, of Tillyfour, ii. 349
M'Farlane, Rev. Duncan, ii. 74
M'Farlan, John W., ii. 126
M'Farlans of Kirkton, ii. 97, 100
M'Farlan, Very Rev. Principal, ii. 75
M'Farlane of Aberfoyle, ii. 168
M'Gil, Rev. Francis, i. 339
Macgregor, Alexr. of Balhaldies, i. 229
Macgregor, James, ii. 143, 148
Macgregor, John, ii. 137
Macgregor, Robert Roy, ii. 136
Macgregor, Robert Og, ii. 141
Macgregor, Ronald, ii. 143
Mac In Doill, Keith, ii. 204
Mackay, John S., i. 286
M'Laren, William, & Sons, ii. 334
Macleod, Rev. Dr. Norman, i. 319

Macpherson, Hugh, i. 287
Macraes of Ross-shire, ii. 162
M'Turk, Robert, i. 349

NAILMAKING, ii. 309
Napier, Sir Charles, ii. 79
Napier, John, of Ballikinrain, ii. 79
Napier, John de, ii. 77
Napier, Lord, i. 289
Napier Family, ii. 358
Nelson & Sons, London Warehouse of, ii. 340
Nestor, ii. 358
Newbottle Abbey, i. 141
New-Year's Day, ii. 387
Nicholas, Prince, ii. 294
Nightshade, Woody, ii. 228
Nimmo, Rev. William, i. 328
Ninian, Saint, i. 375
Ninians, St., ii. 14
Northumbrians, i. 63, 369
Norway, Maiden of, i. 145
Notman, Photographer, ii. 372

OATS, ii. 247
Ochils, ii. 182, 217
Oliphant, Lawrence, i. 371
Ore, Silver, ii. 32
Orr-Ewing, Archibald, ii. 124
Oscar, ii. 191
Oswald, James, of Dryburgh, i. 384
Otter, ii. 233
Ox-eye, Yellow, ii. 226

PALACE, STIRLING CASTLE, i. 68
Paper-making, ii. 336
Parkvale and Hayford Mills, Cambusbarron, ii. 331
Parliament House, Castle, i. 71
Parliament, Houses of, ii. 340
Parliamentary Burghs, Falkirk District, i. 268

Paterson, Rev. John Brown, i. 279
Paton, Messrs., of Tillicoultry, ii. 330
Perth, Houses of, ii. 341
Pestilence, 363
Pheasants, ii. 233, 235, 237
Pimpernel, Scarlet, ii. 226
Pint, Cucoko, ii. 223
Pinus, ii. 220
Pius Antoninus, i. 24
Plantain, Hoary, ii. 229
Plantain, Water, ii. 229
Plean Asylum, i. 382
Ploughing, Subsoil, ii. 244
Police, ii. 24
Police and Improvements Bill, Falkirk, i. 266
Polmaise, ii. 279
Polmont, i. 392; ii. 13, 184
Poor, the, ii. 388
Potato, ii. 250
Ptarmigan, ii. 232
Prentice, Thomas, ii. 256
Prison, Rob Roy's, ii. 216
Primroses, i. 51
Property, County, Annual Value of, ii. 292
Prussian Blue, Manufacture of, ii. 334
Pyroligneous Acid Works, ii. 334

QUADRUPEDS OF PREY, ii. 234, 235
Quarries, Stone, ii. 339
Queen's Haugh, i. 86
Quoit-pitching, ii. 363

RAGMAN ROLL, i. 147
Railways, ii. 32
Railway, Caledonian, ii. 36
Railway, Carron, the First, ii. 297
Railway, Edinburgh and Glasgow, ii. 33, 34
Railway, North British, ii. 35
Ramsay, William, of Barnton and Sauchie, ii. 360
Rankin, R. W., of Rosebank, ii. 343
Raymond, James, of Alva, ii. 3
Rennie, Rev. Dr. R., ii. 74
Richard, Bishop of Dunkeld, ii. 2
Richardson, Professor, of Glasgow, ii. 80
Ridpath, George, ii. 80
Rinderpest, ii. 252
Rintoul, John, Falkirk, ii. 354
River, Channel, Ancient, ii. 179
Roads, ii. 29
Roebuck, Dr. ii. 293
Roes, ii. 233, 234, 235, 237
Rollock, Robert, ii. 81
Rod, Golden, ii. 227
Romans and Fergus II., ii. 191
Rooks, i. 333
Ross, James, of Arnotdale, ii. 335
Roughcastle, i. 7, 38
Rough, John, i. 134
Roughlands, ii. 302
Rounders, ii. 364
Rumbling Bridge, ii. 193
Russel, John, of Mayfield, i. 267

SALMON FISHERY, ii. 199
Saxifrage, Meadow, ii. 228
Schist, ii. 333
Schools, Board, ii. 41
Sea-beaches, Ancient, ii. 177
Sedge, ii. 220
Session Records, St. Ninians, i. 377
Seton-Stewart, Sir H. J., ii. 132
Severus, i. 12, 23, 44.
Shaw, Duncan, of Crathinard, i. 347

INDEX.

Sherriff, John Bell, ii. 131, 263
Shipbuilding, ii. 351
Shire, Derivation of, ii. 20
Shooting, ii. 362
Skating, ii. 371
Skinner, Rev. John, of Bothkennar, ii. 4
Skirva, i. 32
Slamannan, ii. 15, 280
Smith, Robert, & Son, Stirling, ii. 331
Smuggling, ii. 165
Snakeweed, ii. 223
Soils, ii. 242
Song Birds, ii. 238
Sons of the Rock Society, ii. 39
Sowing, ii. 249
Sparling, ii. 200
Speirs, A. G., of Culcreuch, ii. 131
Speirs, Sir Geo. H., of Fintry, ii. 265
Speirs, Peter, of Culcreuch, ii. 29
Speke, the Traveller, ii. 62
Spelter Works, ii. 335
Spirits, Consumption of, ii. 346
Spottiswood, i. 52
Squirrel, ii. 233, 235, 237
Stainton, Joseph, ii. 300
Standalane, ii. 282
Starwort, Sea, ii. 227
Statement, Tabular, Agricultural, ii. 258
Stenhouse, i. 346 ; ii. 284
Stenhousemuir, i. 345 ; ii. 285
Stewart of Appin, ii. 140
Stewart, David, of Stewarthall, ii. 131
Stewart, Sir John, i. 163, 172
Stirling, i. 61, 355 ; ii. 16
Stirlingshire, Population of, ii. 19
Stirlingshire, Area of, ii. 20
Stirling, Andrew, of Muiravonside, ii. 132
Stirling, Ann C., of Glenbervie, ii. 263
Stirling, Sir Chas. E. F., of Glorat, ii. 132
Stirlings of Calder, ii. 96
Stirlings of Craigbarnet, ii. 99
Stirling, First Earl of, ii. 81
Stirling, George, of Glorat, ii. 89
Stirling, James, of Garden, ii. 133
Stirling, John S., of Gargunnock, ii. 133
Stirling, William, of Tarduff, 134
Stove Works, Bonnybridge, ii. 309
Strathblane. i. 316 ; ii. 15
Strikes, ii. 377
Strode, N. W. J., of Candy, ii. 134
Stuart, Charles Edward, i. 89, 228, 241, 243, 398
Stuart, Gilbert, ii. 70
Symington, William, i. 297 ; ii. 81
Surrey, Earl of, i. 156

TACITUS, i. 2, 20
Tappock, i. 52
Tartans, Manufacture of, ii. 329
Temperance Society, Falkirk, ii. 376
Thomas the Rhymer, i. 144
Thomson, George, ii. 342
Thurlow, Lord, ii. 263
Tillicoultry Serge, ii. 327
Todd, John, & Sons, ii. 331
Tortula tortuosa, ii. 224
Torwood Castle, i. 98
Touch House, ii. 291

INDEX.

Tournament, ii. 360
Townhead Loch, Kilsyth, ii. 206
Trees, ii. 221, 224, 229, 230, 231
Trysts, Falkirk, i. 347
Turnip, ii., 250
Twenge, Sir Marmaduke, i. 154
Twisse, Dr., of London, ii. 32

UMFRAVILLE, SIR INGRAM, i. 190
Urbicus, Lollius, i. 2, 11

VALERIAN, WILD, ii. 229
Victoria, Queen, i. 129; ii. 367, 372
Volunteers, Rifle, ii. 365
Voters, County, ii. 42

WAGS and Wits, ii. 377
Wages—
  Calico Printers, ii. 325
  Coach-builders, ii. 345
  Colliers, ii. 320
  Curriers and Tanners, ii. 353
  Ironworkers, ii. 305
  Paper-makers, ii. 339
  Railway Servants, ii. 37
  Quarriers, ii. 341
Wales, Prince of, ii. 294
Wall Legions, i. 24
Wall, Roman, Dimensions of, i. 24
Wallace, Sir William, i. 51, 87, 149, 172; ii. 7
Wallace Monument, i. 372
Wallace Oak, i. 98
Wallace Stone, i. 169
Walker, John, LL.D., ii. 83
Wanzie, The, ii. 181
Watch-tower, Roman, i. 11

Water-lily, White, ii. 222
West-end Park, Glasgow, ii. 202
Westerton, ii. 278
Westerwood, i. 34
Westquarter, ii. 280
Whale, White, ii. 200
Wheat, ii. 246
Whinstone, Eruption of, ii. 171
Whisky, Grain, ii. 345
Wilkie, Gilbert, of Port-Downie, ii. 351
William the Lion, i. 66, 89
Wilson, James, D.D., ii. 83
Wilson, J. & W., Bannockburn, ii. 332
Wilson, William, of Banknock, i. 386
Wilson, William, & Sons, Bannockburn, ii. 332
Wilson, Thomas, of Tophill, i. 293
Wingate, David, ii. 319
Winter-green, ii. 229
Winter Seasons, ii. 368
Wolf Crag, i. 368
Wood, Admiral, i. 214
Woodruff, ii. 225
Woods, ii. 29
Wood, Stitchwood, ii. 229
Woollen Manufactures, ii. 326, 331
Wrestling, ii. 361

YARN Spinning, ii. 326
Yellowlees, Rev. John, ii. 305
York Buildings Company, i. 395

ZETLAND, Earl of, i. 288; ii. 134, 260
Zinc Blende, Manufacture of, ii. 336

www.ingramcontent.com/pod-product-compliance
Lightning Source LLC
Chambersburg PA
CBHW051244300426
44114CB00011B/885